Garfield
LARD OF THE JUNGLE

BY JIM DAVIS

Ballantine Books • **New York**

Published in the United States by Ballantine Books, an imprint of The Random House Publishing Group,
a division of Random House, Inc., New York.

BALLANTINE and colophon are registered trademarks of Random House, Inc.

ISBN 978-0-345-52584-0

Printed in the United States of America

www.ballantinebooks.com

9 8 7 6 5 4 3 2 1

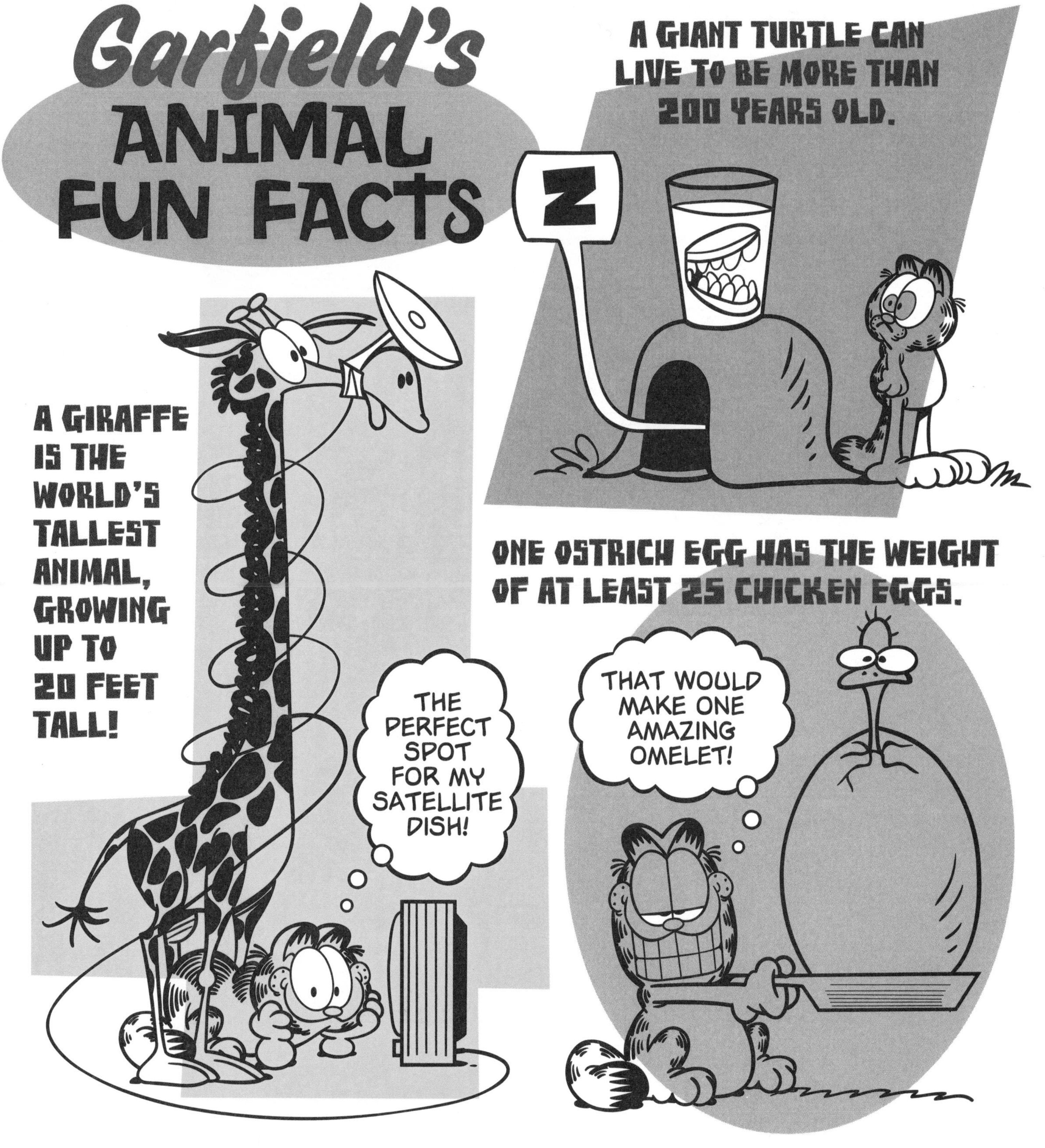
Garfield's
ANIMAL
FUN FACTS
A GIANT TURTLE CAN LIVE TO BE MORE THAN 200 YEARS OLD.
Z
A GIRAFFE IS THE WORLD'S TALLEST ANIMAL, GROWING UP TO 20 FEET TALL!
THE PERFECT SPOT FOR MY SATELLITE DISH!
ONE OSTRICH EGG HAS THE WEIGHT OF AT LEAST 25 CHICKEN EGGS.
THAT WOULD MAKE ONE AMAZING OMELET!

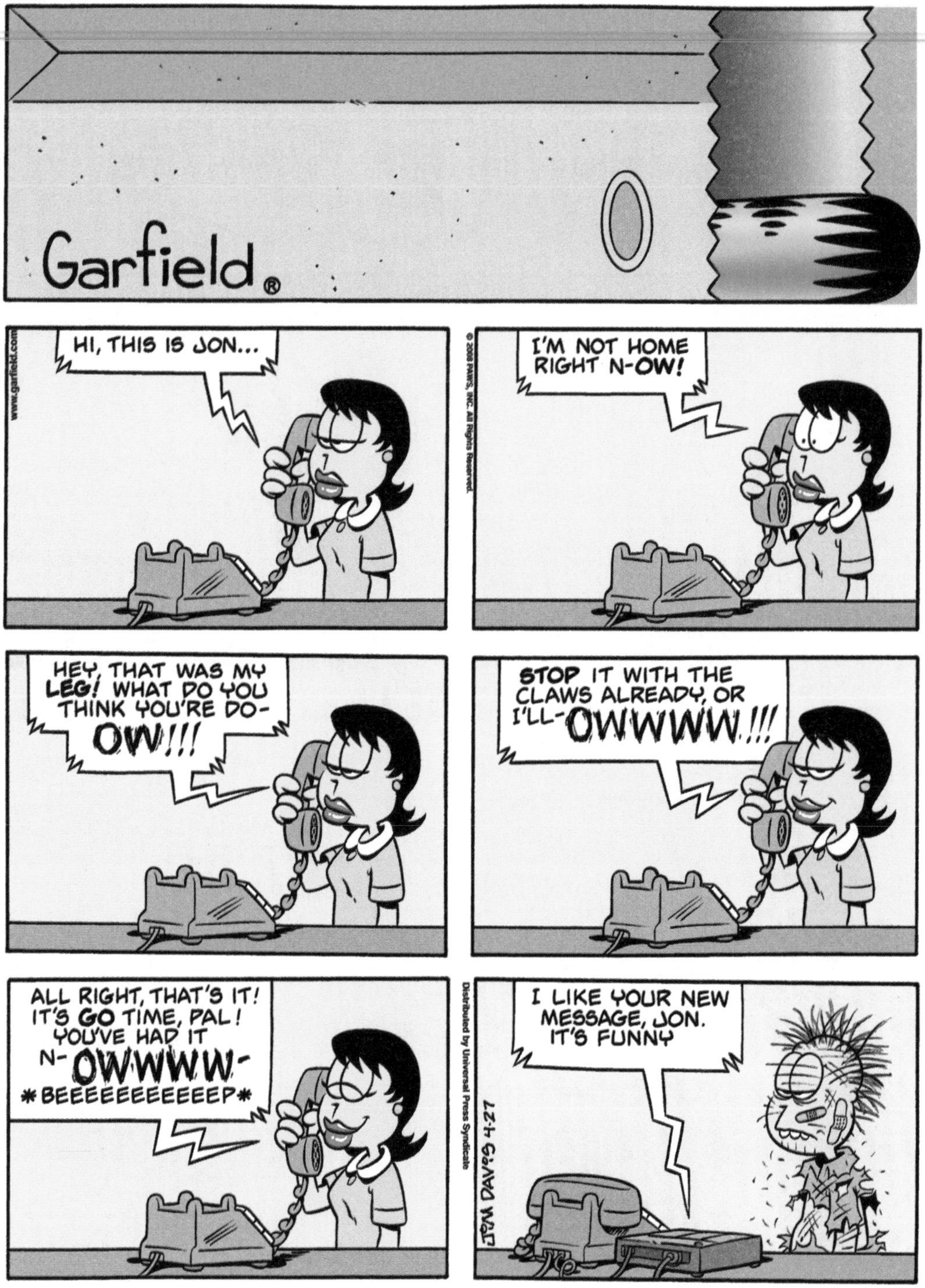
Garfield®
www.garfield.com
HI, THIS IS JON...
© 2008 PAWS, INC. All Rights Reserved.
I'M NOT HOME RIGHT N-OW!
HEY, THAT WAS MY LEG! WHAT DO YOU THINK YOU'RE DO-OW!!!
STOP IT WITH THE CLAWS ALREADY, OR I'LL-OWWWW!!!
ALL RIGHT, THAT'S IT! IT'S GO TIME, PAL! YOU'VE HAD IT N-OWWWW-
BEEEEEEEEEEEP
Distributed by Universal Press Syndicate
JPM DAVIS 4-27
I LIKE YOUR NEW MESSAGE, JON. IT'S FUNNY

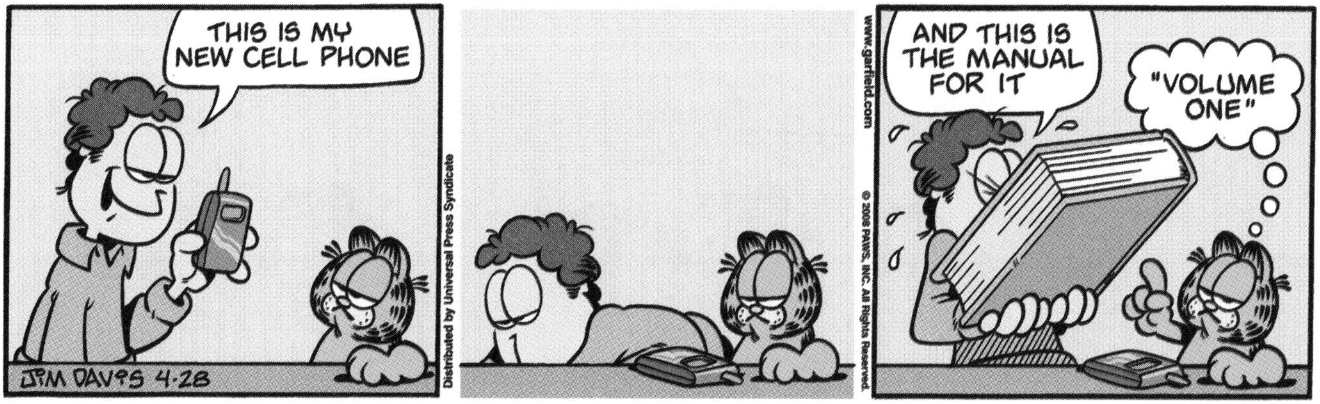
THIS IS MY NEW CELL PHONE
JPM DAVPS 4-28
Distributed by Universal Press Syndicate
www.garfield.com
© 2008 PAWS, INC. All Rights Reserved.
AND THIS IS THE MANUAL FOR IT
"VOLUME ONE"

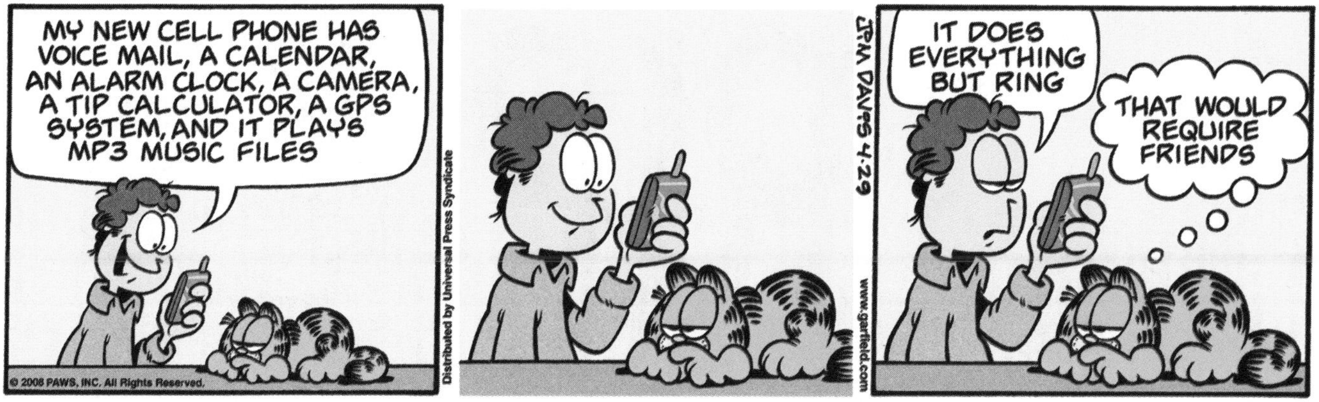
MY NEW CELL PHONE HAS VOICE MAIL, A CALENDAR, AN ALARM CLOCK, A CAMERA, A TIP CALCULATOR, A GPS SYSTEM, AND IT PLAYS MP3 MUSIC FILES
© 2008 PAWS, INC. All Rights Reserved.
Distributed by Universal Press Syndicate
JPM DAVPS 4-29
www.garfield.com
IT DOES EVERYTHING BUT RING
THAT WOULD REQUIRE FRIENDS

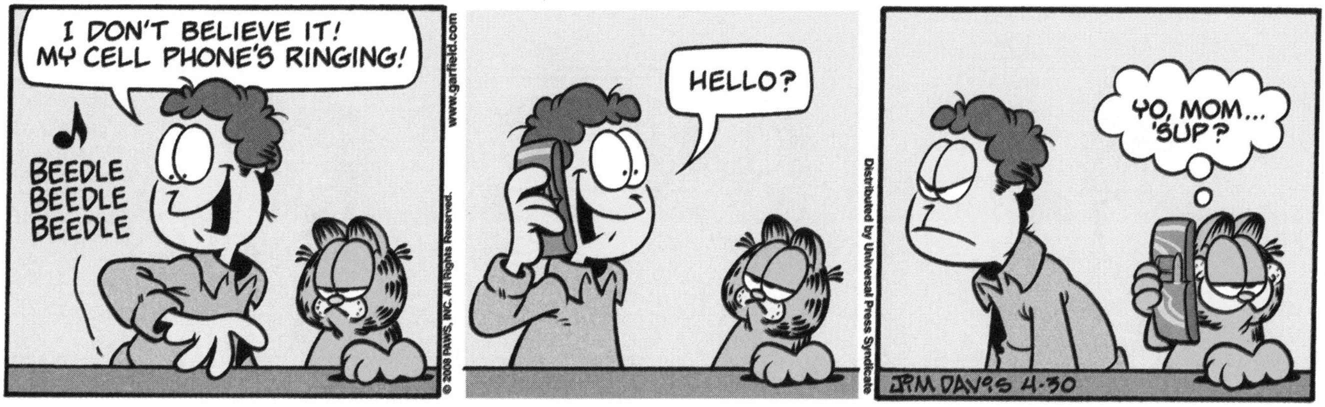
I DON'T BELIEVE IT! MY CELL PHONE'S RINGING!
BEEDLE BEEDLE BEEDLE
www.garfield.com
© 2008 PAWS, INC. All Rights Reserved.
HELLO?
Distributed by Universal Press Syndicate
YO, MOM... 'SUP?
JPM DAVPS 4-30

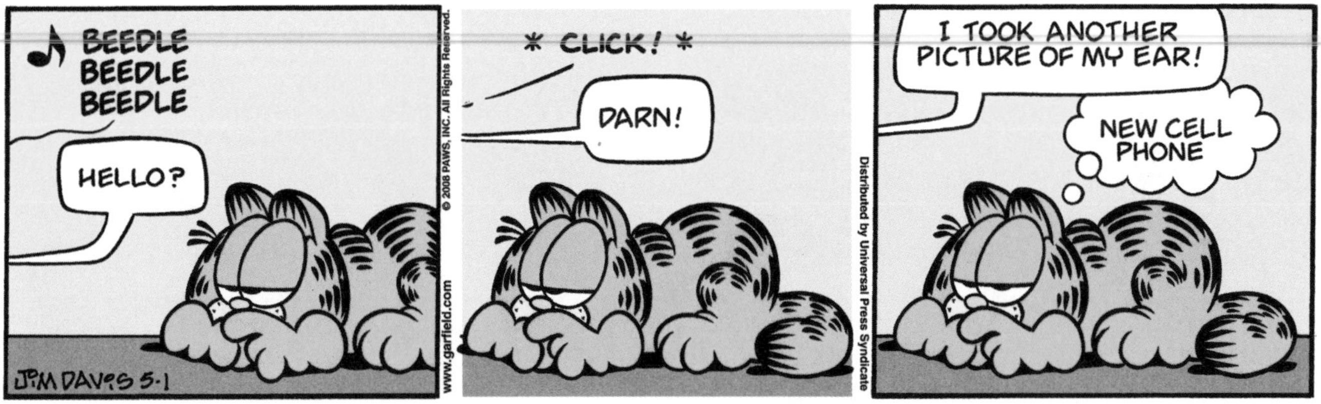
BEEDLE BEEDLE BEEDLE
HELLO?
* CLICK! *
DARN!
I TOOK ANOTHER PICTURE OF MY EAR!
NEW CELL PHONE
JIM DAVIS 5-1
© 2008 PAWS, INC. All Rights Reserved. www.garfield.com
Distributed by Universal Press Syndicate

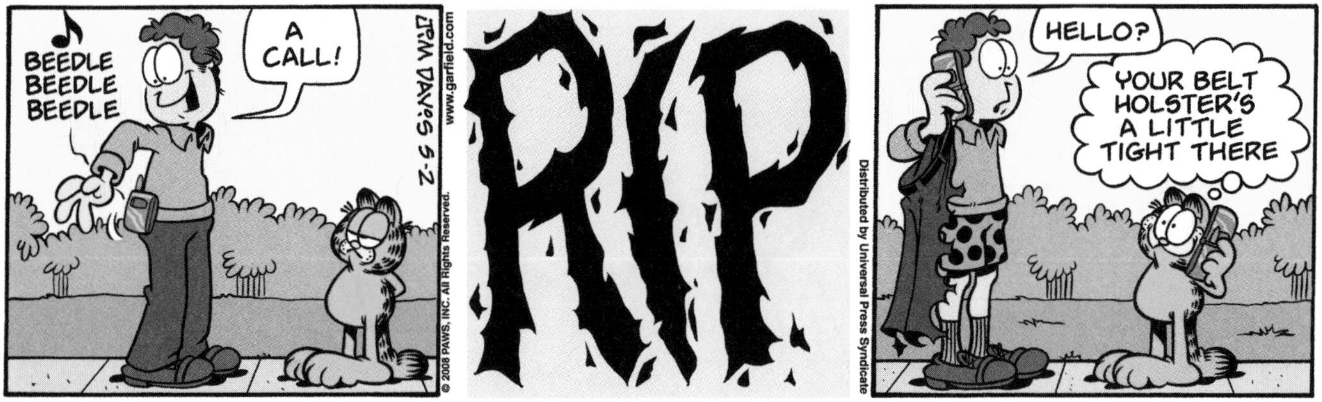
BEEDLE BEEDLE BEEDLE
A CALL!
JIM DAVIS 5-2
© 2008 PAWS, INC. All Rights Reserved. www.garfield.com
RIP
HELLO?
YOUR BELT HOLSTER'S A LITTLE TIGHT THERE
Distributed by Universal Press Syndicate

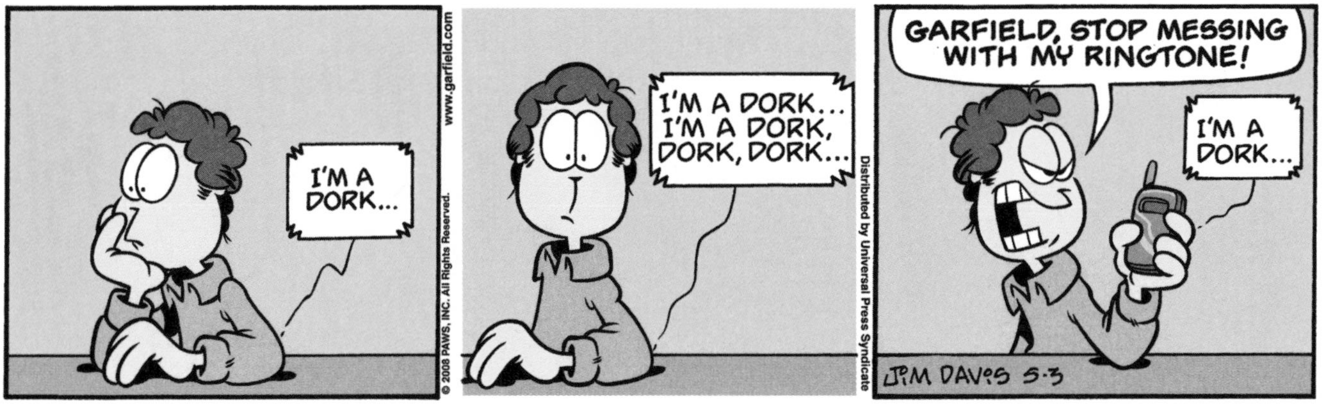
I'M A DORK...
© 2008 PAWS, INC. All Rights Reserved. www.garfield.com
I'M A DORK... I'M A DORK, DORK, DORK...
GARFIELD, STOP MESSING WITH MY RINGTONE!
I'M A DORK...
JIM DAVIS 5-3
Distributed by Universal Press Syndicate

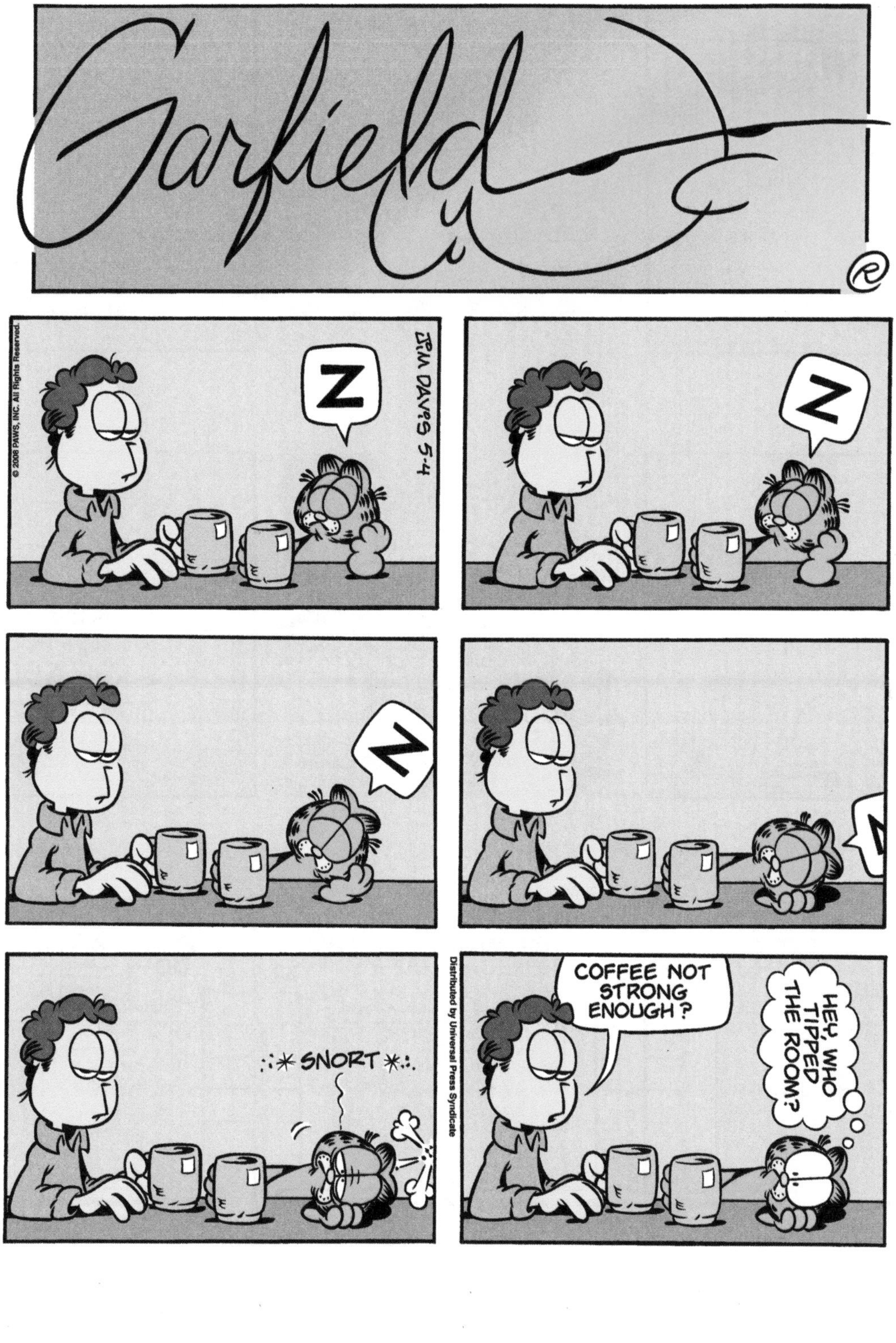
Garfield
JIM DAVIS 5-4
© 2008 PAWS, INC. All Rights Reserved.
Z
Z
Z
SNORT
Distributed by Universal Press Syndicate
COFFEE NOT STRONG ENOUGH?
HEY, WHO TIPPED THE ROOM?

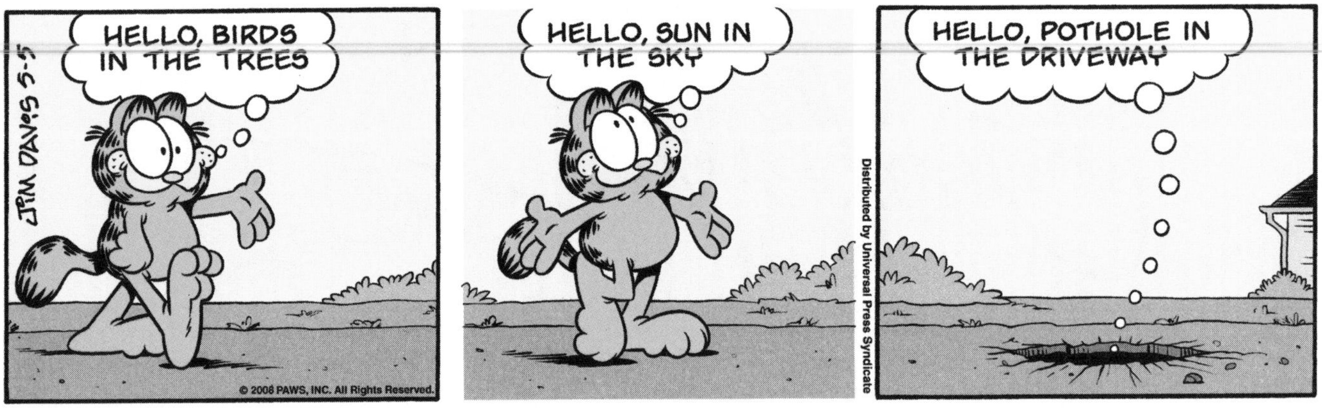
HELLO, BIRDS IN THE TREES
HELLO, SUN IN THE SKY
HELLO, POTHOLE IN THE DRIVEWAY
JIM DAVIS 5-5
© 2008 PAWS, INC. All Rights Reserved.
Distributed by Universal Press Syndicate

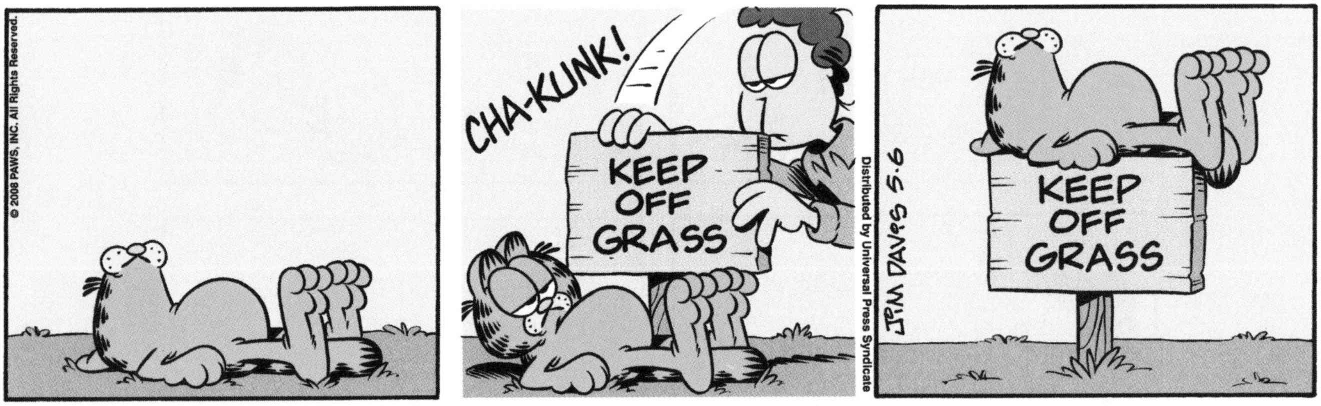
© 2008 PAWS, INC. All Rights Reserved.
CHA-KUNK!
KEEP OFF GRASS
Distributed by Universal Press Syndicate
JIM DAVIS 5-6
KEEP OFF GRASS

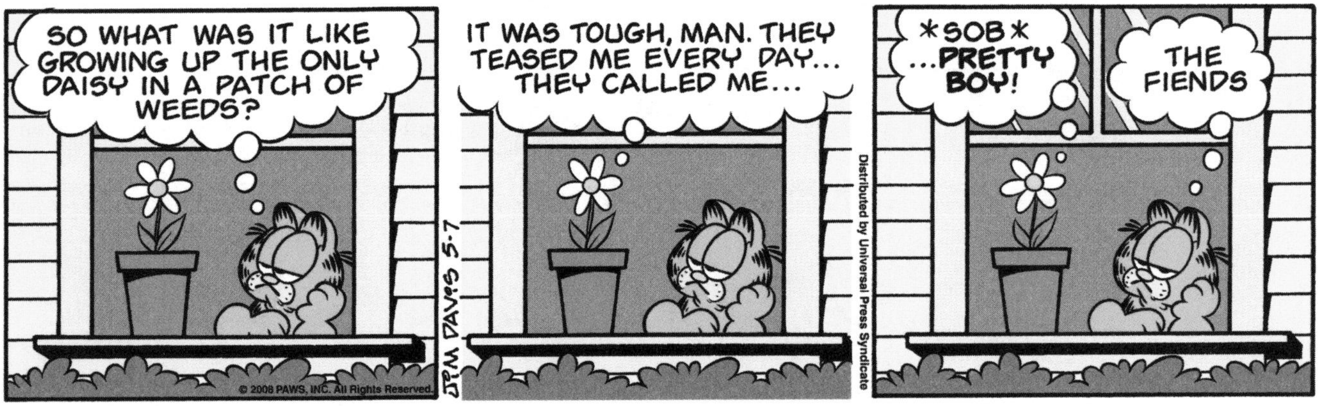
SO WHAT WAS IT LIKE GROWING UP THE ONLY DAISY IN A PATCH OF WEEDS?
© 2008 PAWS, INC. All Rights Reserved.
JIM DAVIS 5-7
IT WAS TOUGH, MAN. THEY TEASED ME EVERY DAY... THEY CALLED ME...
Distributed by Universal Press Syndicate
SOB ...PRETTY BOY!
THE FIENDS

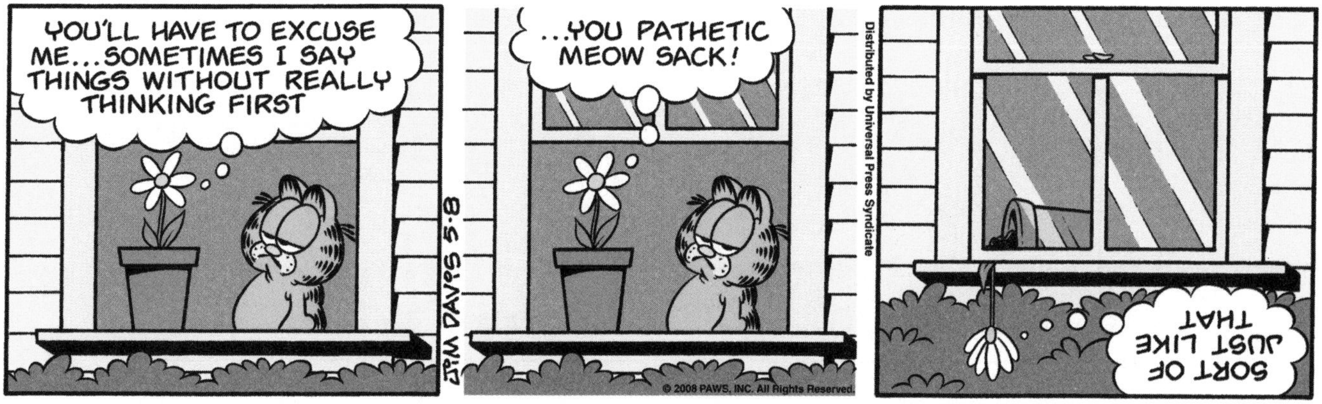
YOU'LL HAVE TO EXCUSE ME...SOMETIMES I SAY THINGS WITHOUT REALLY THINKING FIRST
JIM DAVIS 5-8
...YOU PATHETIC MEOW SACK!
© 2008 PAWS, INC. All Rights Reserved.
Distributed by Universal Press Syndicate
SORT OF JUST LIKE THAT

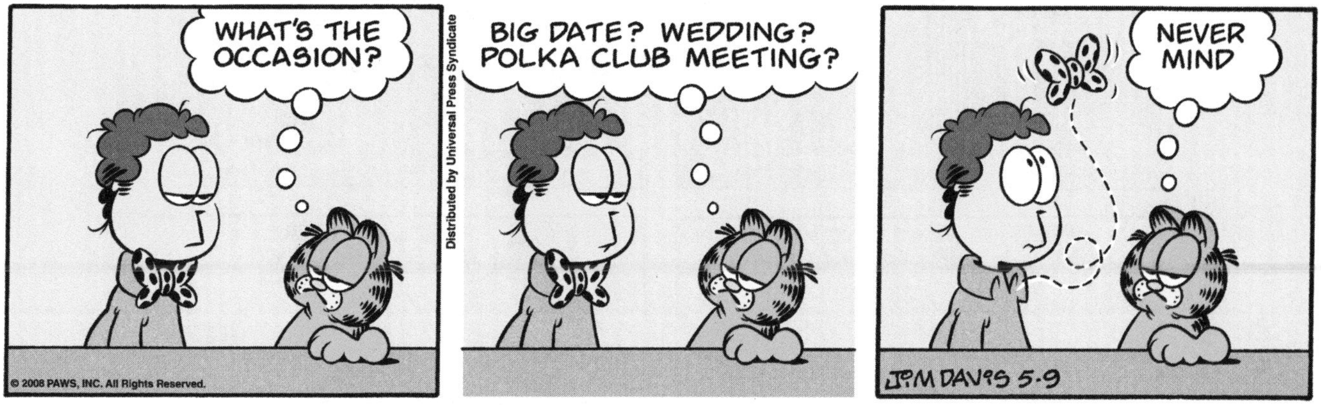
WHAT'S THE OCCASION?
© 2008 PAWS, INC. All Rights Reserved.
Distributed by Universal Press Syndicate
BIG DATE? WEDDING? POLKA CLUB MEETING?
NEVER MIND
JIM DAVIS 5-9

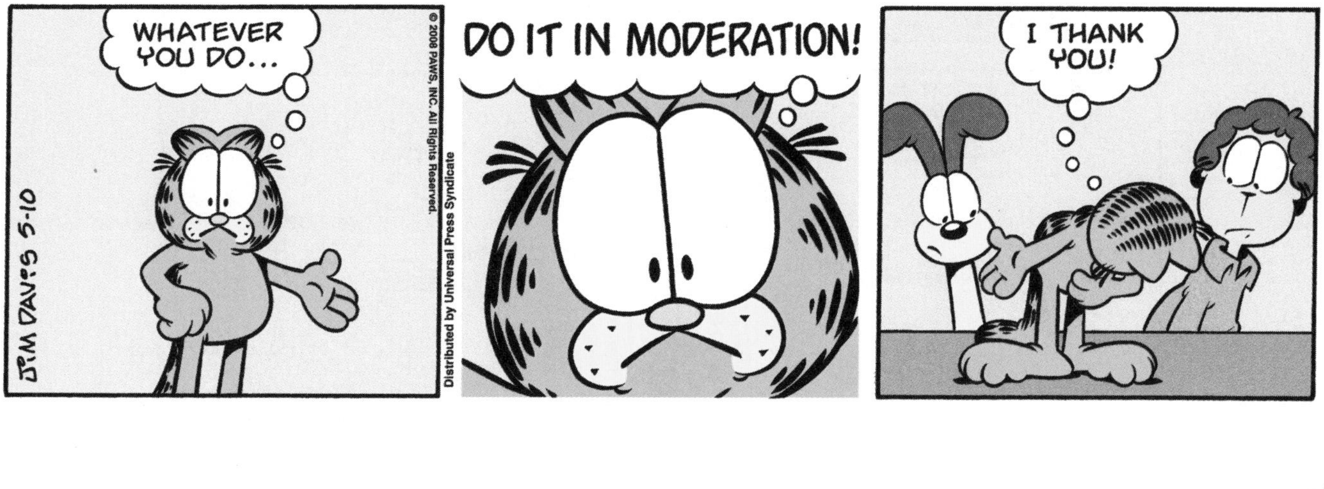
WHATEVER YOU DO...
JIM DAVIS 5-10
© 2008 PAWS, INC. All Rights Reserved.
Distributed by Universal Press Syndicate
DO IT IN MODERATION!
I THANK YOU!

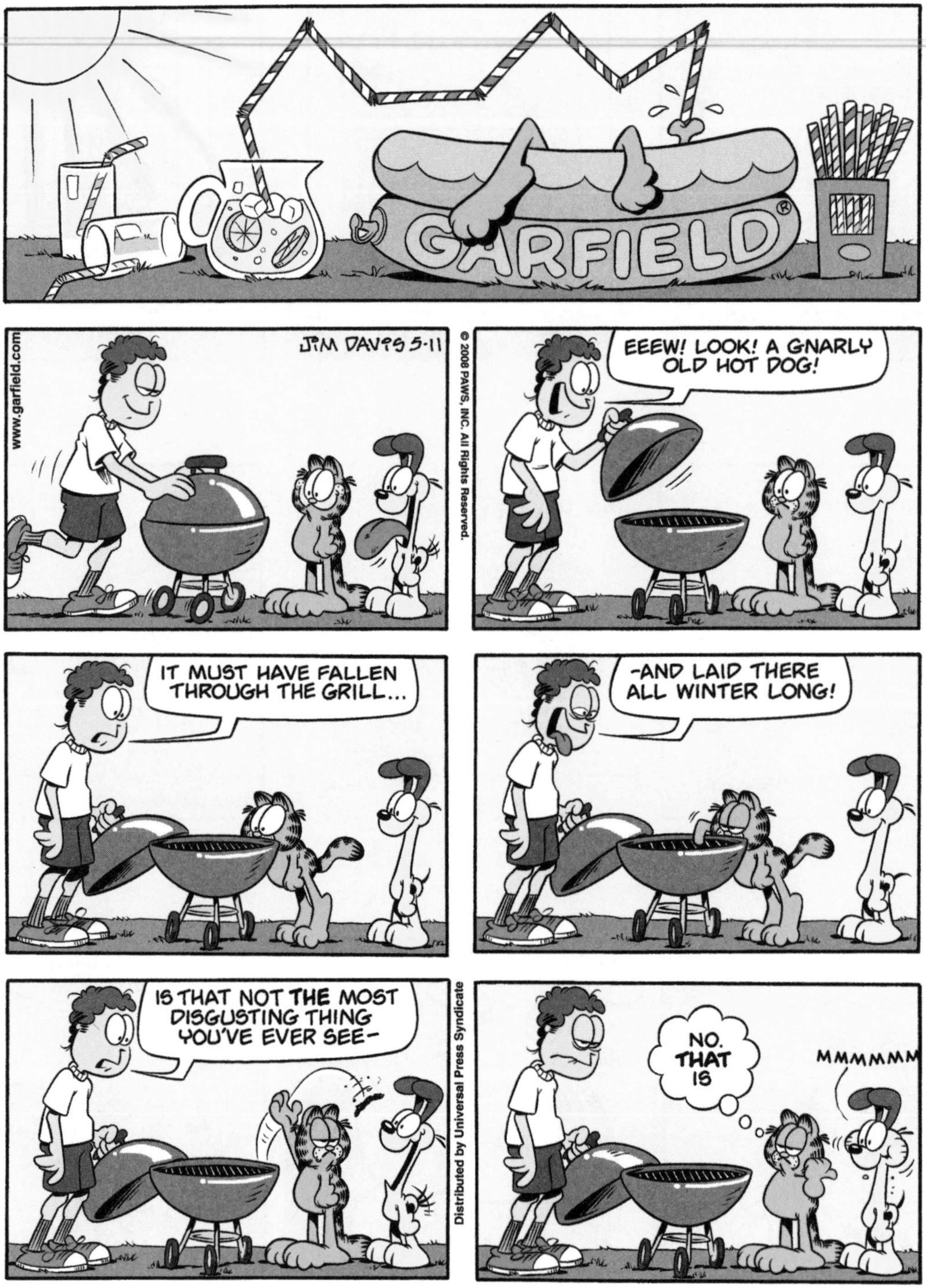
GARFIELD®
www.garfield.com
JIM DAVIS 5-11
© 2008 PAWS, INC. All Rights Reserved.
EEEW! LOOK! A GNARLY OLD HOT DOG!
IT MUST HAVE FALLEN THROUGH THE GRILL...
-AND LAID THERE ALL WINTER LONG!
IS THAT NOT THE MOST DISGUSTING THING YOU'VE EVER SEE-
Distributed by Universal Press Syndicate
NO. THAT IS
MMMMMM

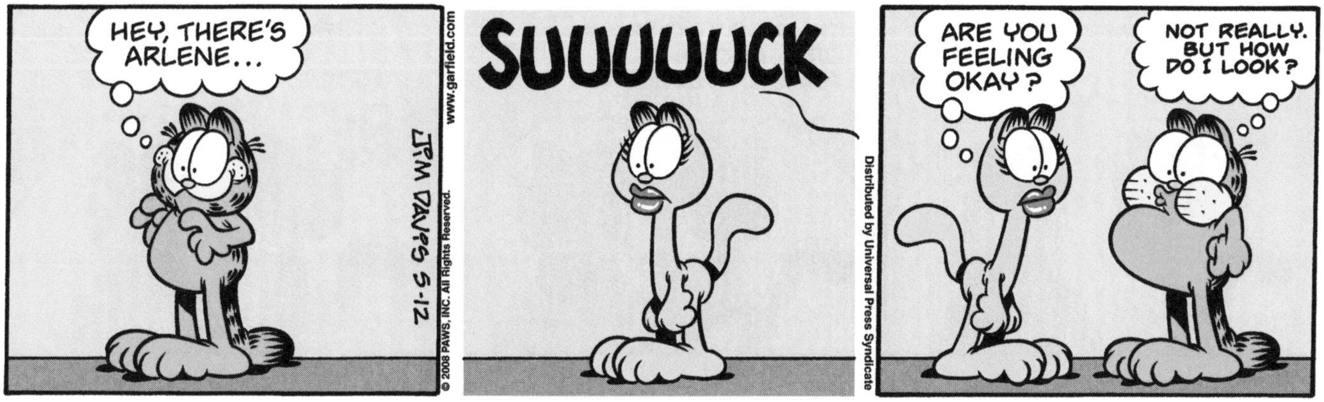
HEY, THERE'S ARLENE...
JPM DAVPS 5-12
www.garfield.com
© 2008 PAWS, INC. All Rights Reserved.
SUUUUUCK
Distributed by Universal Press Syndicate
ARE YOU FEELING OKAY?
NOT REALLY. BUT HOW DO I LOOK?

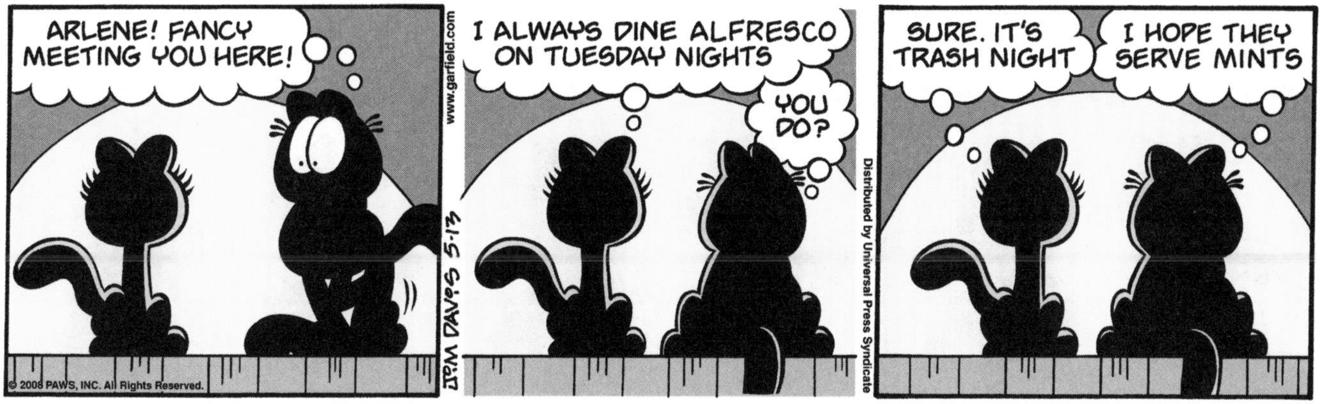
ARLENE! FANCY MEETING YOU HERE!
© 2008 PAWS, INC. All Rights Reserved.
www.garfield.com
JPM DAVPS 5-13
I ALWAYS DINE ALFRESCO ON TUESDAY NIGHTS
YOU DO?
Distributed by Universal Press Syndicate
SURE. IT'S TRASH NIGHT
I HOPE THEY SERVE MINTS

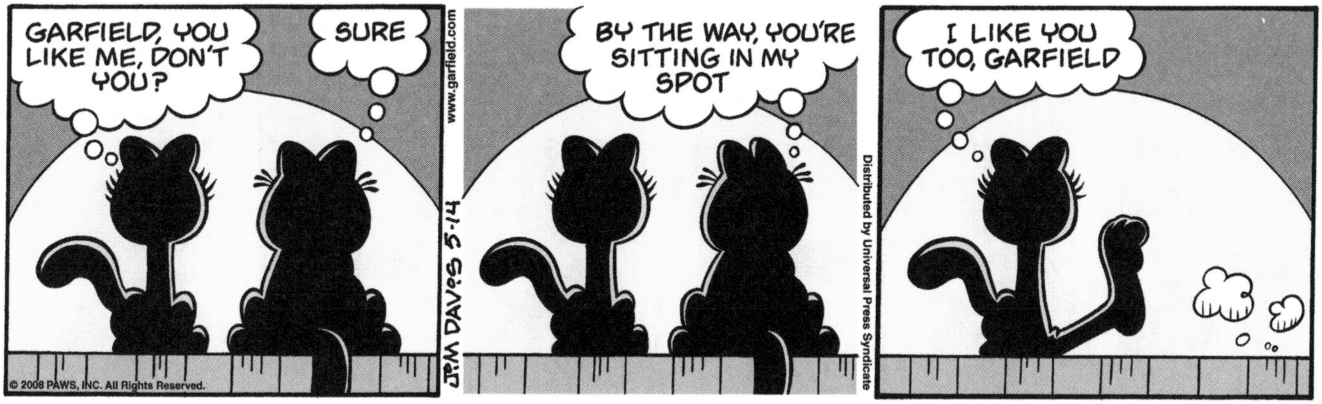
GARFIELD, YOU LIKE ME, DON'T YOU?
SURE
© 2008 PAWS, INC. All Rights Reserved.
www.garfield.com
JPM DAVPS 5-14
BY THE WAY, YOU'RE SITTING IN MY SPOT
Distributed by Universal Press Syndicate
I LIKE YOU TOO, GARFIELD

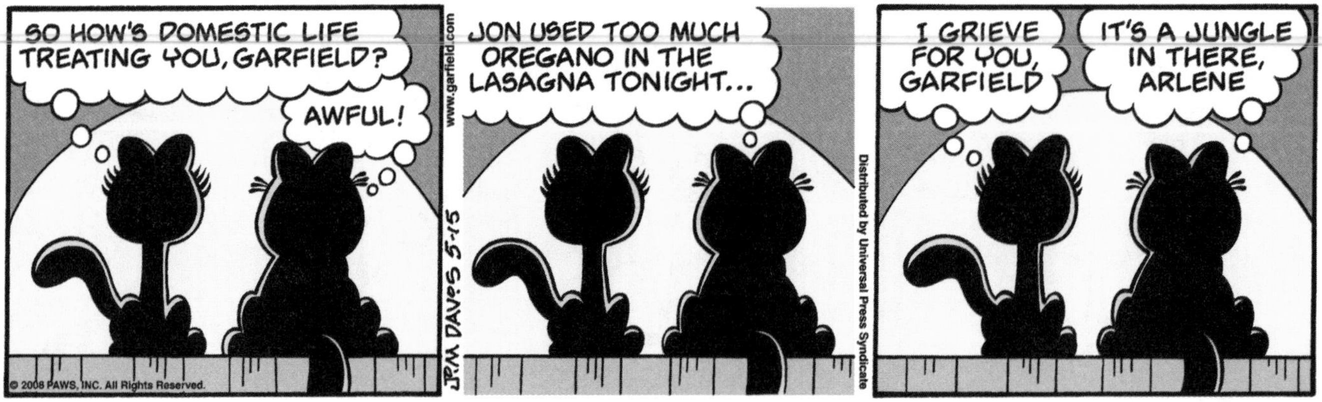
SO HOW'S DOMESTIC LIFE TREATING YOU, GARFIELD?
AWFUL!
JON USED TOO MUCH OREGANO IN THE LASAGNA TONIGHT...
I GREIVE FOR YOU, GARFIELD
IT'S A JUNGLE IN THERE, ARLENE
© 2008 PAWS, INC. All Rights Reserved.
www.garfield.com
JPM DAVPS 5-15
Distributed by Universal Press Syndicate

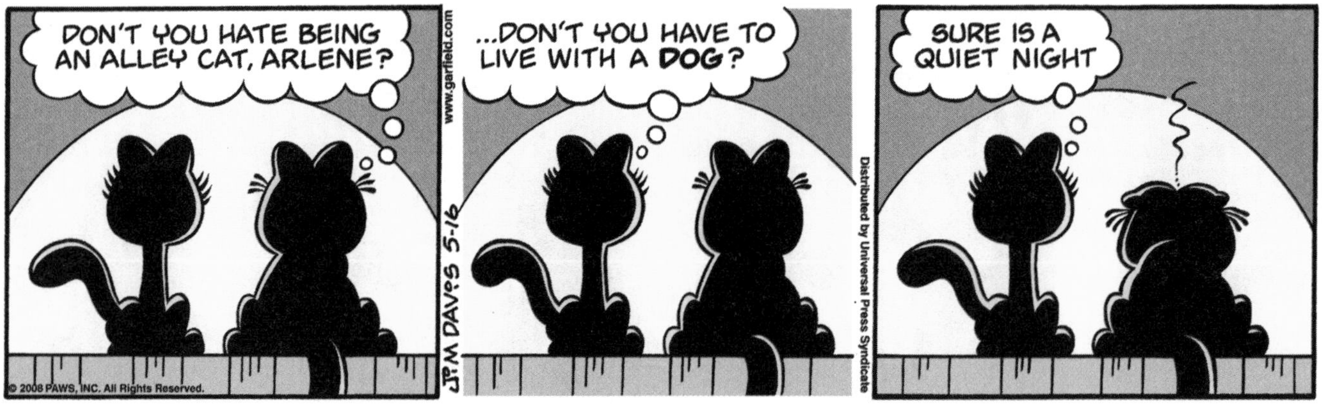
DON'T YOU HATE BEING AN ALLEY CAT, ARLENE?
...DON'T YOU HAVE TO LIVE WITH A DOG?
SURE IS A QUIET NIGHT
© 2008 PAWS, INC. All Rights Reserved.
www.garfield.com
JPM DAVPS 5-16
Distributed by Universal Press Syndicate

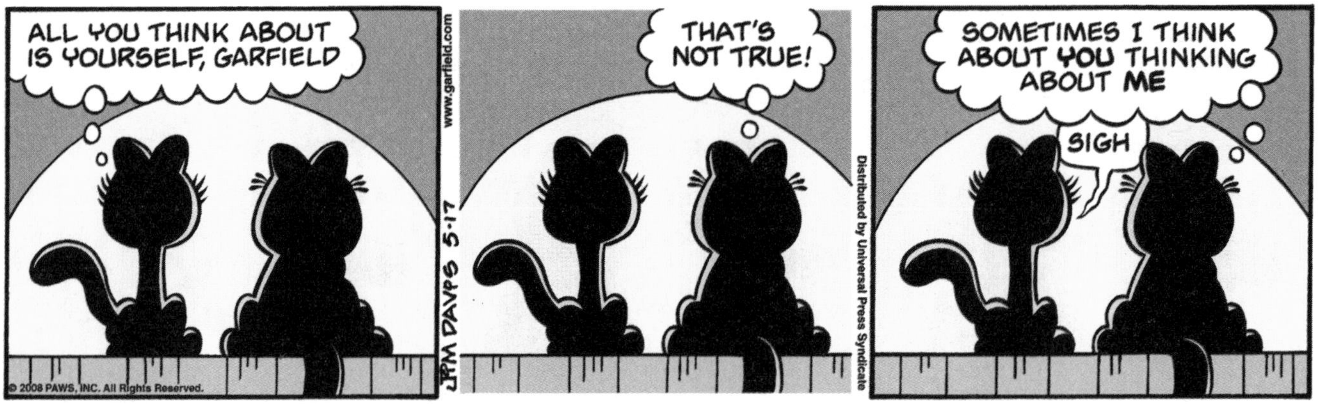
ALL YOU THINK ABOUT IS YOURSELF, GARFIELD
THAT'S NOT TRUE!
SOMETIMES I THINK ABOUT YOU THINKING ABOUT ME
SIGH
© 2008 PAWS, INC. All Rights Reserved.
www.garfield.com
JPM DAVPS 5-17
Distributed by Universal Press Syndicate

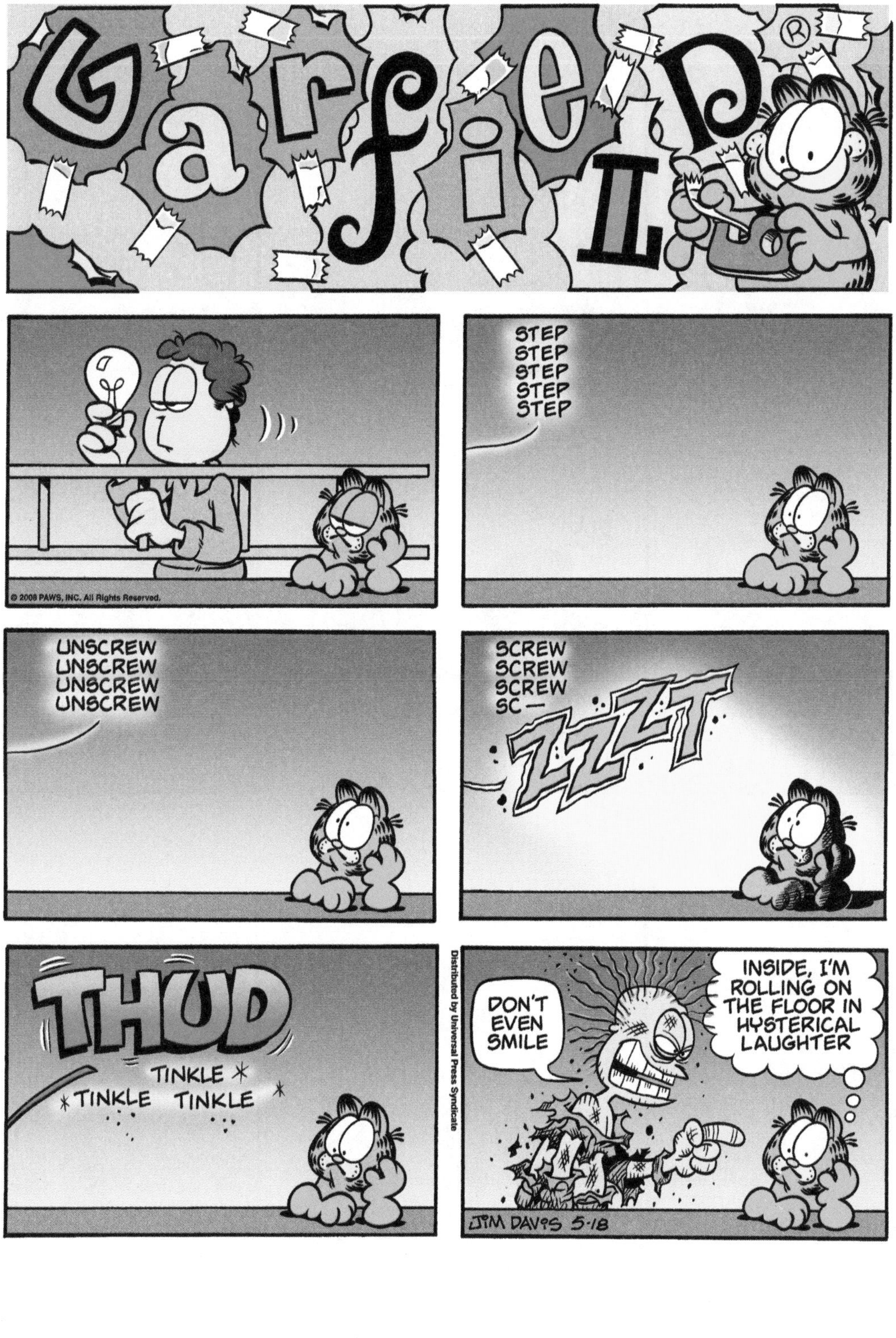

GARFIELD
© 2008 PAWS, INC. All Rights Reserved.
STEP
STEP
STEP
STEP
STEP
UNSCREW
UNSCREW
UNSCREW
UNSCREW
SCREW
SCREW
SCREW
SC—
ZZZZT
THUD
TINKLE
TINKLE TINKLE
Distributed by Universal Press Syndicate
DON'T EVEN SMILE
INSIDE, I'M ROLLING ON THE FLOOR IN HYSTERICAL LAUGHTER
JIM DAVIS 5-18

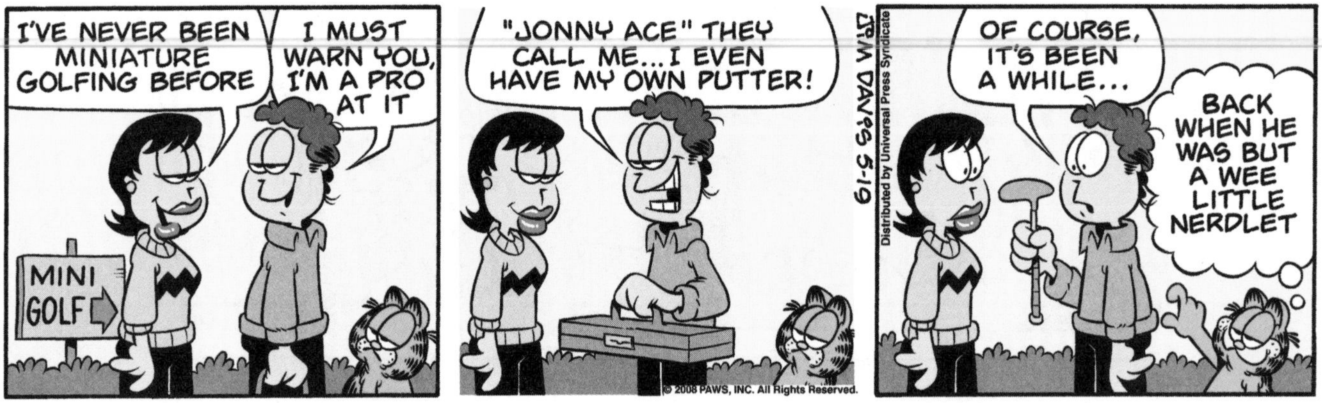
I'VE NEVER BEEN MINIATURE GOLFING BEFORE
I MUST WARN YOU, I'M A PRO AT IT
MINI GOLF
"JONNY ACE" THEY CALL ME... I EVEN HAVE MY OWN PUTTER!
JIM DAVIS 5-19
© 2008 PAWS, INC. All Rights Reserved.
Distributed by Universal Press Syndicate
OF COURSE, IT'S BEEN A WHILE...
BACK WHEN HE WAS BUT A WEE LITTLE NERDLET

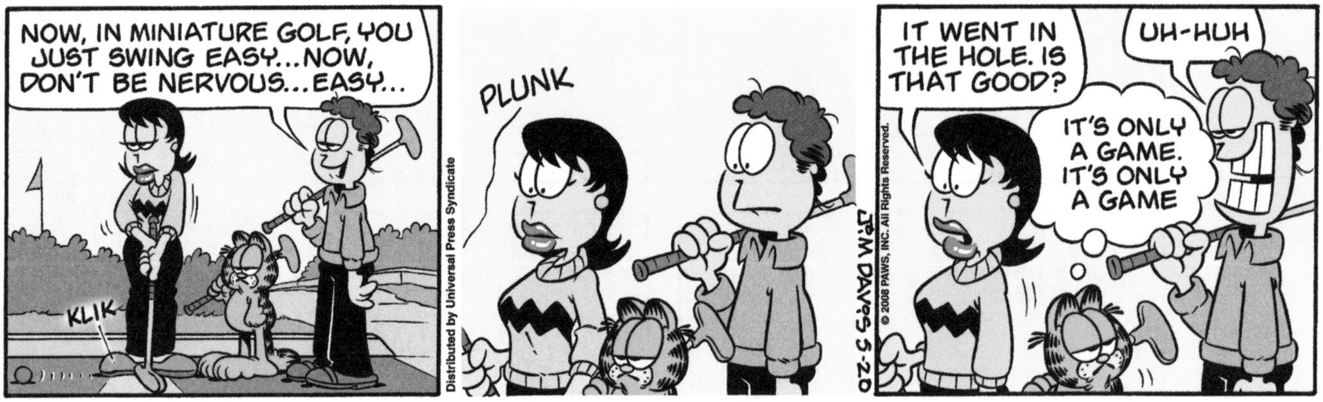
NOW, IN MINIATURE GOLF, YOU JUST SWING EASY... NOW, DON'T BE NERVOUS... EASY...
KLIK
Distributed by Universal Press Syndicate
PLUNK
JIM DAVIS 5-20
© 2008 PAWS, INC. All Rights Reserved.
IT WENT IN THE HOLE. IS THAT GOOD?
UH-HUH
IT'S ONLY A GAME. IT'S ONLY A GAME

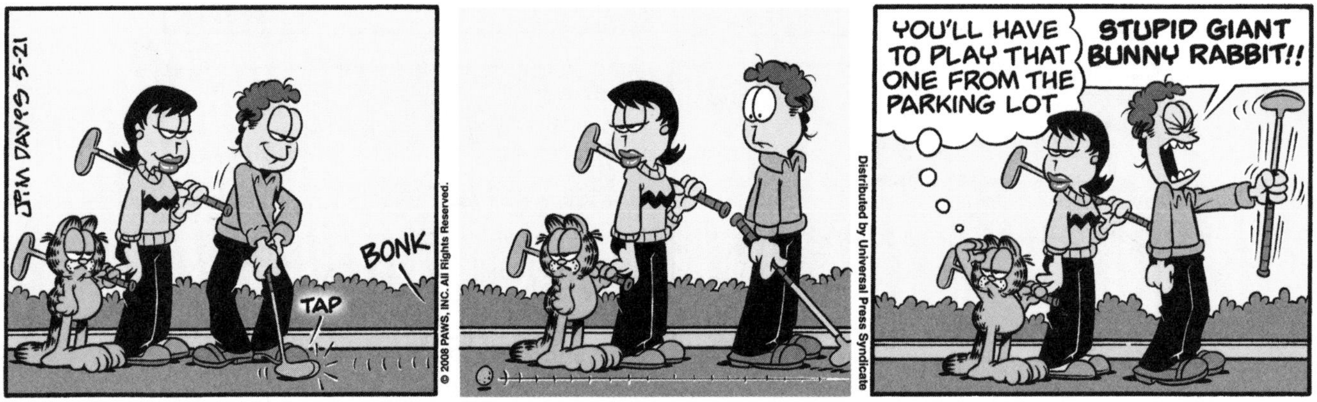
JIM DAVIS 5-21
BONK
TAP
© 2008 PAWS, INC. All Rights Reserved.
Distributed by Universal Press Syndicate
YOU'LL HAVE TO PLAY THAT ONE FROM THE PARKING LOT
STUPID GIANT BUNNY RABBIT!!

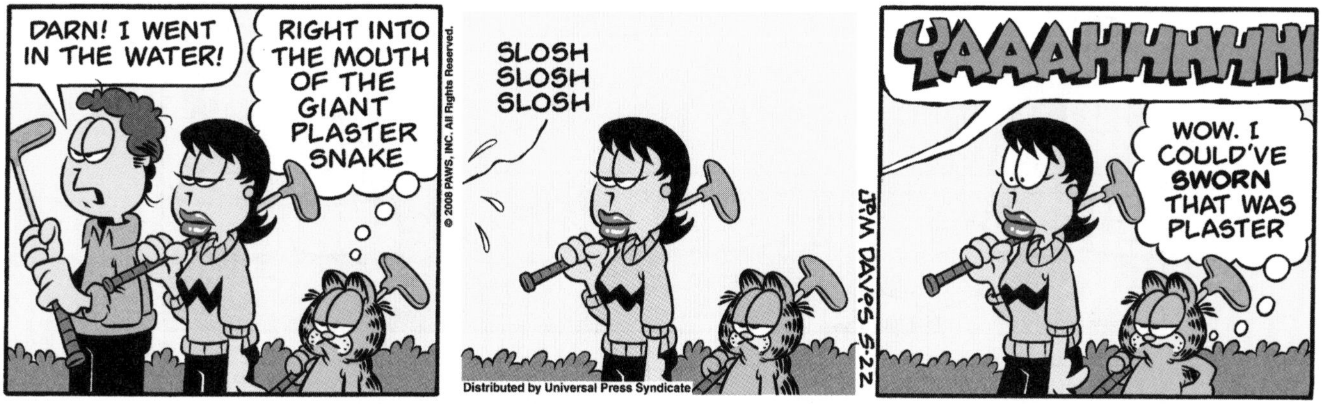
DARN! I WENT IN THE WATER!
RIGHT INTO THE MOUTH OF THE GIANT PLASTER SNAKE
SLOSH SLOSH SLOSH
YAAAHHHHH!
WOW. I COULD'VE **SWORN** THAT WAS PLASTER
JIM DAVIS 5-22
© 2008 PAWS, INC. All Rights Reserved.
Distributed by Universal Press Syndicate

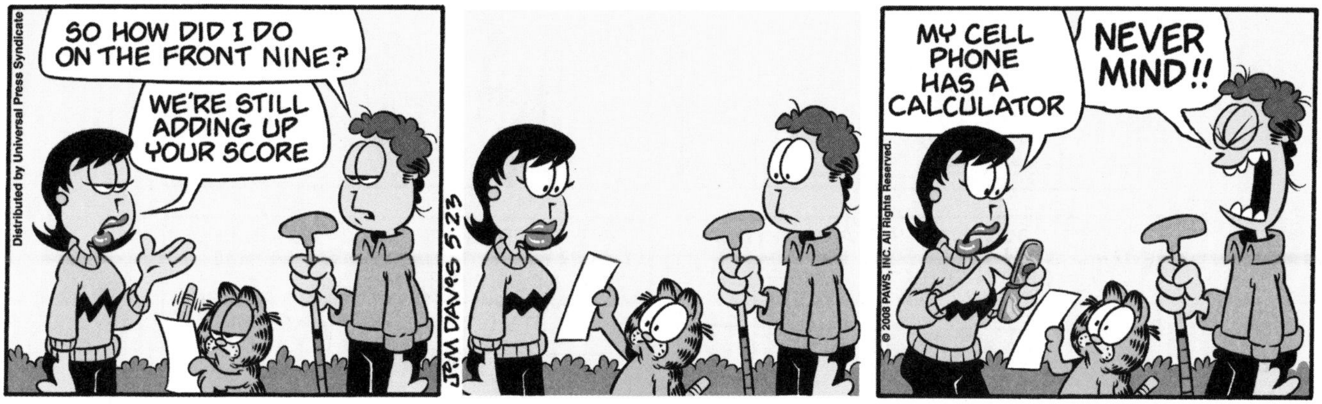
SO HOW DID I DO ON THE FRONT NINE?
WE'RE STILL ADDING UP YOUR SCORE
MY CELL PHONE HAS A CALCULATOR
NEVER MIND!!
JIM DAVIS 5-23
Distributed by Universal Press Syndicate
© 2008 PAWS, INC. All Rights Reserved.

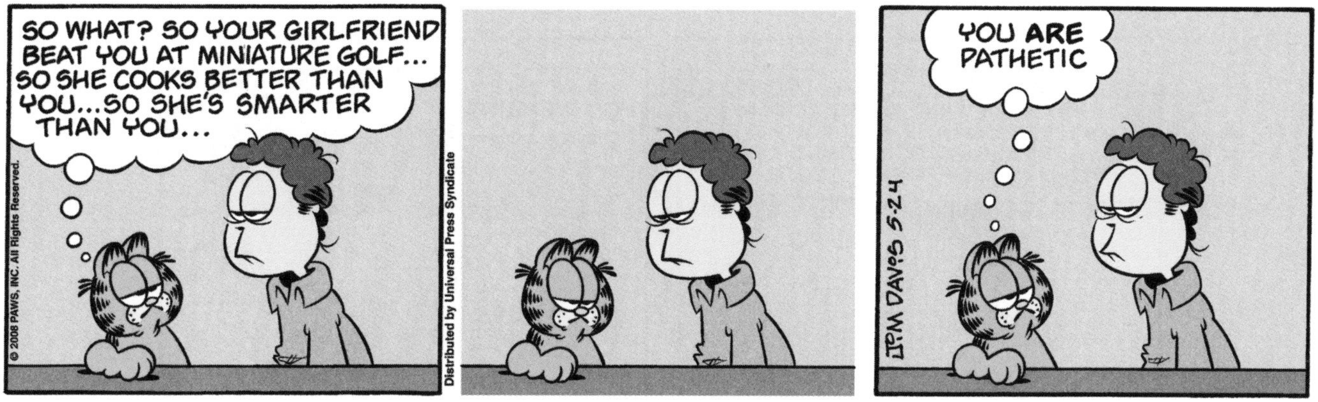
SO WHAT? SO YOUR GIRLFRIEND BEAT YOU AT MINIATURE GOLF... SO SHE COOKS BETTER THAN YOU...SO SHE'S SMARTER THAN YOU...
YOU **ARE** PATHETIC
JIM DAVIS 5-24
© 2008 PAWS, INC. All Rights Reserved.
Distributed by Universal Press Syndicate

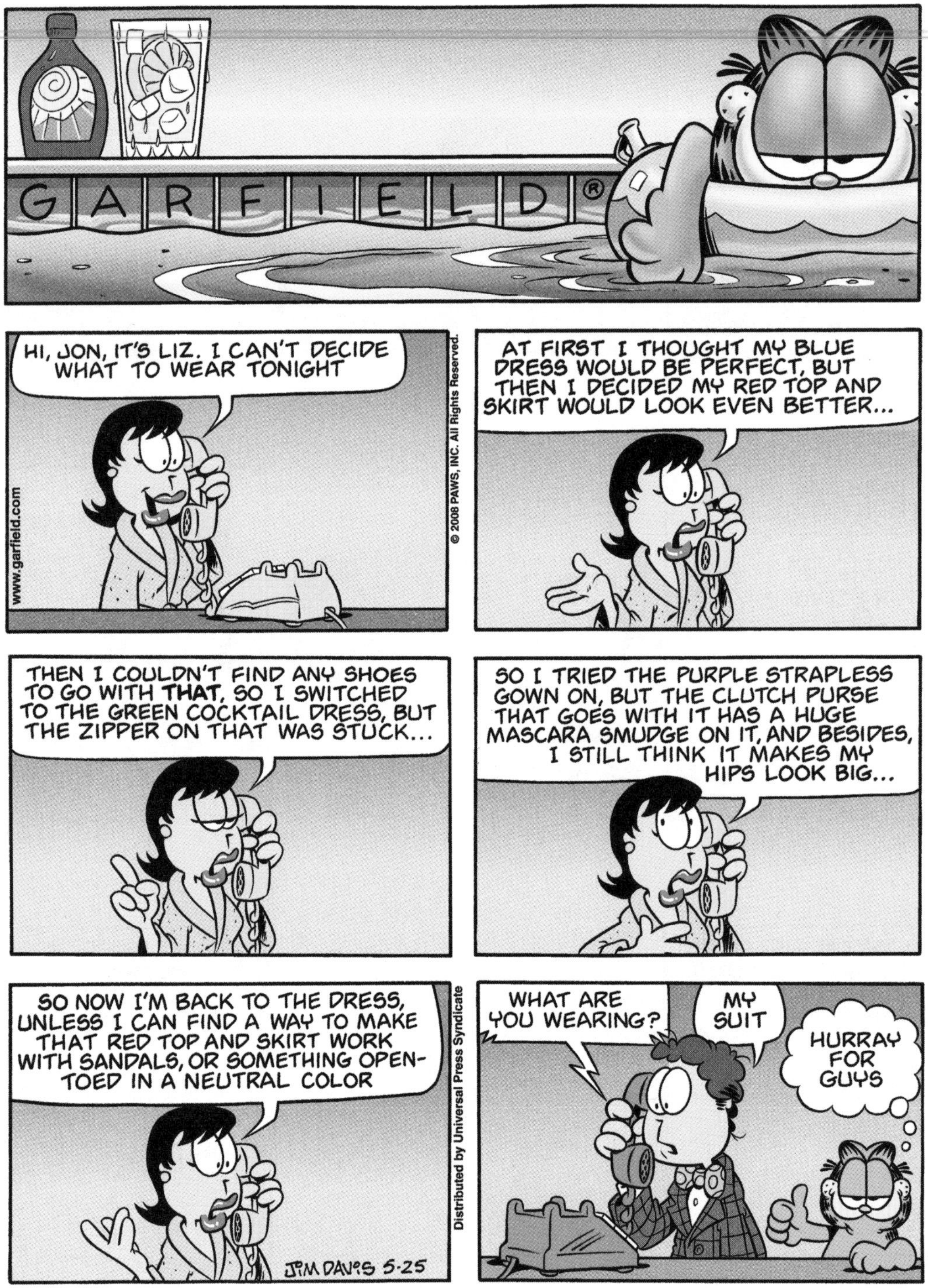
GARFIELD®
HI, JON, IT'S LIZ. I CAN'T DECIDE WHAT TO WEAR TONIGHT
www.garfield.com
© 2008 PAWS, INC. All Rights Reserved.
AT FIRST I THOUGHT MY BLUE DRESS WOULD BE PERFECT, BUT THEN I DECIDED MY RED TOP AND SKIRT WOULD LOOK EVEN BETTER...
THEN I COULDN'T FIND ANY SHOES TO GO WITH THAT, SO I SWITCHED TO THE GREEN COCKTAIL DRESS, BUT THE ZIPPER ON THAT WAS STUCK...
SO I TRIED THE PURPLE STRAPLESS GOWN ON, BUT THE CLUTCH PURSE THAT GOES WITH IT HAS A HUGE MASCARA SMUDGE ON IT, AND BESIDES, I STILL THINK IT MAKES MY HIPS LOOK BIG...
SO NOW I'M BACK TO THE DRESS, UNLESS I CAN FIND A WAY TO MAKE THAT RED TOP AND SKIRT WORK WITH SANDALS, OR SOMETHING OPEN-TOED IN A NEUTRAL COLOR
JIM DAVIS 5-25
Distributed by Universal Press Syndicate
WHAT ARE YOU WEARING?
MY SUIT
HURRAY FOR GUYS

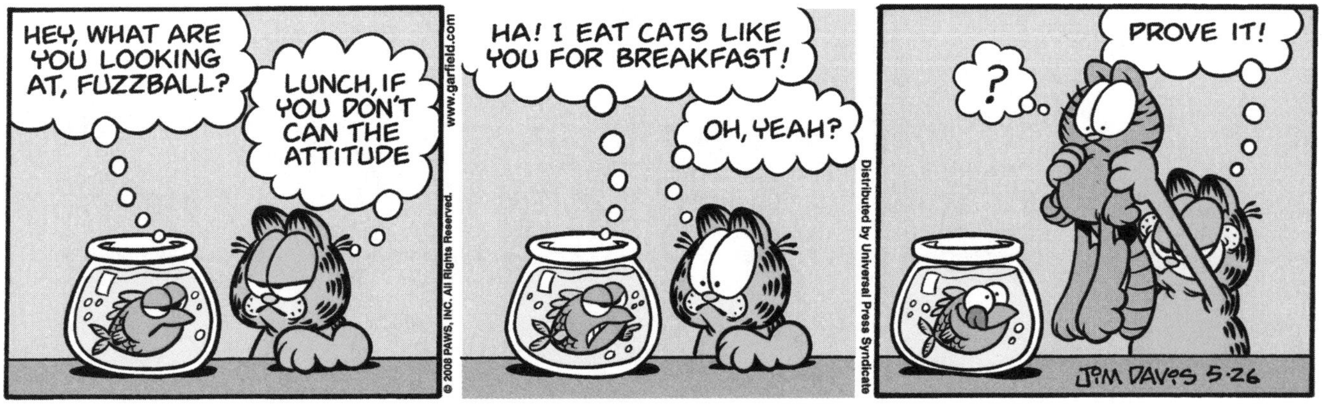
HEY, WHAT ARE YOU LOOKING AT, FUZZBALL?
LUNCH, IF YOU DON'T CAN THE ATTITUDE
© 2008 PAWS, INC. All Rights Reserved. www.garfield.com
HA! I EAT CATS LIKE YOU FOR BREAKFAST!
OH, YEAH?
Distributed by Universal Press Syndicate
?
PROVE IT!
JIM DAVIS 5-26

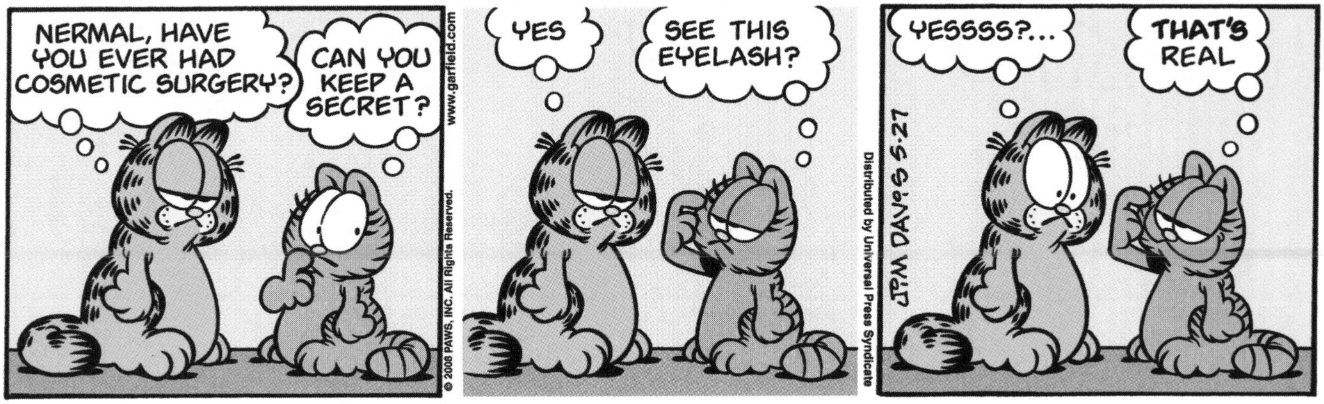
NERMAL, HAVE YOU EVER HAD COSMETIC SURGERY?
CAN YOU KEEP A SECRET?
© 2008 PAWS, INC. All Rights Reserved. www.garfield.com
YES
SEE THIS EYELASH?
Distributed by Universal Press Syndicate
JIM DAVIS 5-27
YESSSS?...
THAT'S REAL

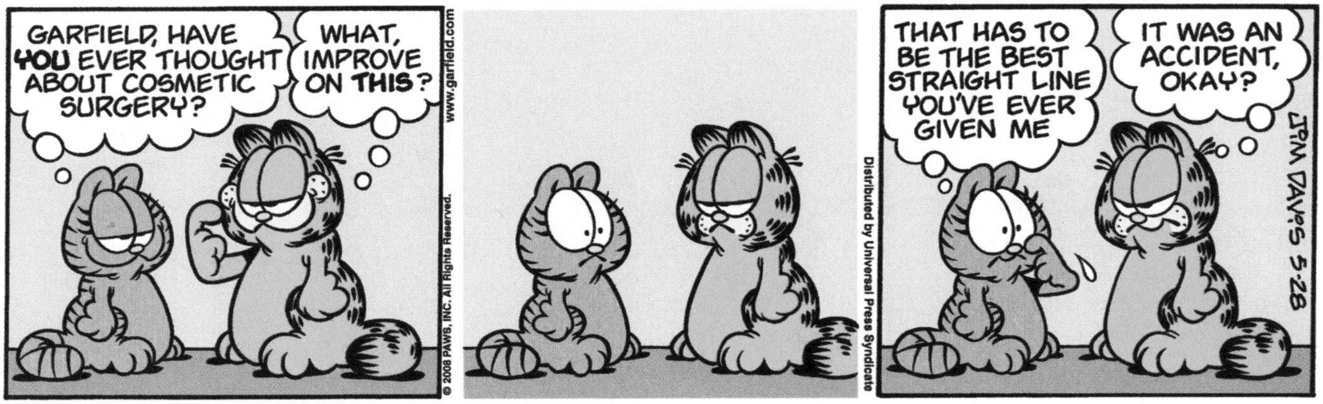
GARFIELD, HAVE **YOU** EVER THOUGHT ABOUT COSMETIC SURGERY?
WHAT, IMPROVE ON **THIS**?
© 2008 PAWS, INC. All Rights Reserved. www.garfield.com
Distributed by Universal Press Syndicate
THAT HAS TO BE THE BEST STRAIGHT LINE YOU'VE EVER GIVEN ME
IT WAS AN ACCIDENT, OKAY?
JIM DAVIS 5-28

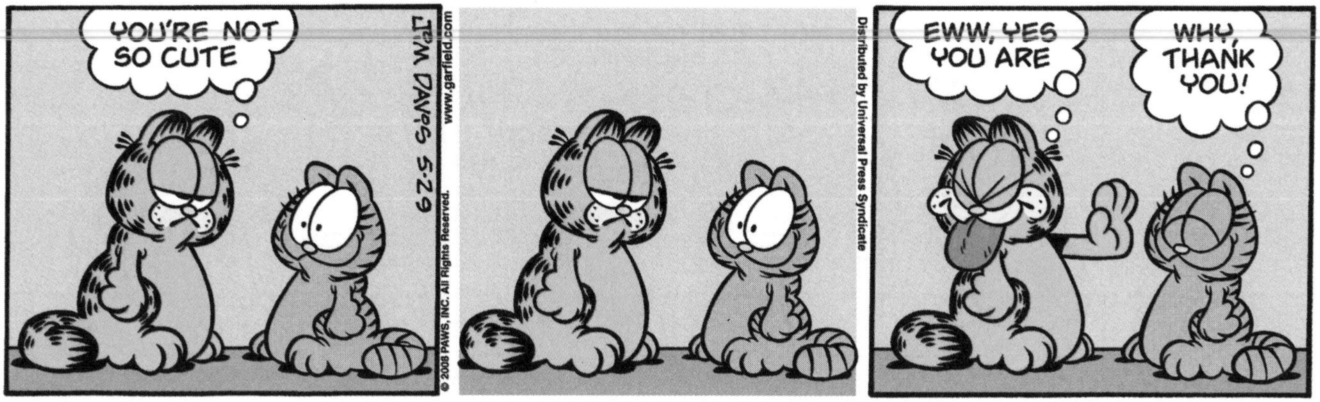
YOU'RE NOT SO CUTE
JIM DAVIS 5-29
www.garfield.com
© 2008 PAWS, INC. All Rights Reserved.
Distributed by Universal Press Syndicate
EWW, YES YOU ARE
WHY, THANK YOU!

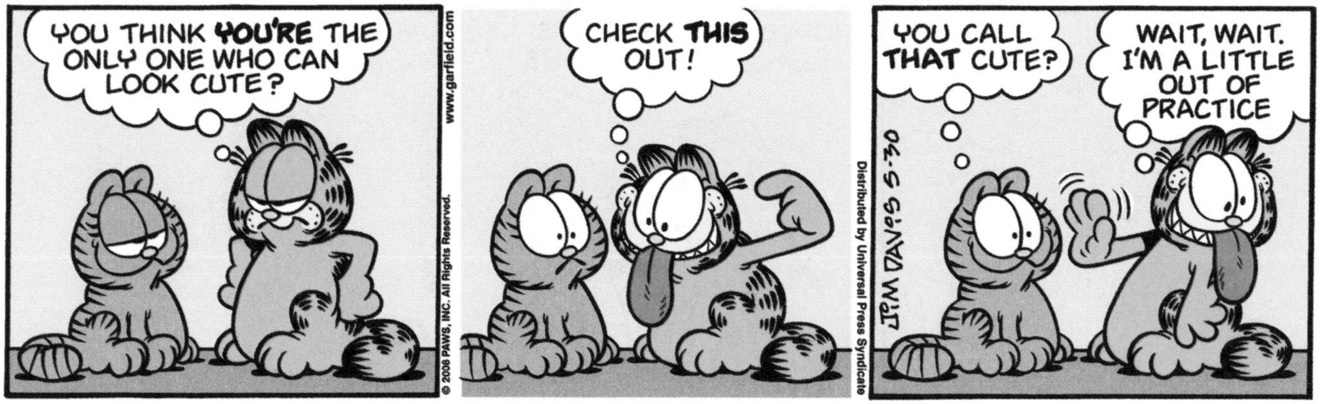
YOU THINK **YOU'RE** THE ONLY ONE WHO CAN LOOK CUTE?
www.garfield.com
© 2008 PAWS, INC. All Rights Reserved.
CHECK **THIS** OUT!
Distributed by Universal Press Syndicate
YOU CALL **THAT** CUTE?
WAIT, WAIT. I'M A LITTLE OUT OF PRACTICE
JIM DAVIS 5-30

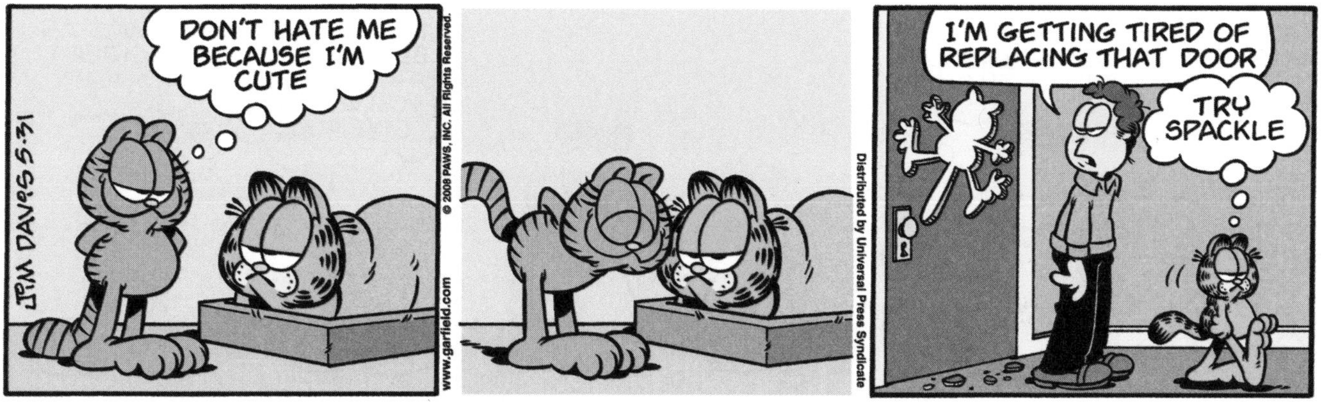
DON'T HATE ME BECAUSE I'M CUTE
JIM DAVIS 5-31
© 2008 PAWS, INC. All Rights Reserved.
www.garfield.com
Distributed by Universal Press Syndicate
I'M GETTING TIRED OF REPLACING THAT DOOR
TRY SPACKLE

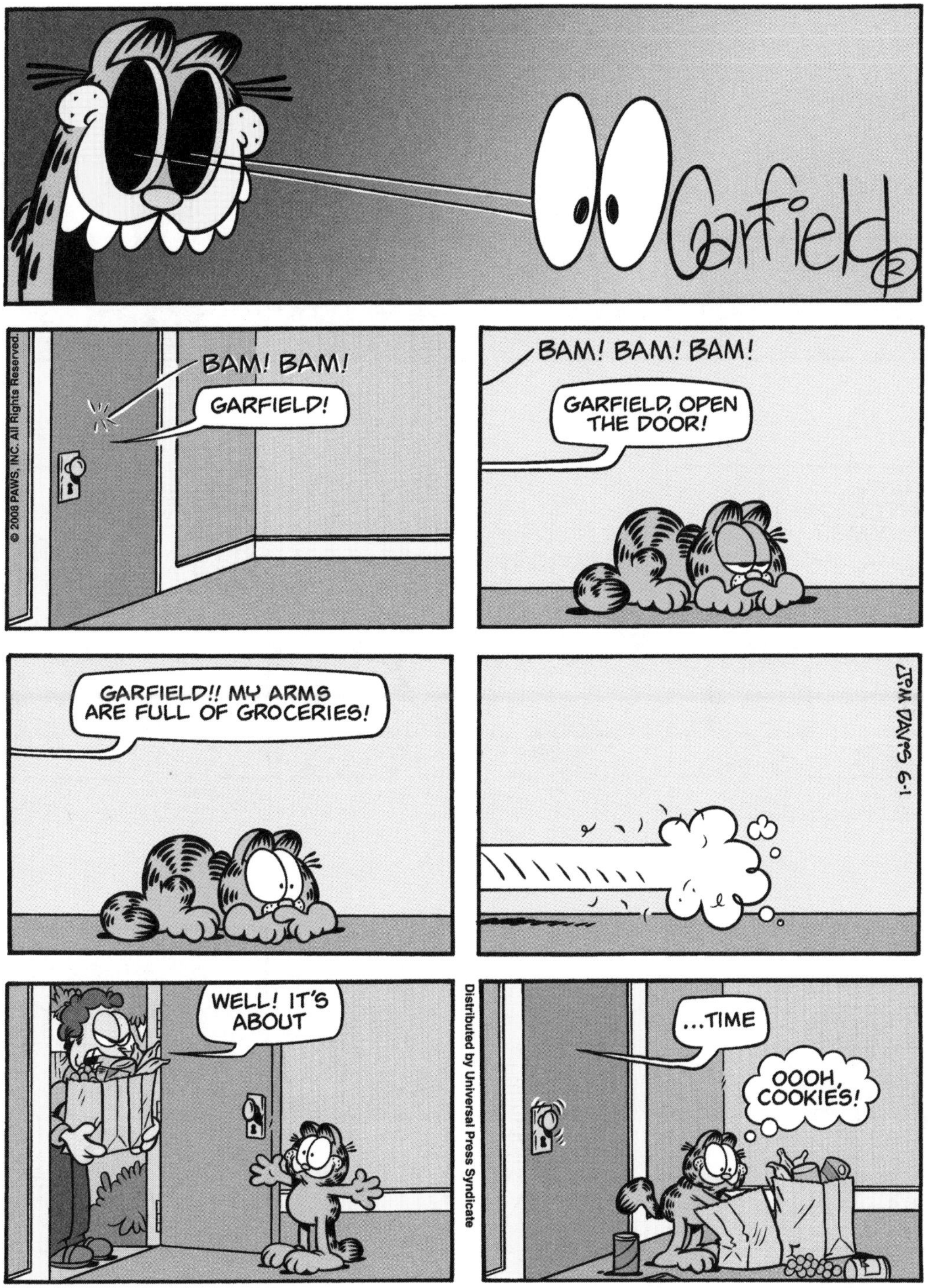
Garfield
© 2008 PAWS, INC. All Rights Reserved.
BAM! BAM!
GARFIELD!
BAM! BAM! BAM!
GARFIELD, OPEN THE DOOR!
GARFIELD!! MY ARMS ARE FULL OF GROCERIES!
JPM DAVPS 6-1
Distributed by Universal Press Syndicate
WELL! IT'S ABOUT
...TIME
OOOH, COOKIES!

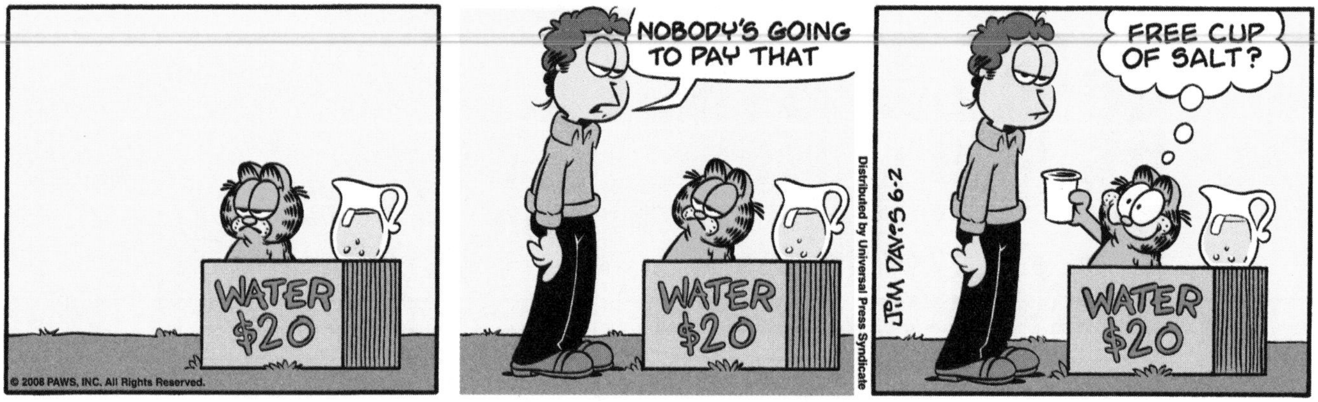
WATER $20
© 2008 PAWS, INC. All Rights Reserved.
NOBODY'S GOING TO PAY THAT
Distributed by Universal Press Syndicate
JIM DAVIS 6-2
FREE CUP OF SALT?

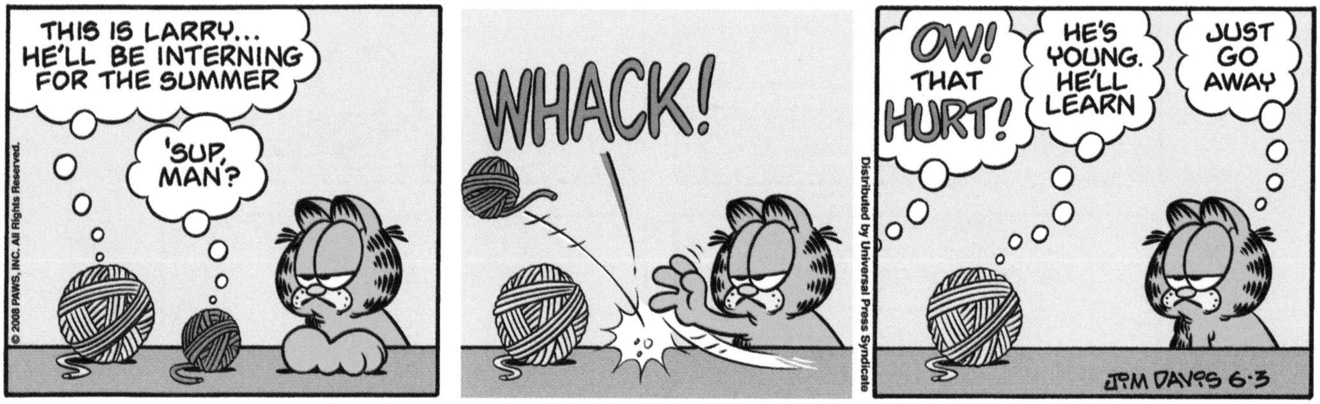
© 2008 PAWS, INC. All Rights Reserved.
THIS IS LARRY... HE'LL BE INTERNING FOR THE SUMMER
'SUP, MAN?
WHACK!
Distributed by Universal Press Syndicate
OW! THAT HURT!
HE'S YOUNG. HE'LL LEARN
JUST GO AWAY
JIM DAVIS 6-3

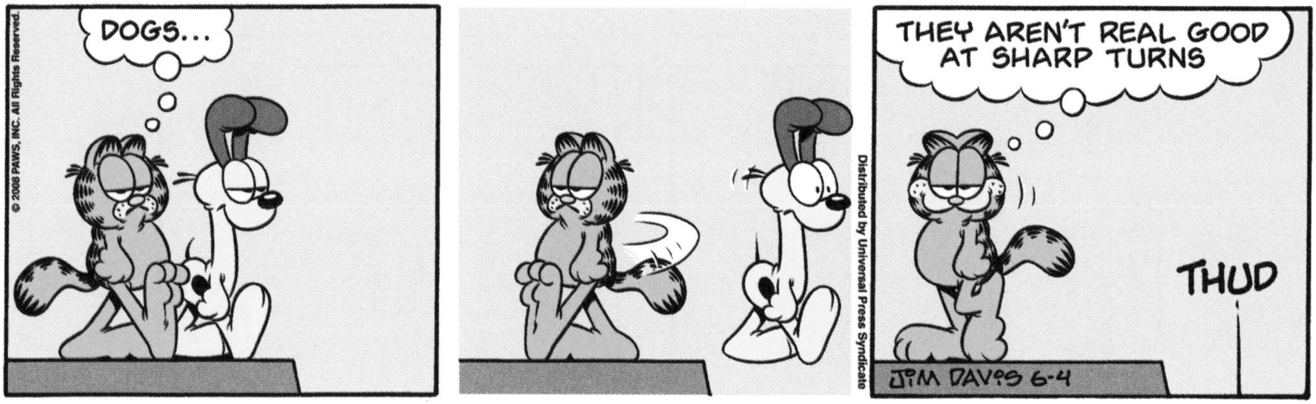
© 2008 PAWS, INC. All Rights Reserved.
DOGS...
Distributed by Universal Press Syndicate
THEY AREN'T REAL GOOD AT SHARP TURNS
THUD
JIM DAVIS 6-4

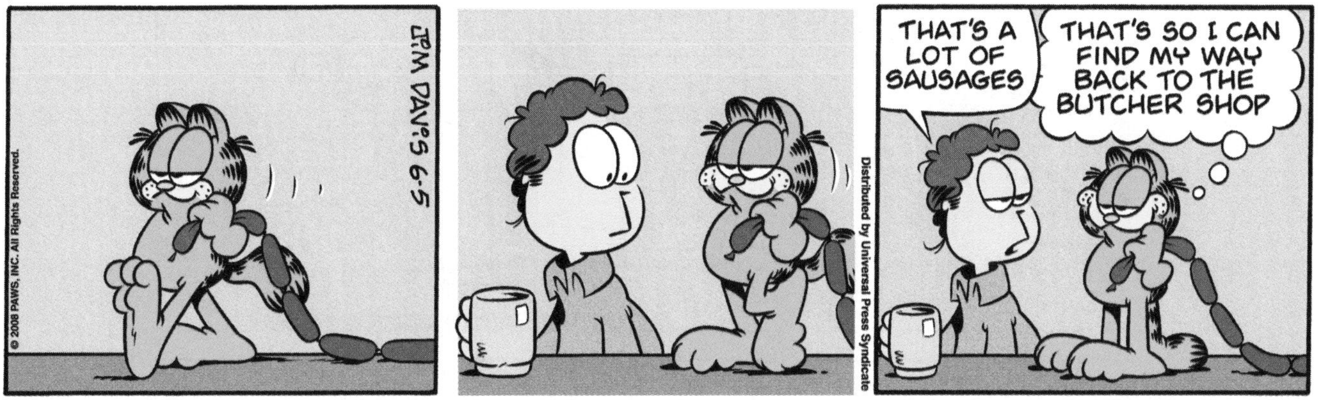
© 2008 PAWS, INC. All Rights Reserved.
JIM DAVIS 6-5
Distributed by Universal Press Syndicate
THAT'S A LOT OF SAUSAGES
THAT'S SO I CAN FIND MY WAY BACK TO THE BUTCHER SHOP

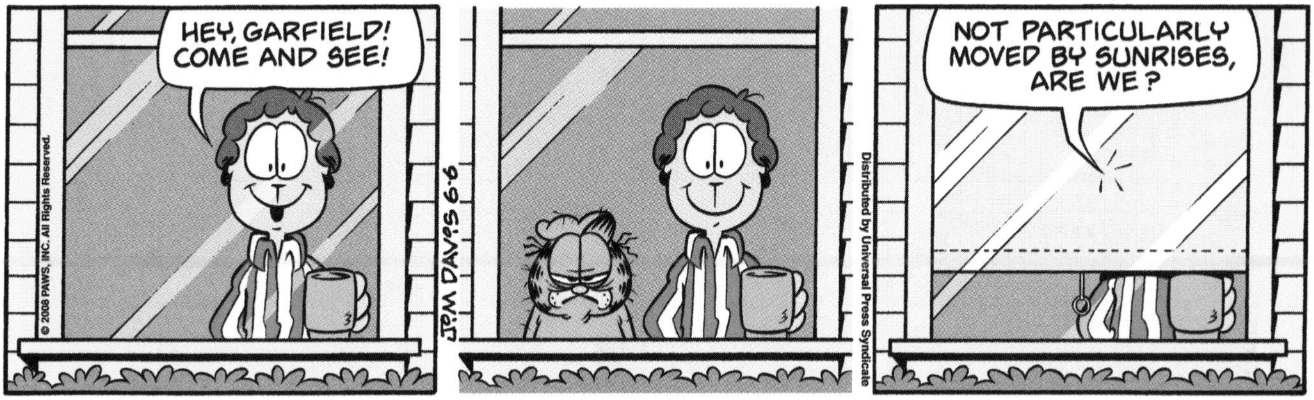
HEY, GARFIELD! COME AND SEE!
© 2008 PAWS, INC. All Rights Reserved.
JIM DAVIS 6-6
Distributed by Universal Press Syndicate
NOT PARTICULARLY MOVED BY SUNRISES, ARE WE?

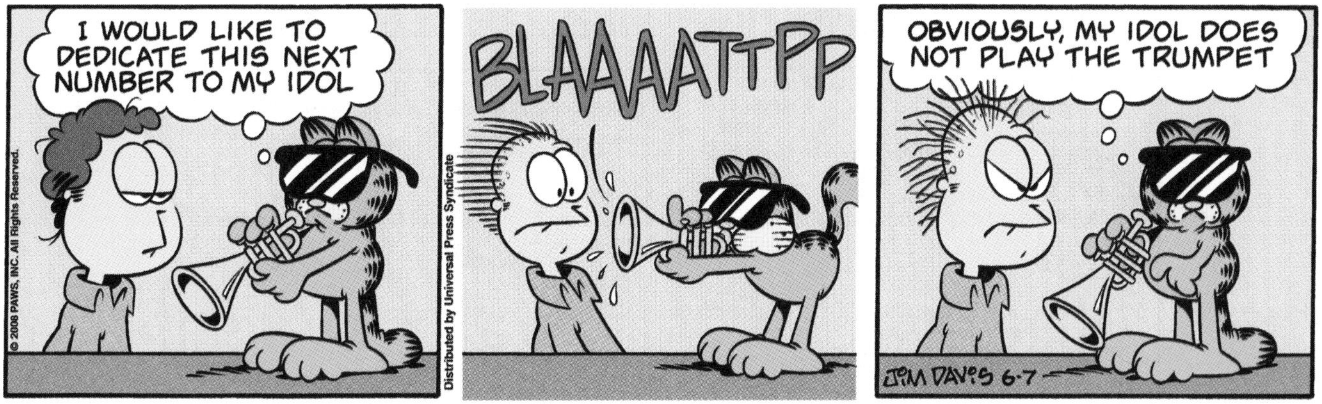
I WOULD LIKE TO DEDICATE THIS NEXT NUMBER TO MY IDOL
© 2008 PAWS, INC. All Rights Reserved.
Distributed by Universal Press Syndicate
BLAAAAATTPP
OBVIOUSLY, MY IDOL DOES NOT PLAY THE TRUMPET
JIM DAVIS 6-7

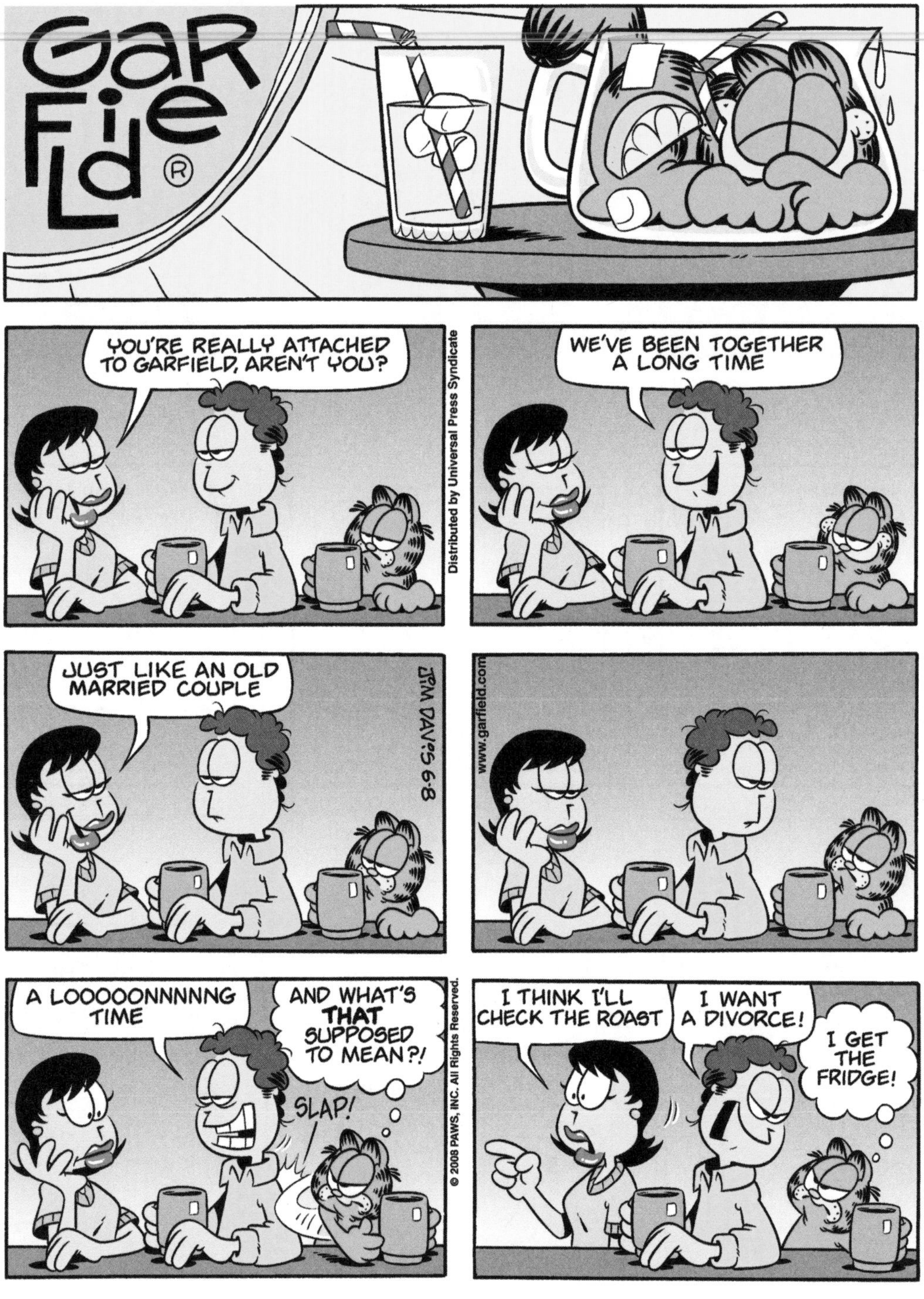
GARFIELD®
YOU'RE REALLY ATTACHED TO GARFIELD, AREN'T YOU?
WE'VE BEEN TOGETHER A LONG TIME
JUST LIKE AN OLD MARRIED COUPLE
A LOOOOONNNNNG TIME
AND WHAT'S THAT SUPPOSED TO MEAN?!
SLAP!
I THINK I'LL CHECK THE ROAST
I WANT A DIVORCE!
I GET THE FRIDGE!
JPM DAVIS 6-8
Distributed by Universal Press Syndicate
www.garfield.com
© 2008 PAWS, INC. All Rights Reserved.

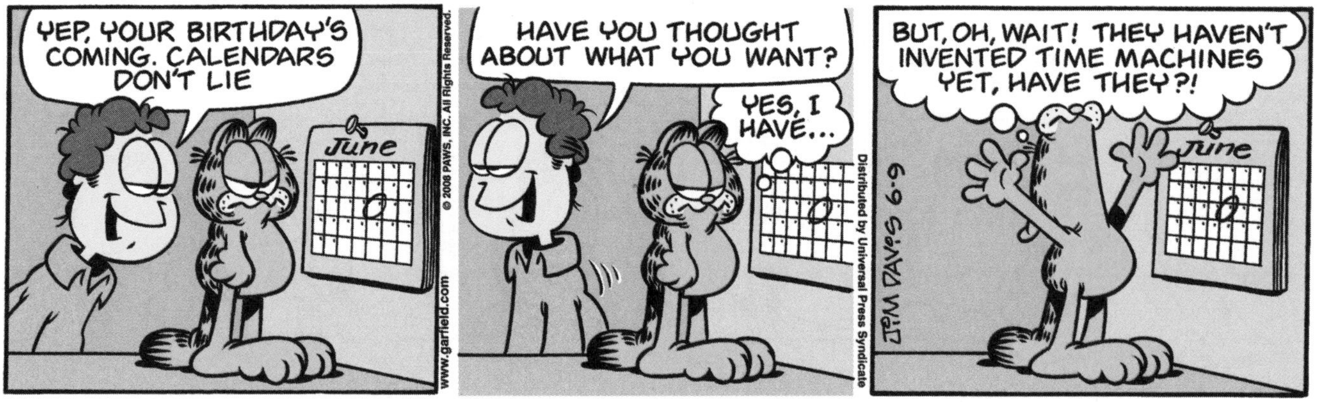
YEP, YOUR BIRTHDAY'S COMING. CALENDARS DON'T LIE
June
HAVE YOU THOUGHT ABOUT WHAT YOU WANT?
YES, I HAVE...
BUT, OH, WAIT! THEY HAVEN'T INVENTED TIME MACHINES YET, HAVE THEY?!
June
JIM DAVIS 6-9
© 2008 PAWS, INC. All Rights Reserved. www.garfield.com
Distributed by Universal Press Syndicate

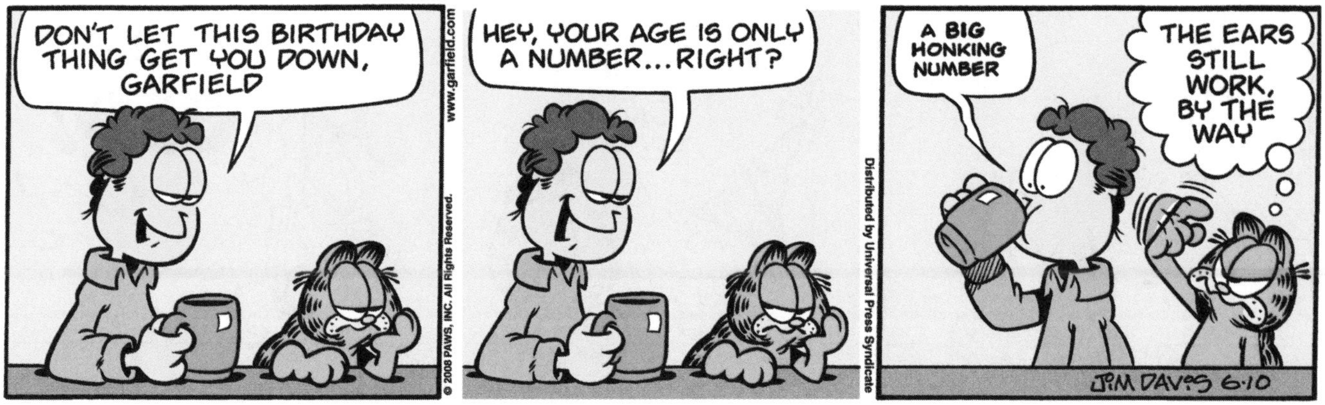
DON'T LET THIS BIRTHDAY THING GET YOU DOWN, GARFIELD
HEY, YOUR AGE IS ONLY A NUMBER... RIGHT?
A BIG HONKING NUMBER
THE EARS STILL WORK, BY THE WAY
JIM DAVIS 6-10
© 2008 PAWS, INC. All Rights Reserved. www.garfield.com
Distributed by Universal Press Syndicate

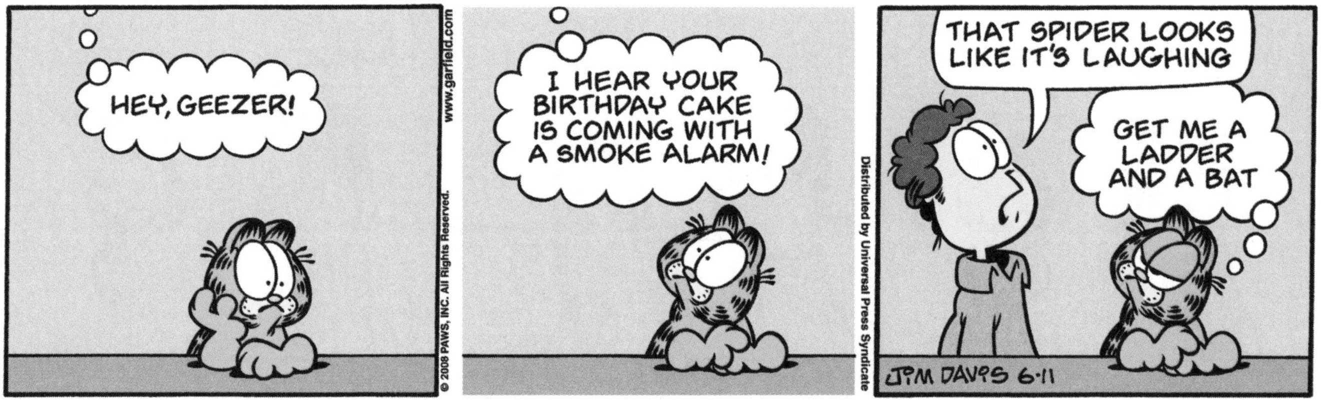
HEY, GEEZER!
I HEAR YOUR BIRTHDAY CAKE IS COMING WITH A SMOKE ALARM!
THAT SPIDER LOOKS LIKE IT'S LAUGHING
GET ME A LADDER AND A BAT
JIM DAVIS 6-11
© 2008 PAWS, INC. All Rights Reserved. www.garfield.com
Distributed by Universal Press Syndicate

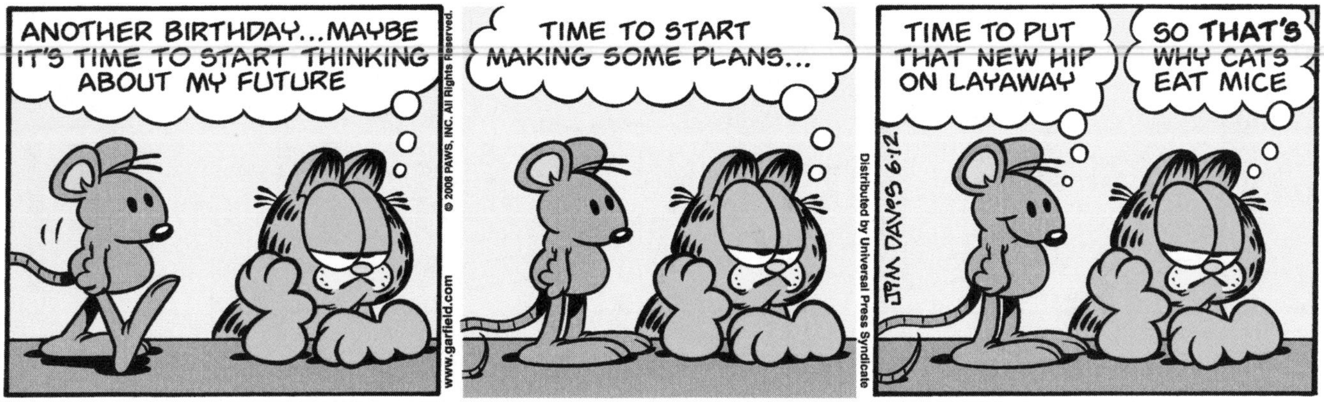
ANOTHER BIRTHDAY...MAYBE IT'S TIME TO START THINKING ABOUT MY FUTURE
TIME TO START MAKING SOME PLANS...
TIME TO PUT THAT NEW HIP ON LAYAWAY
SO THAT'S WHY CATS EAT MICE
JIM DAVIS 6·12
© 2008 PAWS, INC. All Rights Reserved.
www.garfield.com
Distributed by Universal Press Syndicate

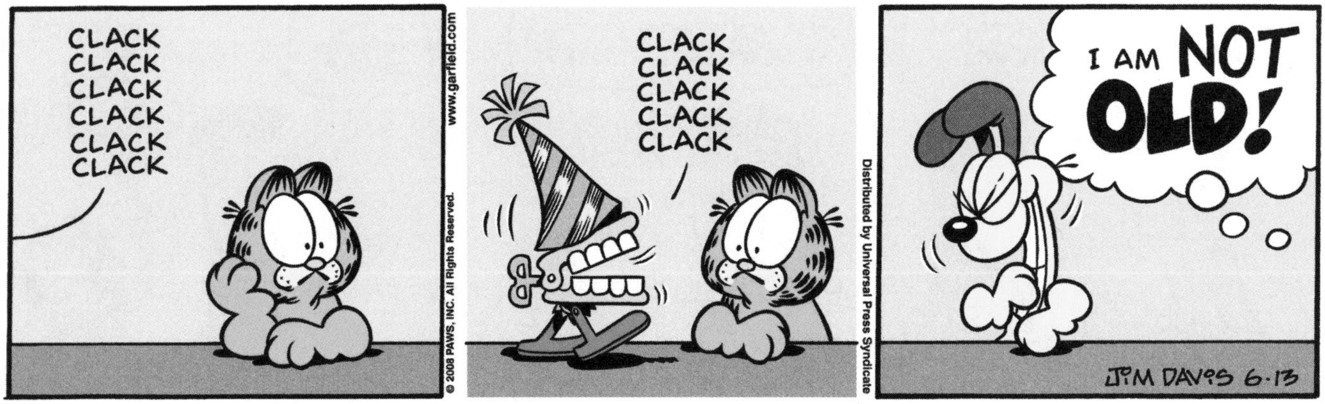
CLACK CLACK CLACK CLACK CLACK CLACK
CLACK CLACK CLACK CLACK CLACK
I AM NOT OLD!
JIM DAVIS 6·13
© 2008 PAWS, INC. All Rights Reserved.
www.garfield.com
Distributed by Universal Press Syndicate

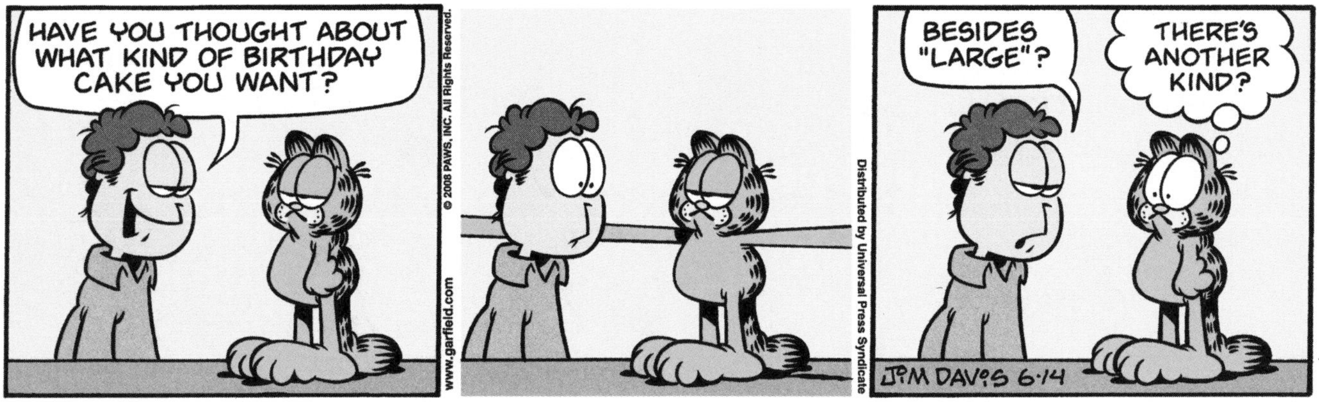
HAVE YOU THOUGHT ABOUT WHAT KIND OF BIRTHDAY CAKE YOU WANT?
BESIDES "LARGE"?
THERE'S ANOTHER KIND?
JIM DAVIS 6·14
© 2008 PAWS, INC. All Rights Reserved.
www.garfield.com
Distributed by Universal Press Syndicate

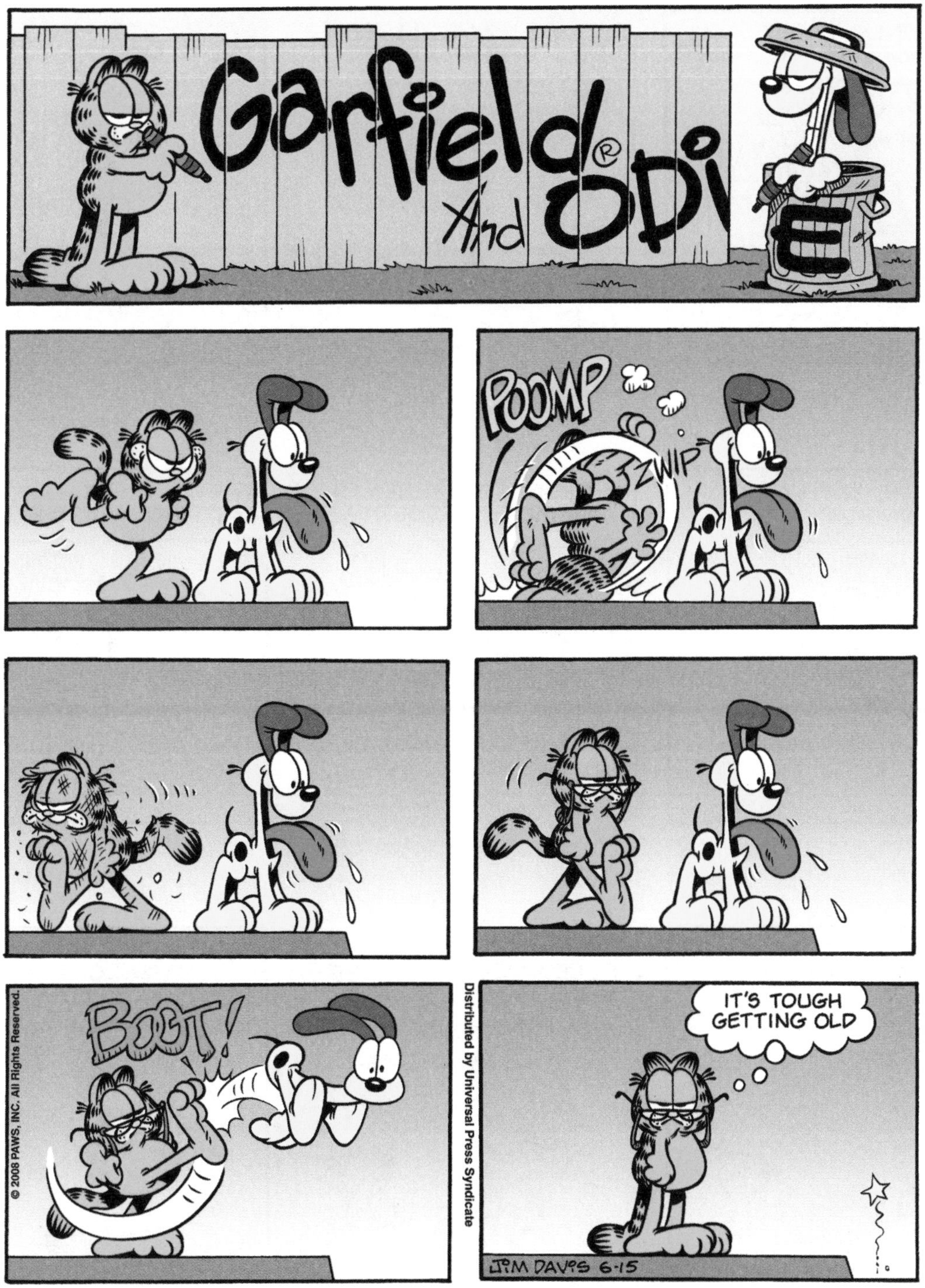
Garfield® And ODIE
POOMP
ZWIP
BOOT!
IT'S TOUGH GETTING OLD
JIM DAVIS 6-15
© 2008 PAWS, INC. All Rights Reserved.
Distributed by Universal Press Syndicate

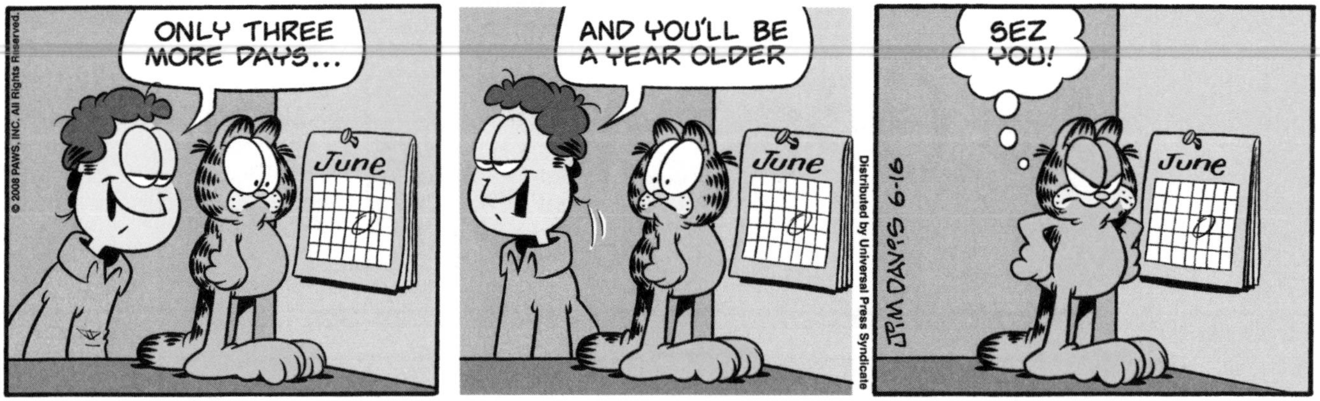
© 2008 PAWS, INC. All Rights Reserved.
ONLY THREE MORE DAYS...
AND YOU'LL BE A YEAR OLDER
Distributed by Universal Press Syndicate
June
SEZ YOU!
JIM DAVIS 6-16

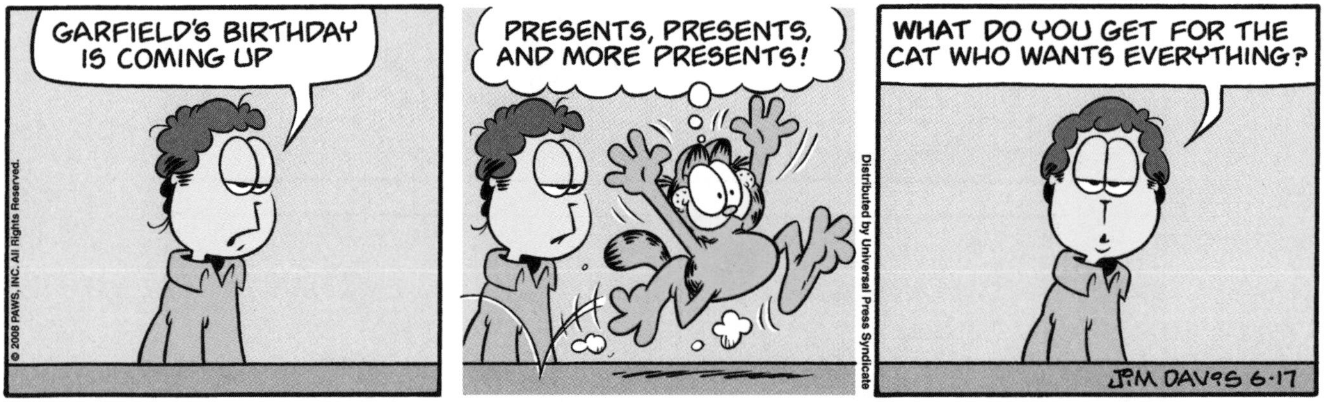
© 2008 PAWS, INC. All Rights Reserved.
GARFIELD'S BIRTHDAY IS COMING UP
PRESENTS, PRESENTS, AND MORE PRESENTS!
Distributed by Universal Press Syndicate
WHAT DO YOU GET FOR THE CAT WHO WANTS EVERYTHING?
JIM DAVIS 6-17

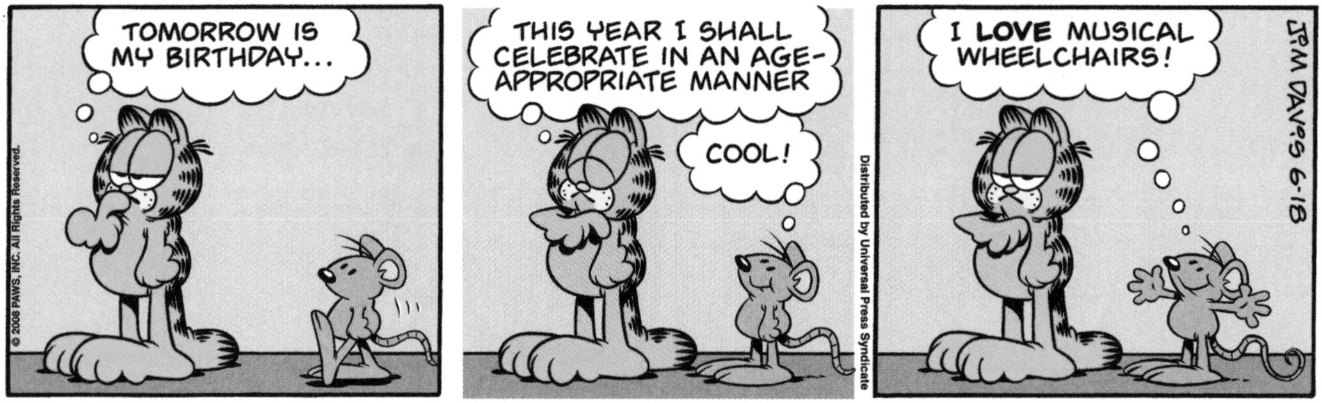
© 2008 PAWS, INC. All Rights Reserved.
TOMORROW IS MY BIRTHDAY...
THIS YEAR I SHALL CELEBRATE IN AN AGE-APPROPRIATE MANNER
COOL!
Distributed by Universal Press Syndicate
I **LOVE** MUSICAL WHEELCHAIRS!
JIM DAVIS 6-18

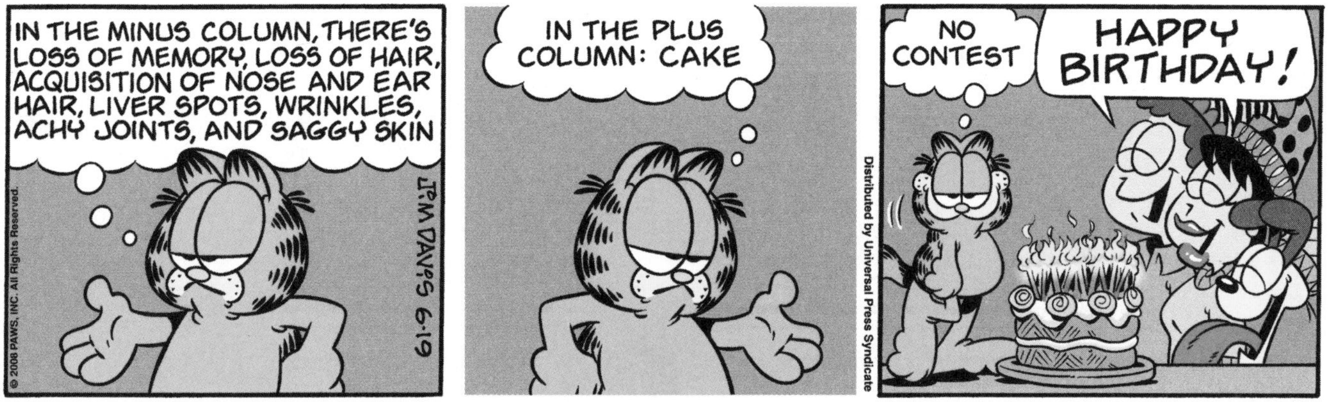
IN THE MINUS COLUMN, THERE'S LOSS OF MEMORY, LOSS OF HAIR, ACQUISITION OF NOSE AND EAR HAIR, LIVER SPOTS, WRINKLES, ACHY JOINTS, AND SAGGY SKIN
JIM DAVIS 6-19
© 2008 PAWS, INC. All Rights Reserved.
IN THE PLUS COLUMN: CAKE
NO CONTEST
HAPPY BIRTHDAY!
Distributed by Universal Press Syndicate

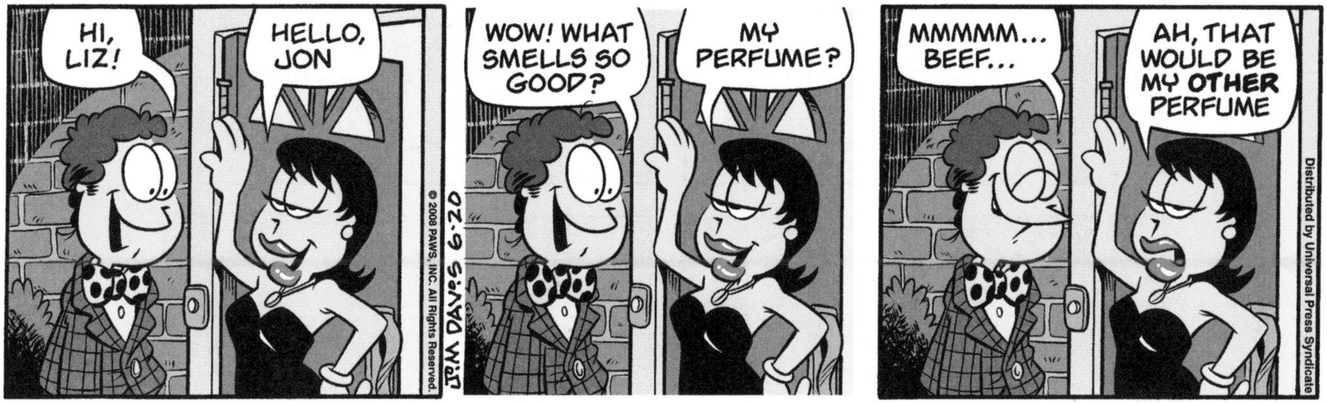
HI, LIZ!
HELLO, JON
JIM DAVIS 6-20
© 2008 PAWS, INC. All Rights Reserved.
WOW! WHAT SMELLS SO GOOD?
MY PERFUME?
MMMMM... BEEF...
AH, THAT WOULD BE MY **OTHER** PERFUME
Distributed by Universal Press Syndicate

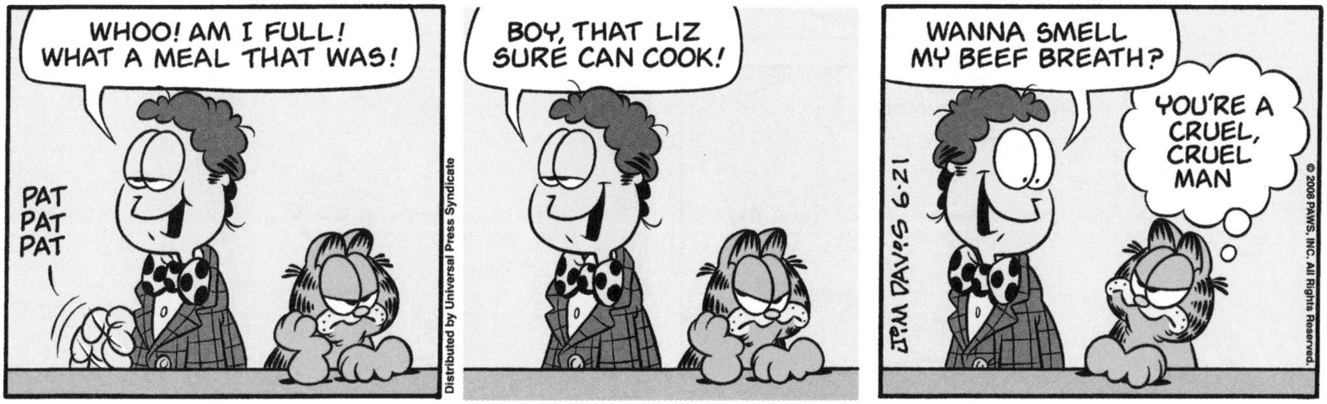
WHOO! AM I FULL! WHAT A MEAL THAT WAS!
PAT PAT PAT
Distributed by Universal Press Syndicate
BOY, THAT LIZ SURE CAN COOK!
WANNA SMELL MY BEEF BREATH?
YOU'RE A CRUEL, CRUEL MAN
JIM DAVIS 6-21
© 2008 PAWS, INC. All Rights Reserved.

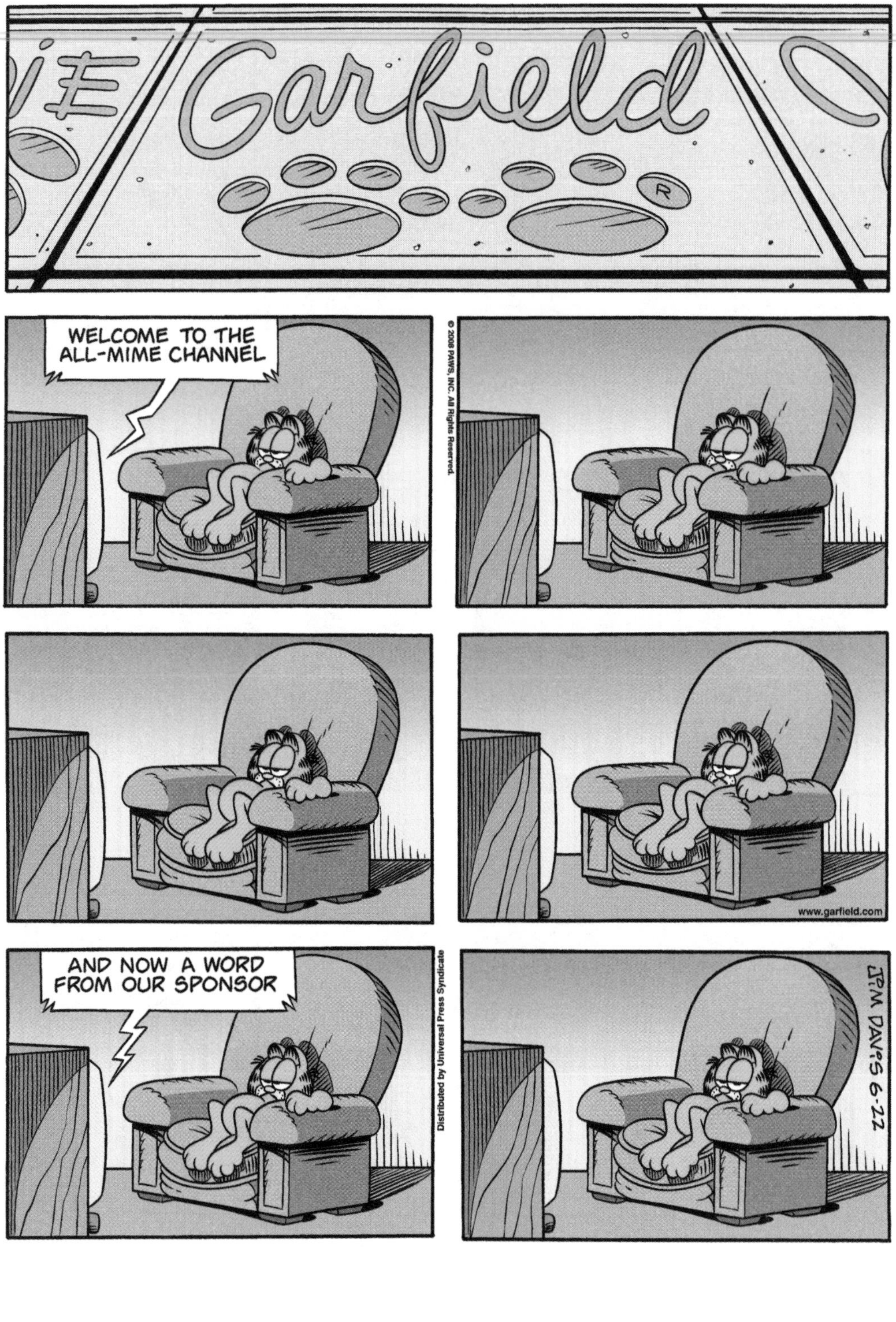
Garfield
WELCOME TO THE ALL-MIME CHANNEL
© 2008 PAWS, INC. All Rights Reserved.
www.garfield.com
AND NOW A WORD FROM OUR SPONSOR
Distributed by Universal Press Syndicate
JPM DAVIS 6-22

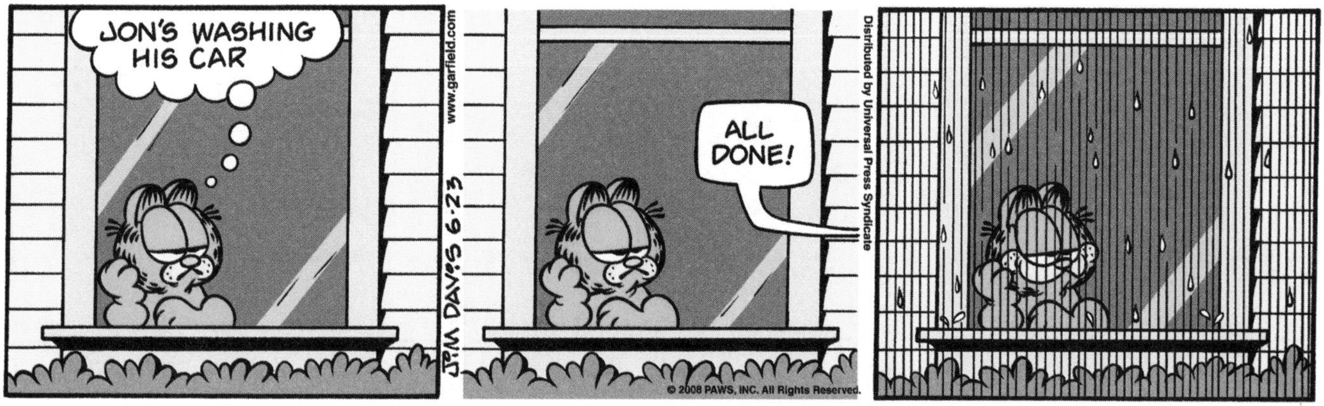
JON'S WASHING HIS CAR
ALL DONE!
JIM DAVIS 6-23
www.garfield.com
Distributed by Universal Press Syndicate
© 2008 PAWS, INC. All Rights Reserved.

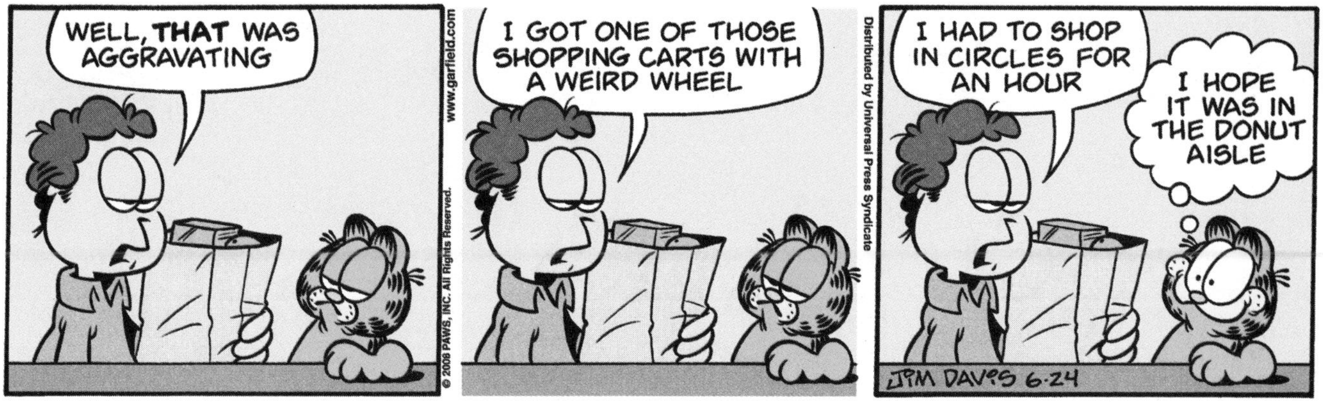
WELL, **THAT** WAS AGGRAVATING
I GOT ONE OF THOSE SHOPPING CARTS WITH A WEIRD WHEEL
I HAD TO SHOP IN CIRCLES FOR AN HOUR
I HOPE IT WAS IN THE DONUT AISLE
JIM DAVIS 6-24
www.garfield.com
© 2008 PAWS, INC. All Rights Reserved.
Distributed by Universal Press Syndicate

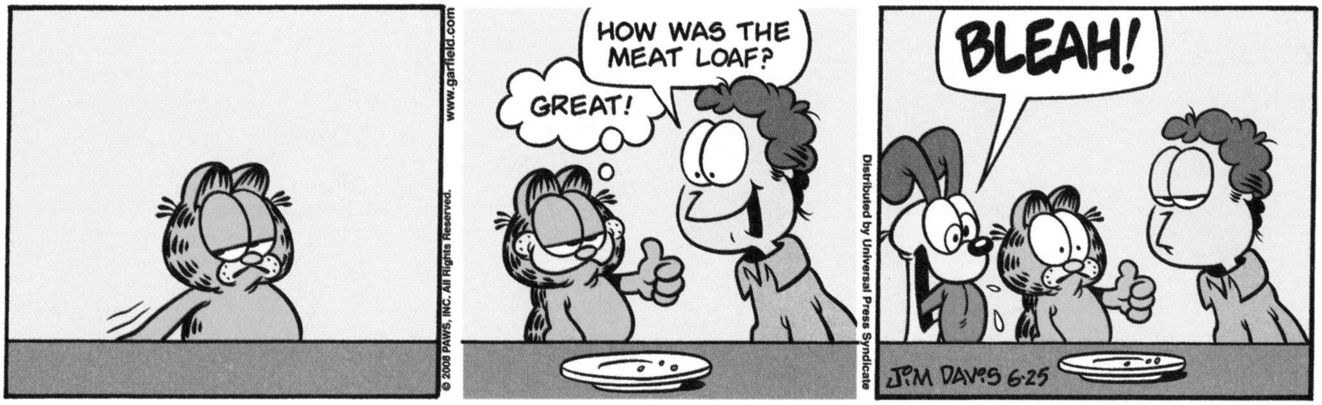
HOW WAS THE MEAT LOAF?
GREAT!
BLEAH!
JIM DAVIS 6-25
www.garfield.com
© 2008 PAWS, INC. All Rights Reserved.
Distributed by Universal Press Syndicate

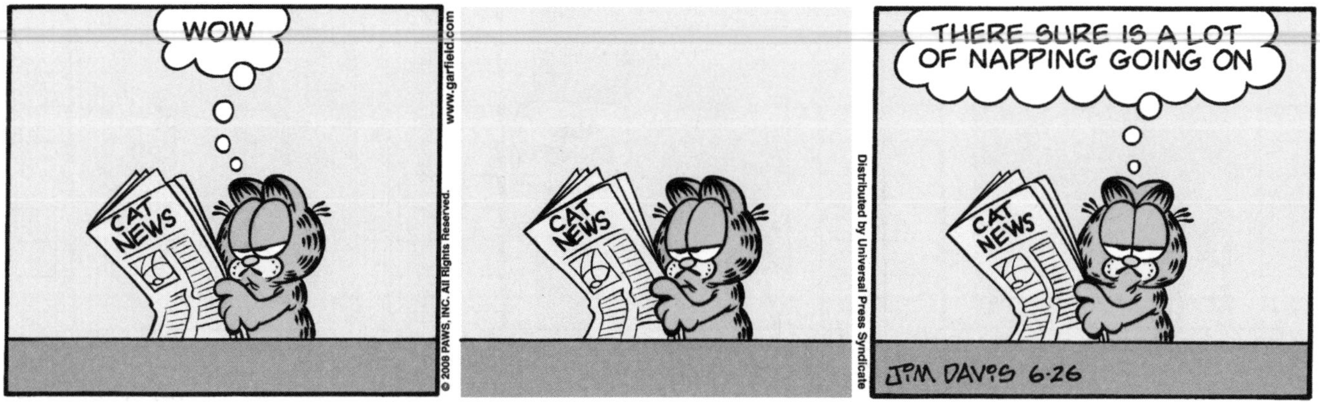
WOW
CAT NEWS
www.garfield.com
© 2008 PAWS, INC. All Rights Reserved.
Distributed by Universal Press Syndicate
THERE SURE IS A LOT OF NAPPING GOING ON
JIM DAVIS 6-26

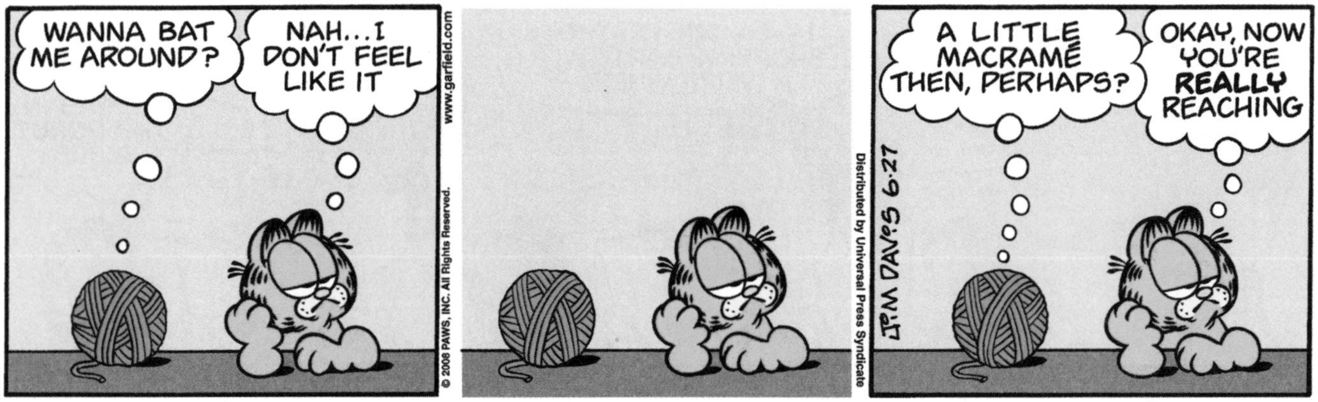
WANNA BAT ME AROUND?
NAH...I DON'T FEEL LIKE IT
www.garfield.com
© 2008 PAWS, INC. All Rights Reserved.
Distributed by Universal Press Syndicate
JIM DAVIS 6-27
A LITTLE MACRAMÉ THEN, PERHAPS?
OKAY, NOW YOU'RE **REALLY** REACHING

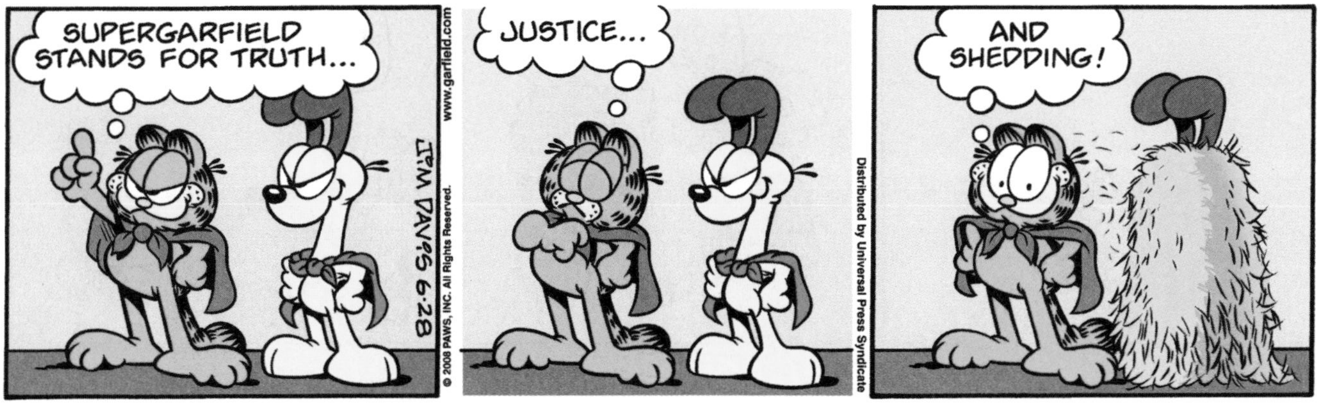
SUPERGARFIELD STANDS FOR TRUTH...
JIM DAVIS 6-28
www.garfield.com
© 2008 PAWS, INC. All Rights Reserved.
JUSTICE...
Distributed by Universal Press Syndicate
AND SHEDDING!

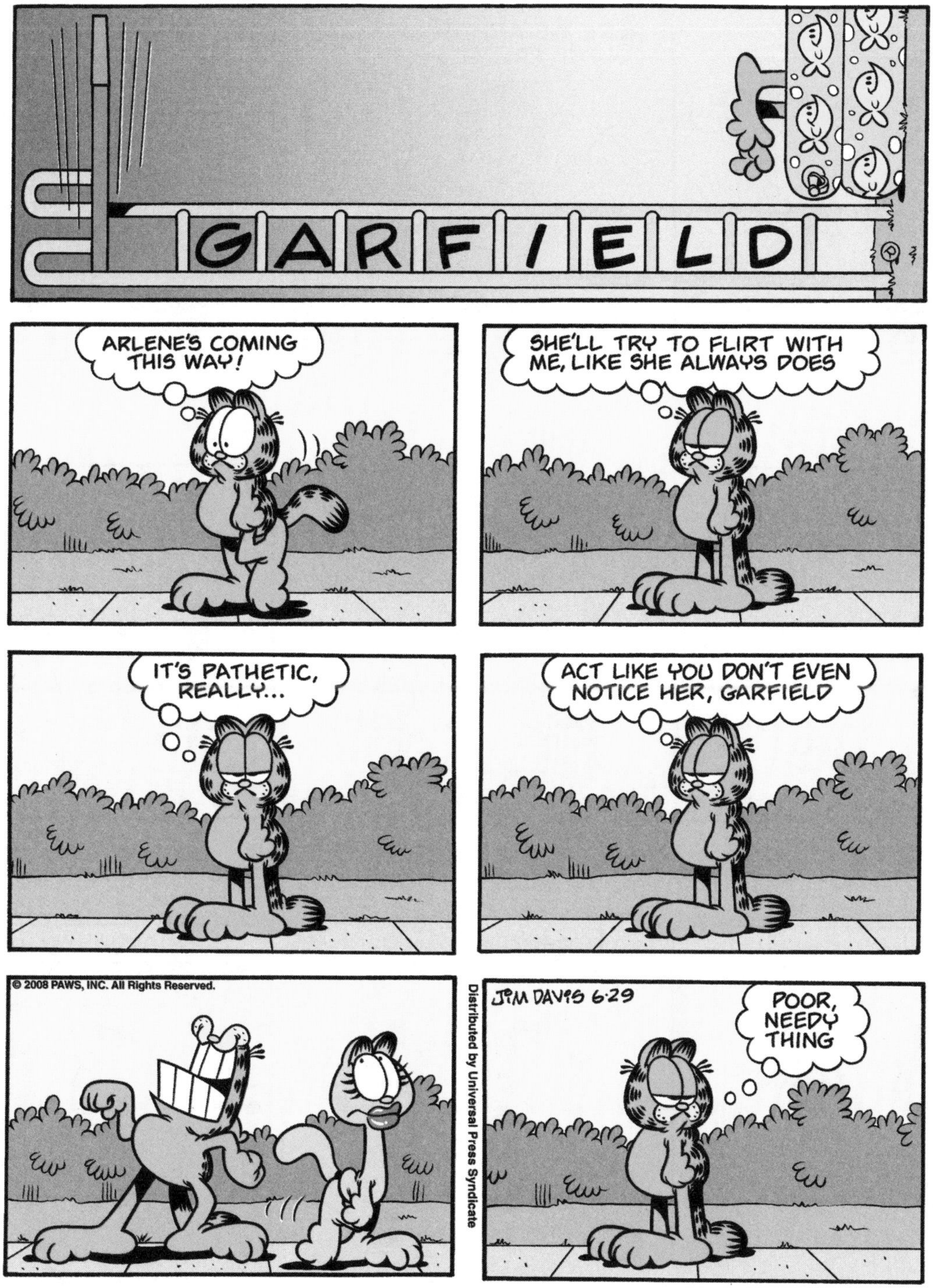
GARFIELD
ARLENE'S COMING THIS WAY!
SHE'LL TRY TO FLIRT WITH ME, LIKE SHE ALWAYS DOES
IT'S PATHETIC, REALLY...
ACT LIKE YOU DON'T EVEN NOTICE HER, GARFIELD
© 2008 PAWS, INC. All Rights Reserved.
Distributed by Universal Press Syndicate
JIM DAVIS 6·29
POOR, NEEDY THING

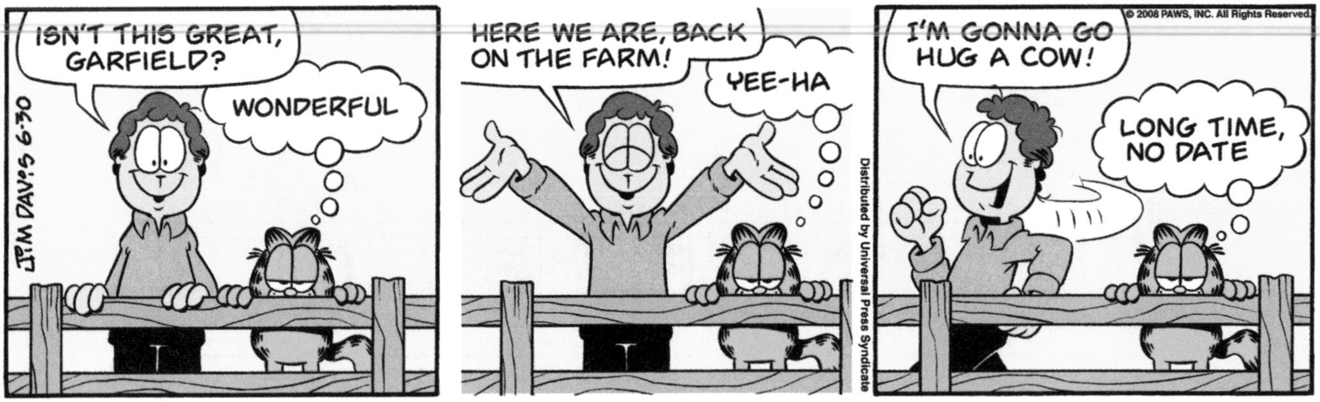
ISN'T THIS GREAT, GARFIELD?
WONDERFUL
HERE WE ARE, BACK ON THE FARM!
YEE-HA
I'M GONNA GO HUG A COW!
LONG TIME, NO DATE
JIM DAVIS 6-30
© 2008 PAWS, INC. All Rights Reserved.
Distributed by Universal Press Syndicate

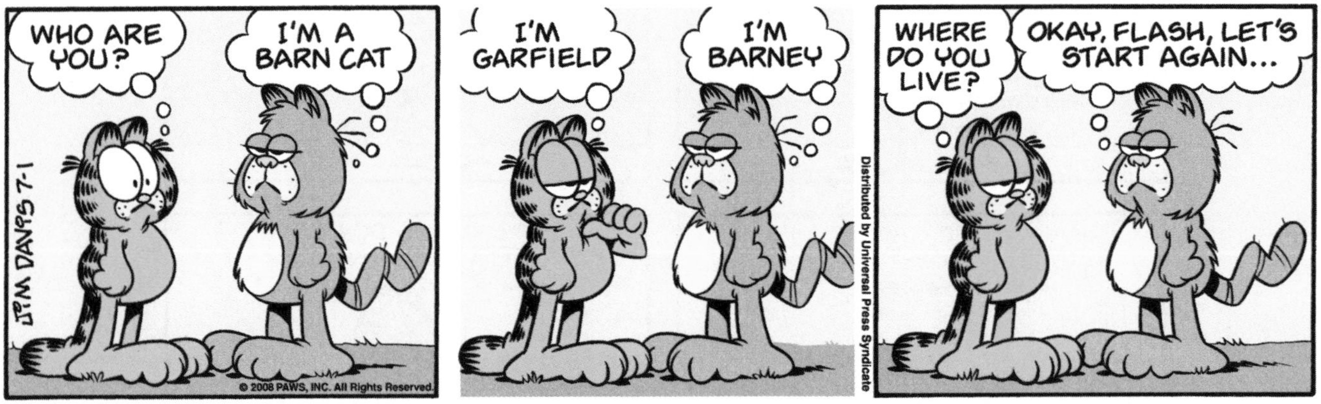
WHO ARE YOU?
I'M A BARN CAT
I'M GARFIELD
I'M BARNEY
WHERE DO YOU LIVE?
OKAY, FLASH, LET'S START AGAIN...
JIM DAVIS 7-1
© 2008 PAWS, INC. All Rights Reserved.
Distributed by Universal Press Syndicate

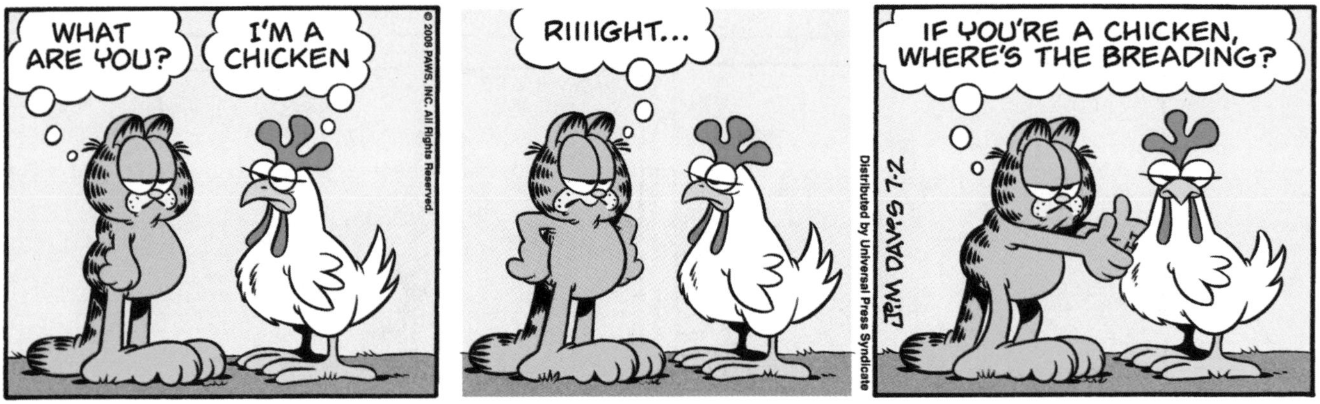
WHAT ARE YOU?
I'M A CHICKEN
RIIIIGHT...
IF YOU'RE A CHICKEN, WHERE'S THE BREADING?
JIM DAVIS 7-2
© 2008 PAWS, INC. All Rights Reserved.
Distributed by Universal Press Syndicate

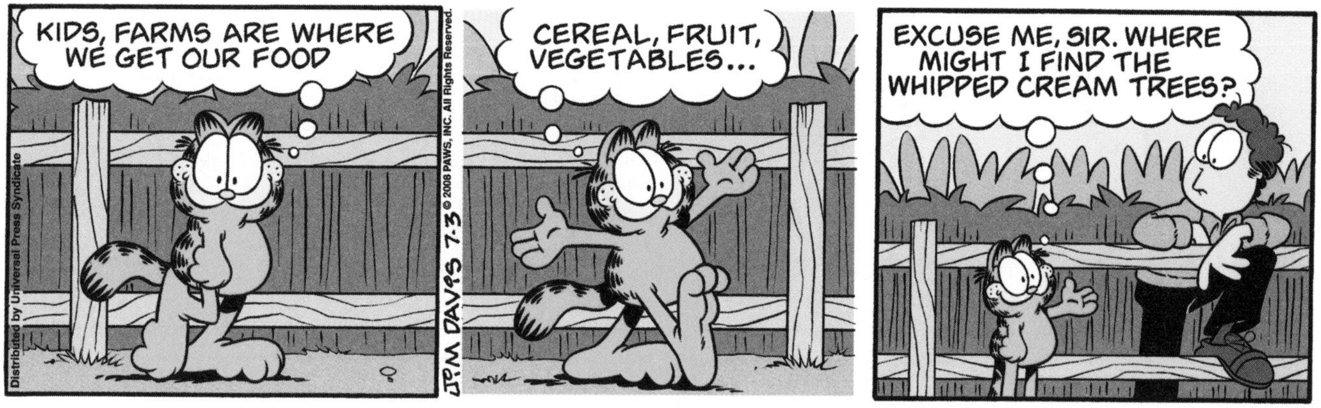
KIDS, FARMS ARE WHERE WE GET OUR FOOD
CEREAL, FRUIT, VEGETABLES...
EXCUSE ME, SIR. WHERE MIGHT I FIND THE WHIPPED CREAM TREES?
Distributed by Universal Press Syndicate
JIM DAVIS 7-3 © 2008 PAWS, INC. All Rights Reserved.

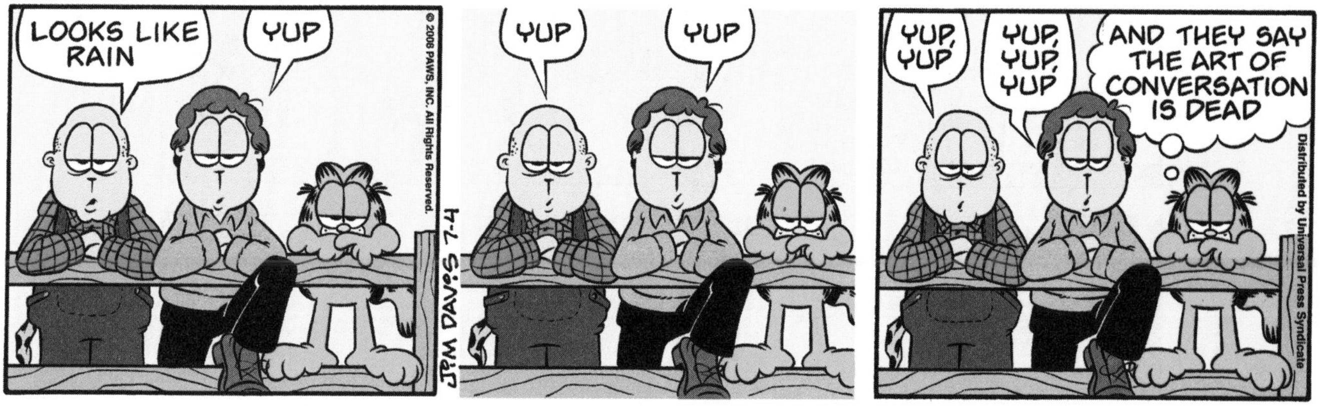
LOOKS LIKE RAIN
YUP
YUP
YUP
YUP, YUP
YUP, YUP, YUP
AND THEY SAY THE ART OF CONVERSATION IS DEAD
© 2008 PAWS, INC. All Rights Reserved.
JIM DAVIS 7-4
Distributed by Universal Press Syndicate

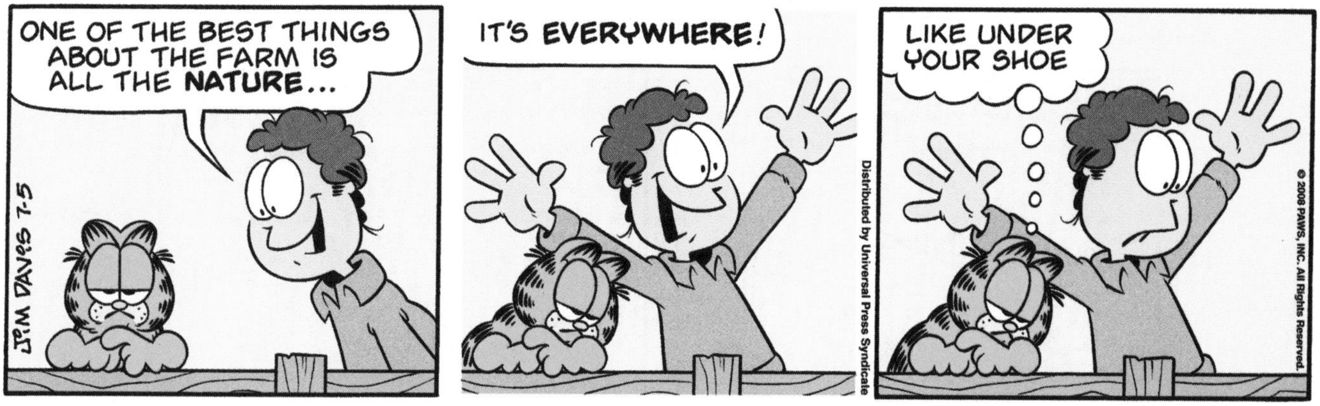
ONE OF THE BEST THINGS ABOUT THE FARM IS ALL THE NATURE...
IT'S EVERYWHERE!
LIKE UNDER YOUR SHOE
JIM DAVIS 7-5
Distributed by Universal Press Syndicate
© 2008 PAWS, INC. All Rights Reserved.

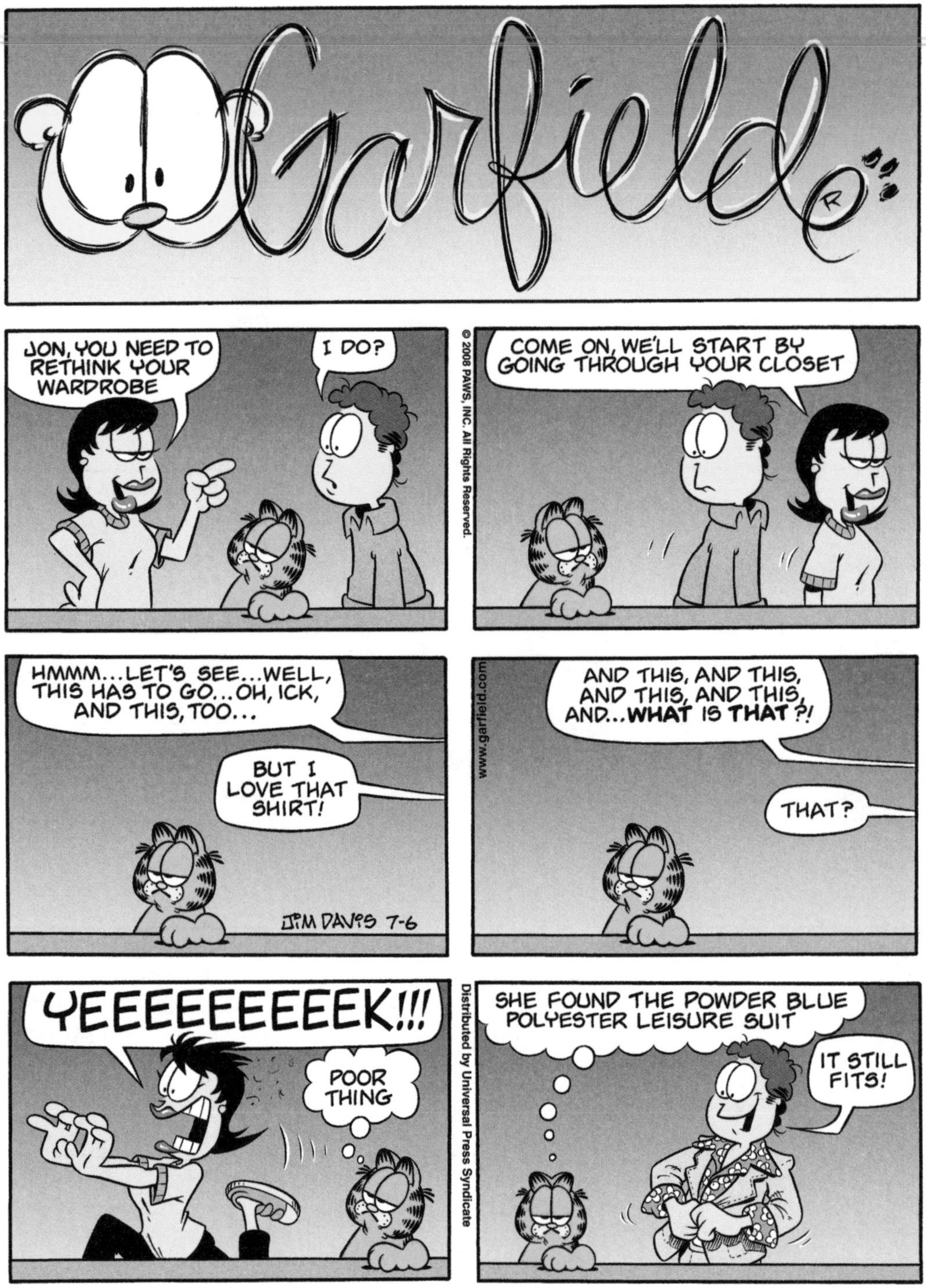
Garfield
JON, YOU NEED TO RETHINK YOUR WARDROBE
I DO?
© 2008 PAWS, INC. All Rights Reserved.
COME ON, WE'LL START BY GOING THROUGH YOUR CLOSET
HMMM...LET'S SEE...WELL, THIS HAS TO GO...OH, ICK, AND THIS, TOO...
BUT I LOVE THAT SHIRT!
JIM DAVIS 7-6
www.garfield.com
AND THIS, AND THIS, AND THIS, AND THIS, AND...WHAT IS THAT?!
THAT?
YEEEEEEEEEK!!!
POOR THING
Distributed by Universal Press Syndicate
SHE FOUND THE POWDER BLUE POLYESTER LEISURE SUIT
IT STILL FITS!

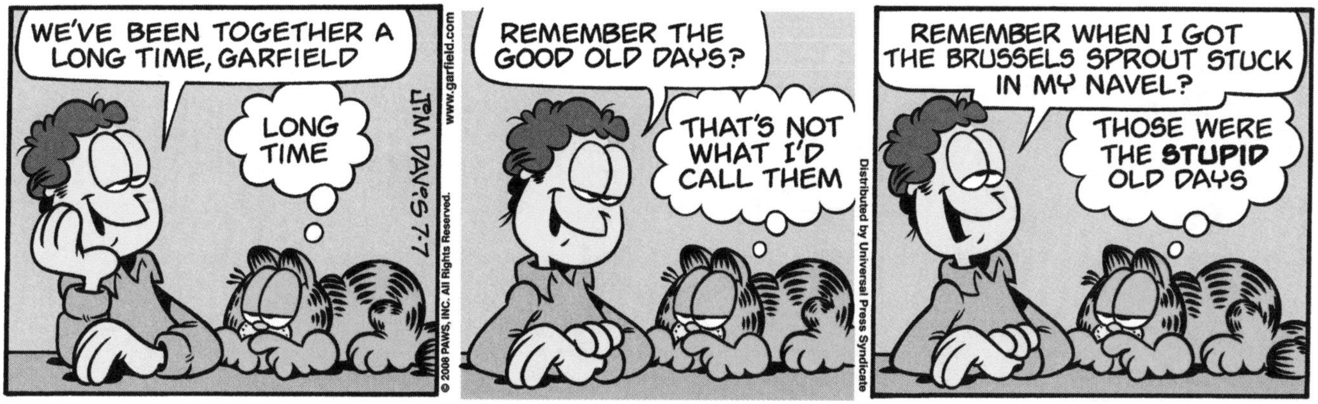
WE'VE BEEN TOGETHER A LONG TIME, GARFIELD
LONG TIME
JIM DAVIS 7-7
© 2008 PAWS, INC. All Rights Reserved.
www.garfield.com
REMEMBER THE GOOD OLD DAYS?
THAT'S NOT WHAT I'D CALL THEM
Distributed by Universal Press Syndicate
REMEMBER WHEN I GOT THE BRUSSELS SPROUT STUCK IN MY NAVEL?
THOSE WERE THE **STUPID** OLD DAYS

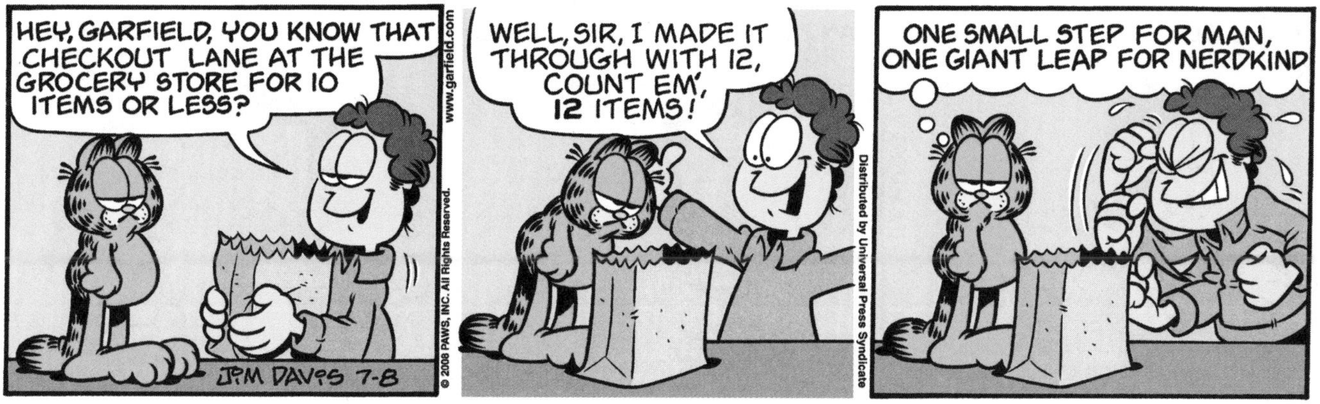
HEY, GARFIELD, YOU KNOW THAT CHECKOUT LANE AT THE GROCERY STORE FOR 10 ITEMS OR LESS?
JIM DAVIS 7-8
© 2008 PAWS, INC. All Rights Reserved.
www.garfield.com
WELL, SIR, I MADE IT THROUGH WITH 12, COUNT EM', **12** ITEMS!
Distributed by Universal Press Syndicate
ONE SMALL STEP FOR MAN, ONE GIANT LEAP FOR NERDKIND

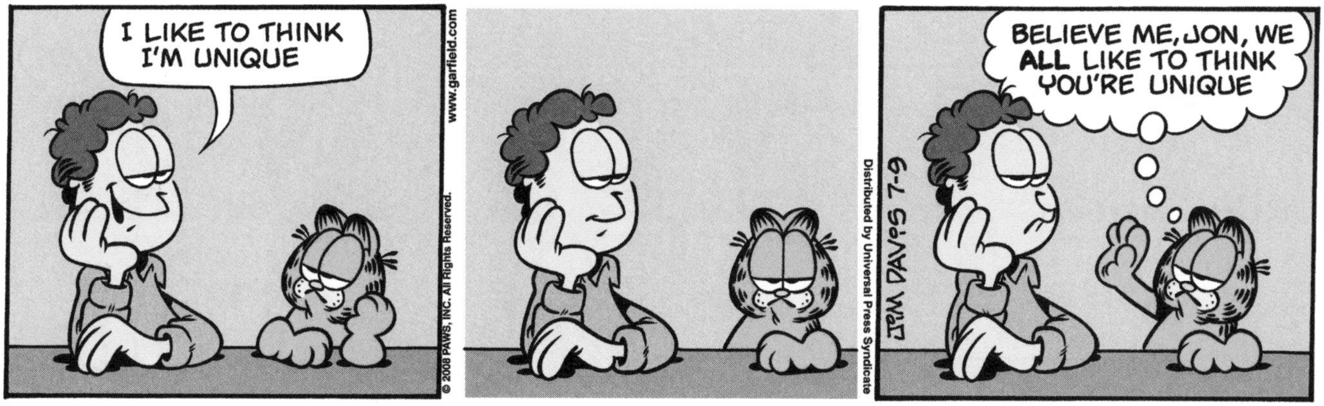
I LIKE TO THINK I'M UNIQUE
© 2008 PAWS, INC. All Rights Reserved.
www.garfield.com
JIM DAVIS 7-9
Distributed by Universal Press Syndicate
BELIEVE ME, JON, WE **ALL** LIKE TO THINK YOU'RE UNIQUE

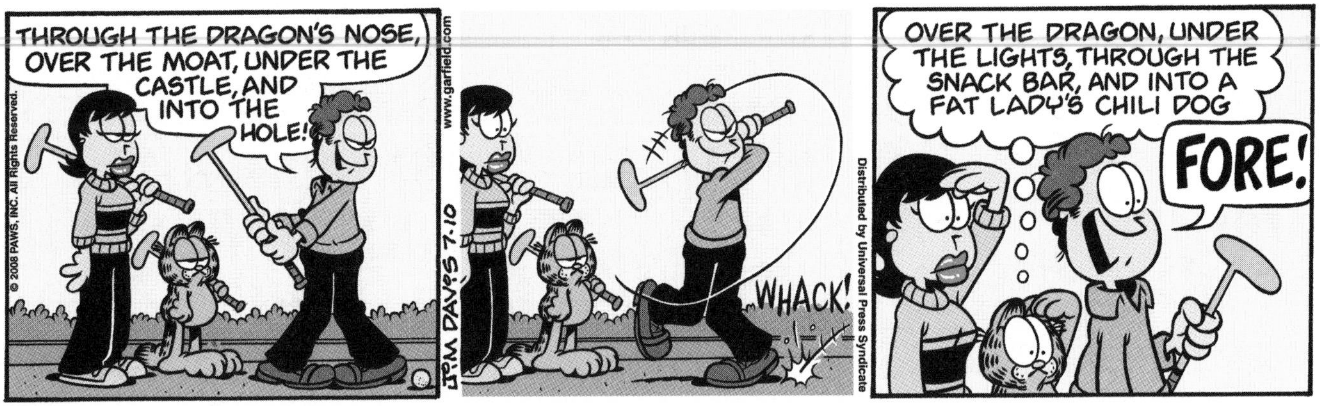
THROUGH THE DRAGON'S NOSE, OVER THE MOAT, UNDER THE CASTLE, AND INTO THE HOLE!
© 2008 PAWS, INC. All Rights Reserved.
www.garfield.com
JIM DAVIS 7-10
WHACK!
Distributed by Universal Press Syndicate
OVER THE DRAGON, UNDER THE LIGHTS, THROUGH THE SNACK BAR, AND INTO A FAT LADY'S CHILI DOG
FORE!

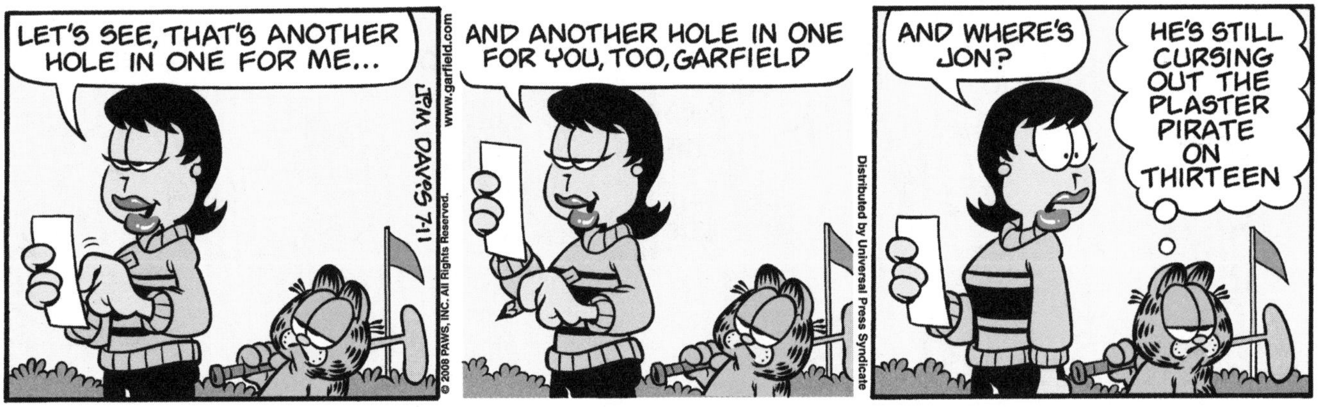
LET'S SEE, THAT'S ANOTHER HOLE IN ONE FOR ME...
JIM DAVIS 7-11
www.garfield.com
© 2008 PAWS, INC. All Rights Reserved.
AND ANOTHER HOLE IN ONE FOR YOU, TOO, GARFIELD
Distributed by Universal Press Syndicate
AND WHERE'S JON?
HE'S STILL CURSING OUT THE PLASTER PIRATE ON THIRTEEN

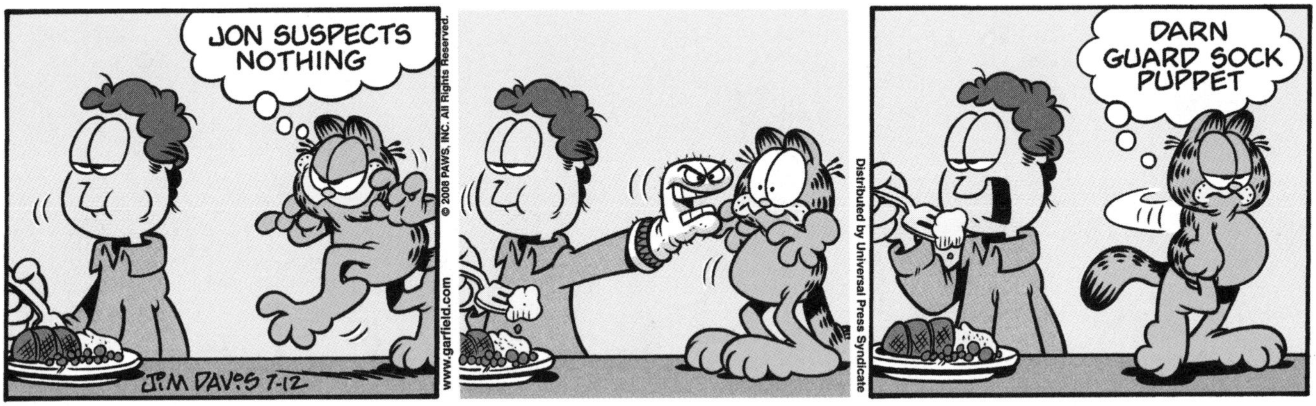
JON SUSPECTS NOTHING
JIM DAVIS 7-12
www.garfield.com
© 2008 PAWS, INC. All Rights Reserved.
Distributed by Universal Press Syndicate
DARN GUARD SOCK PUPPET

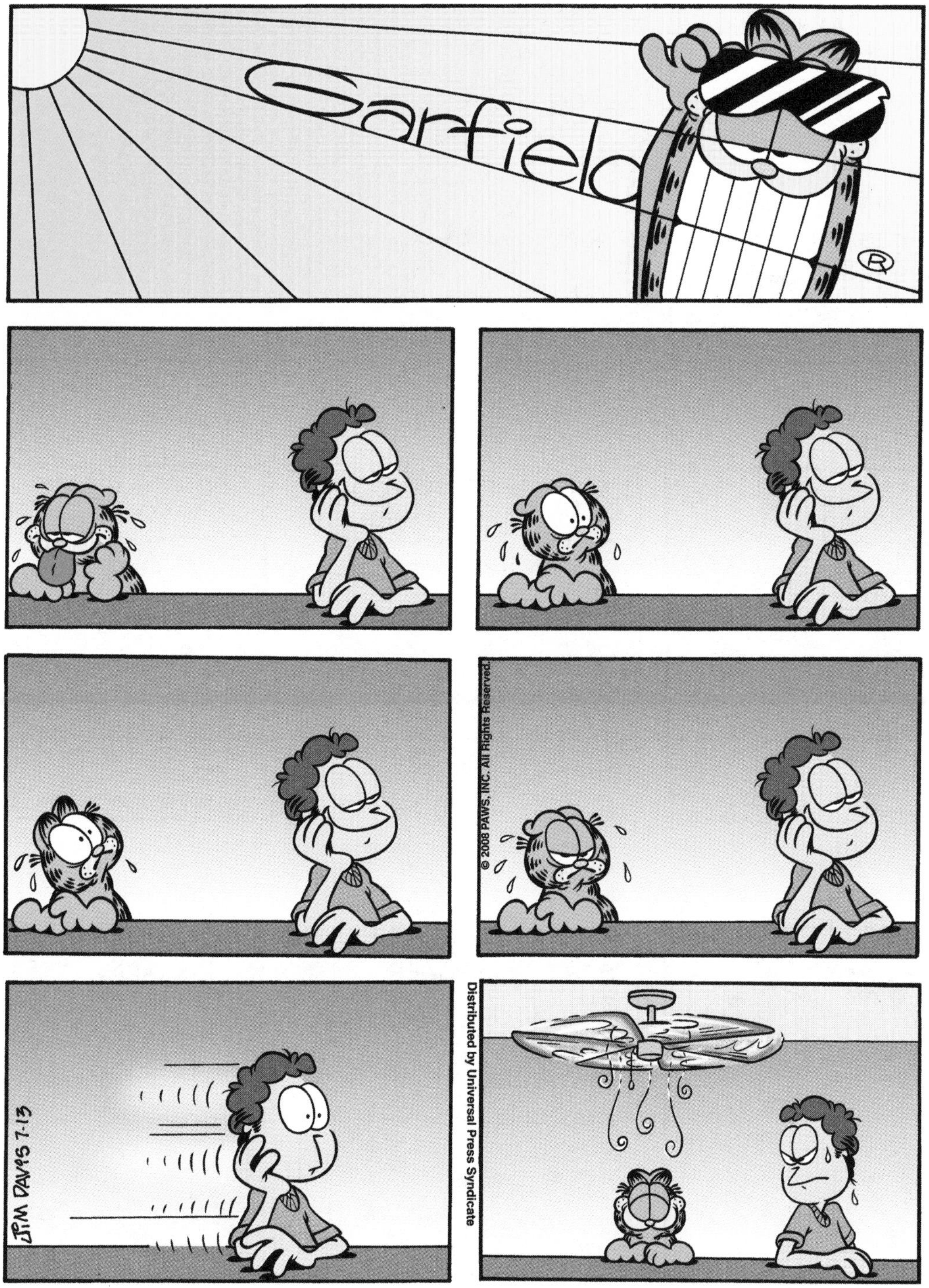
Garfield®
© 2008 PAWS, INC. All Rights Reserved.
Distributed by Universal Press Syndicate
JPM DAVIS 7-13

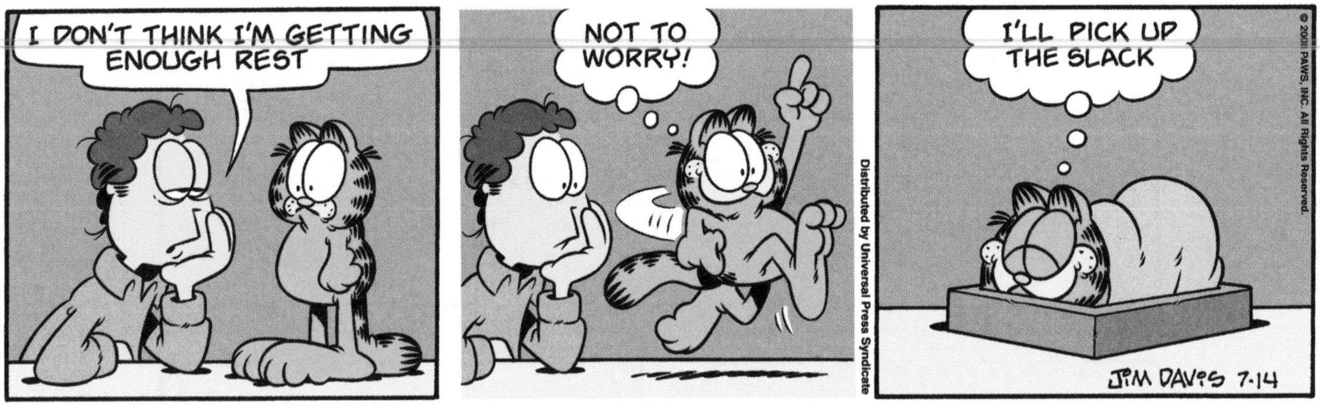
I DON'T THINK I'M GETTING ENOUGH REST
NOT TO WORRY!
I'LL PICK UP THE SLACK
JIM DAVIS 7-14
Distributed by Universal Press Syndicate
© 2008 PAWS, INC. All Rights Reserved.

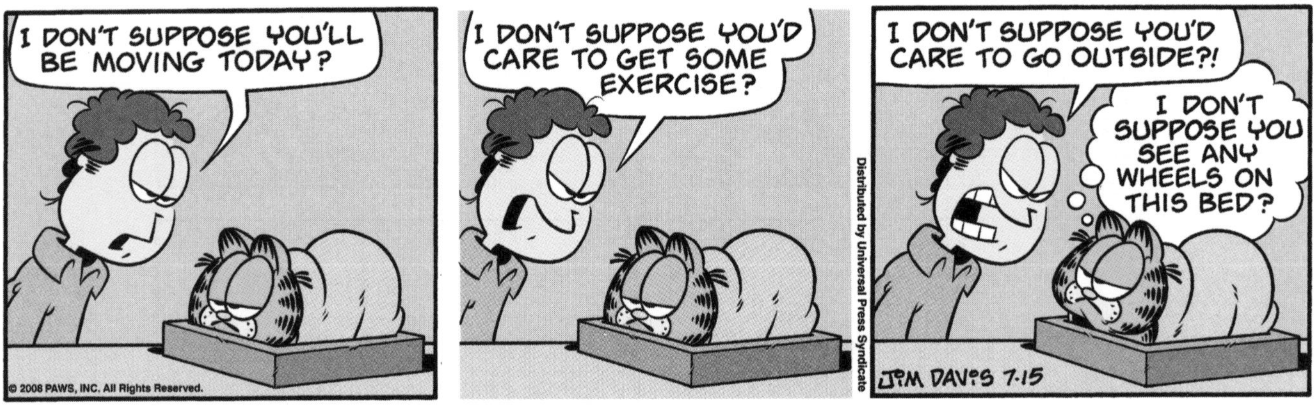
I DON'T SUPPOSE YOU'LL BE MOVING TODAY?
I DON'T SUPPOSE YOU'D CARE TO GET SOME EXERCISE?
I DON'T SUPPOSE YOU'D CARE TO GO OUTSIDE?!
I DON'T SUPPOSE YOU SEE ANY WHEELS ON THIS BED?
JIM DAVIS 7-15
© 2008 PAWS, INC. All Rights Reserved.
Distributed by Universal Press Syndicate

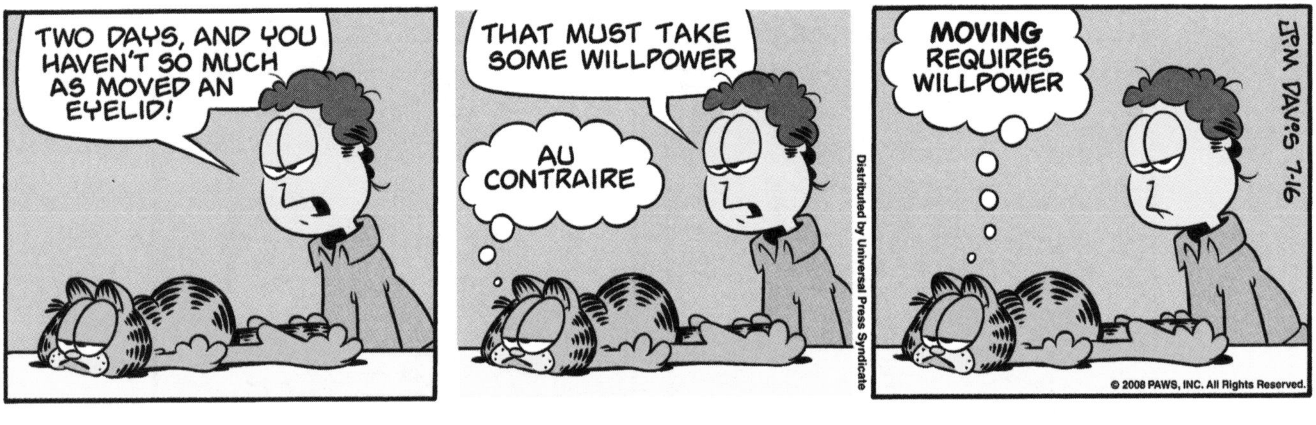
TWO DAYS, AND YOU HAVEN'T SO MUCH AS MOVED AN EYELID!
THAT MUST TAKE SOME WILLPOWER
AU CONTRAIRE
MOVING REQUIRES WILLPOWER
JIM DAVIS 7-16
Distributed by Universal Press Syndicate
© 2008 PAWS, INC. All Rights Reserved.

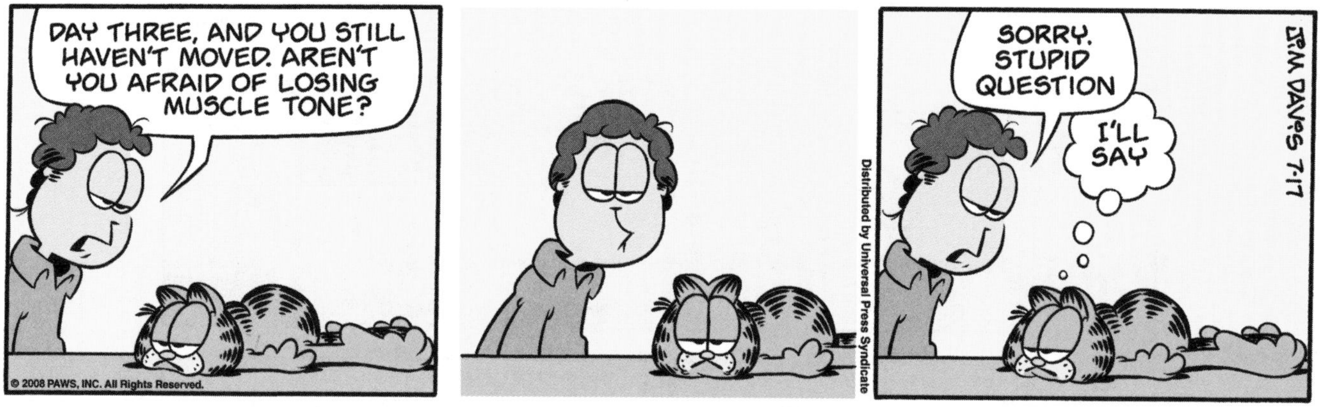
DAY THREE, AND YOU STILL HAVEN'T MOVED. AREN'T YOU AFRAID OF LOSING MUSCLE TONE?
SORRY. STUPID QUESTION
I'LL SAY
JIM DAVIS 7-17
© 2008 PAWS, INC. All Rights Reserved.
Distributed by Universal Press Syndicate

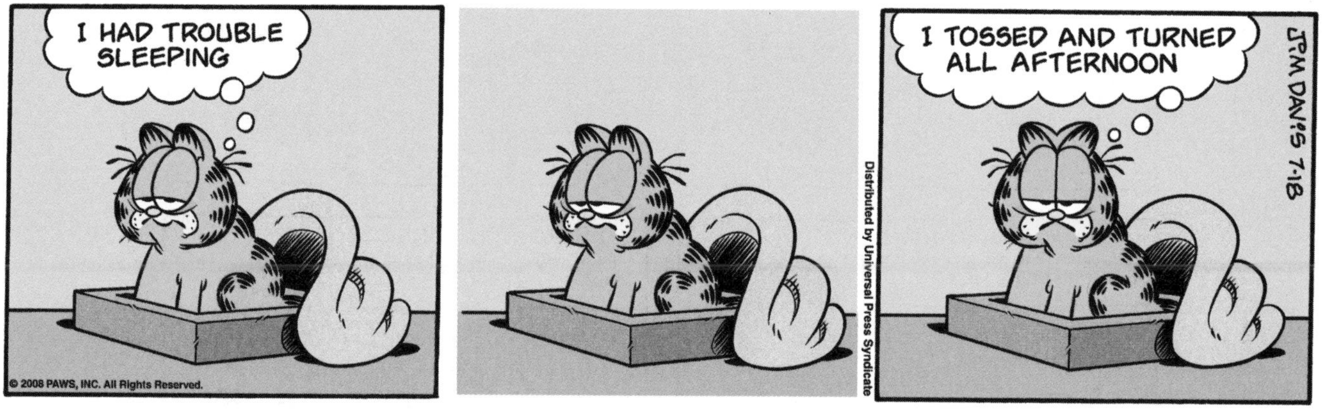
I HAD TROUBLE SLEEPING
I TOSSED AND TURNED ALL AFTERNOON
JIM DAVIS 7-18
© 2008 PAWS, INC. All Rights Reserved.
Distributed by Universal Press Syndicate

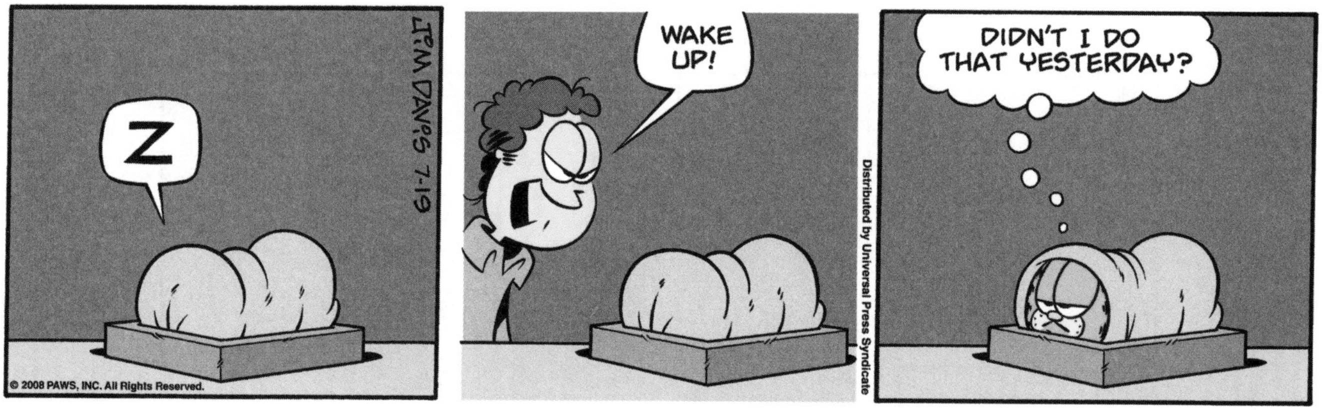
Z
WAKE UP!
DIDN'T I DO THAT YESTERDAY?
JIM DAVIS 7-19
© 2008 PAWS, INC. All Rights Reserved.
Distributed by Universal Press Syndicate

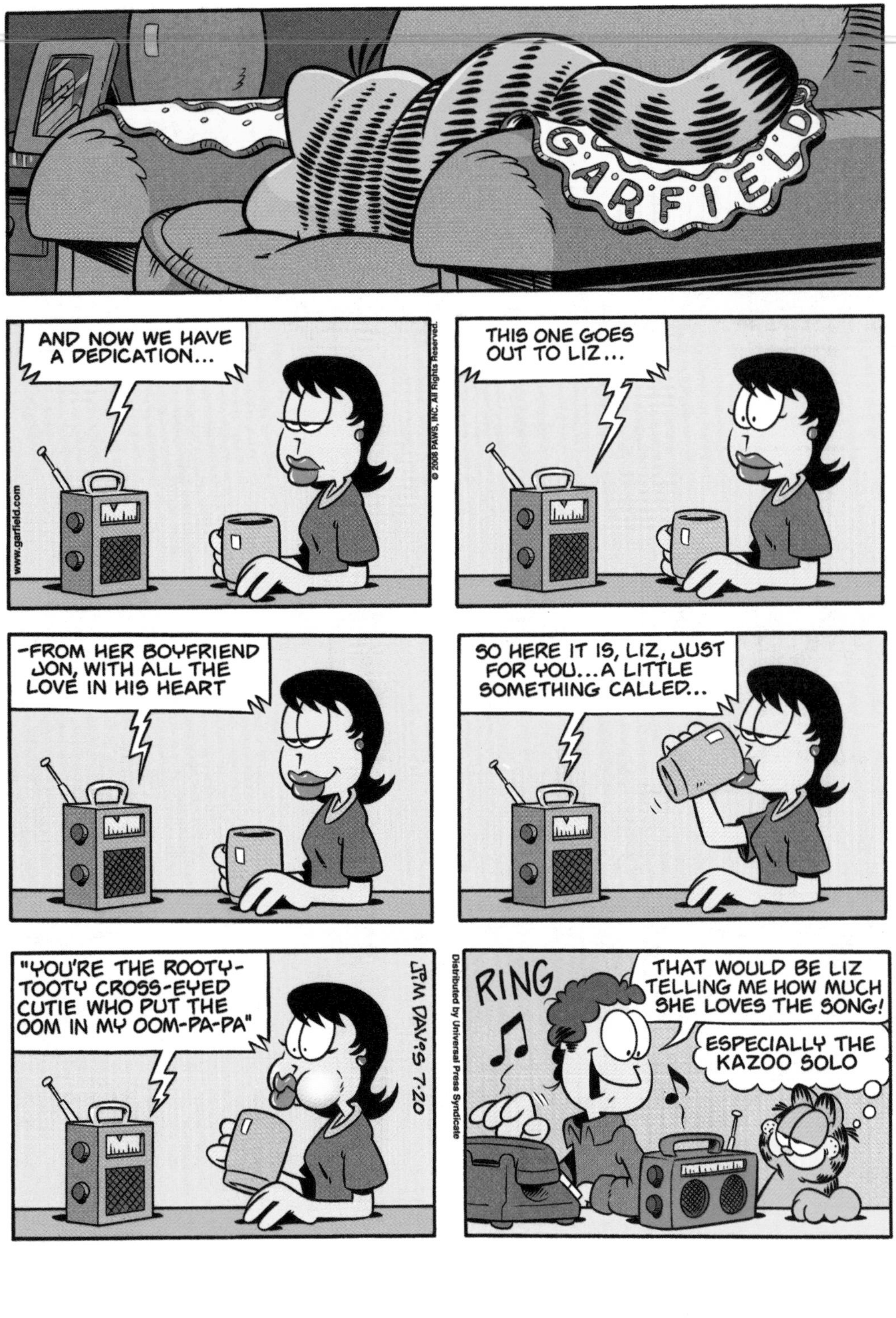
GARFIELD
AND NOW WE HAVE A DEDICATION...
www.garfield.com
© 2008 PAWS, INC. All Rights Reserved.
THIS ONE GOES OUT TO LIZ...
-FROM HER BOYFRIEND JON, WITH ALL THE LOVE IN HIS HEART
SO HERE IT IS, LIZ, JUST FOR YOU...A LITTLE SOMETHING CALLED...
"YOU'RE THE ROOTY-TOOTY CROSS-EYED CUTIE WHO PUT THE OOM IN MY OOM-PA-PA"
JIM DAVIS 7-20
Distributed by Universal Press Syndicate
RING
THAT WOULD BE LIZ TELLING ME HOW MUCH SHE LOVES THE SONG!
ESPECIALLY THE KAZOO SOLO

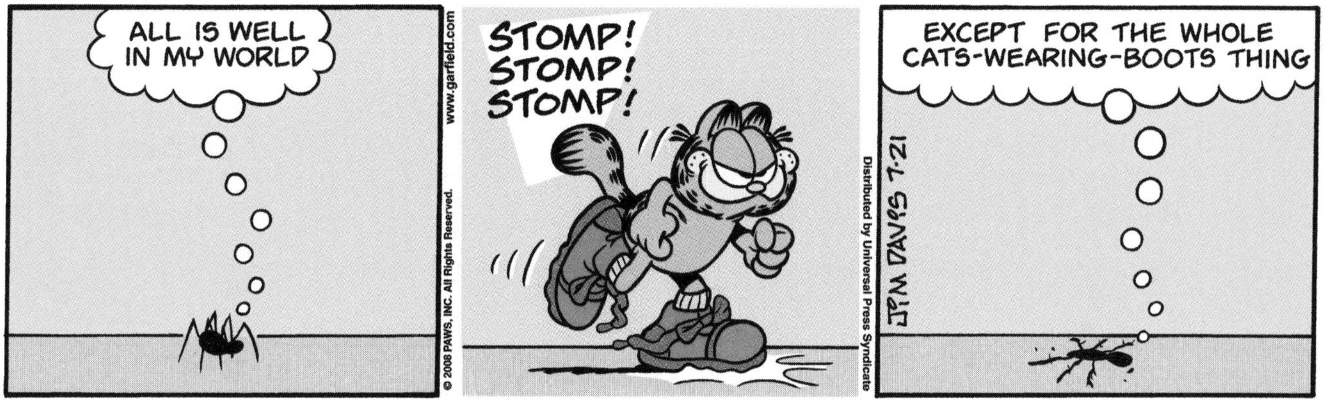
ALL IS WELL IN MY WORLD
© 2008 PAWS, INC. All Rights Reserved.
www.garfield.com
STOMP! STOMP! STOMP!
Distributed by Universal Press Syndicate
JIM DAVIS 7-21
EXCEPT FOR THE WHOLE CATS-WEARING-BOOTS THING

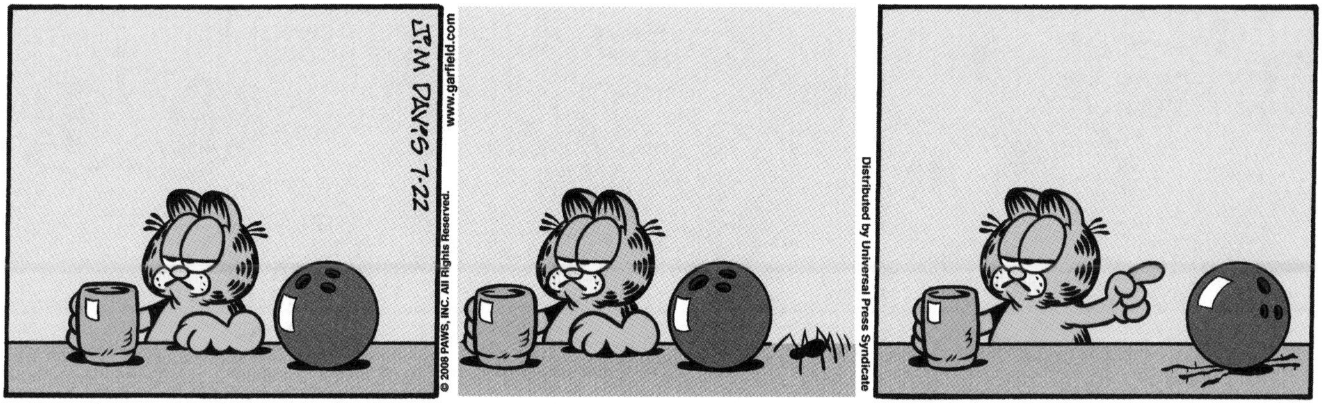
JIM DAVIS 7-22
© 2008 PAWS, INC. All Rights Reserved.
www.garfield.com
Distributed by Universal Press Syndicate

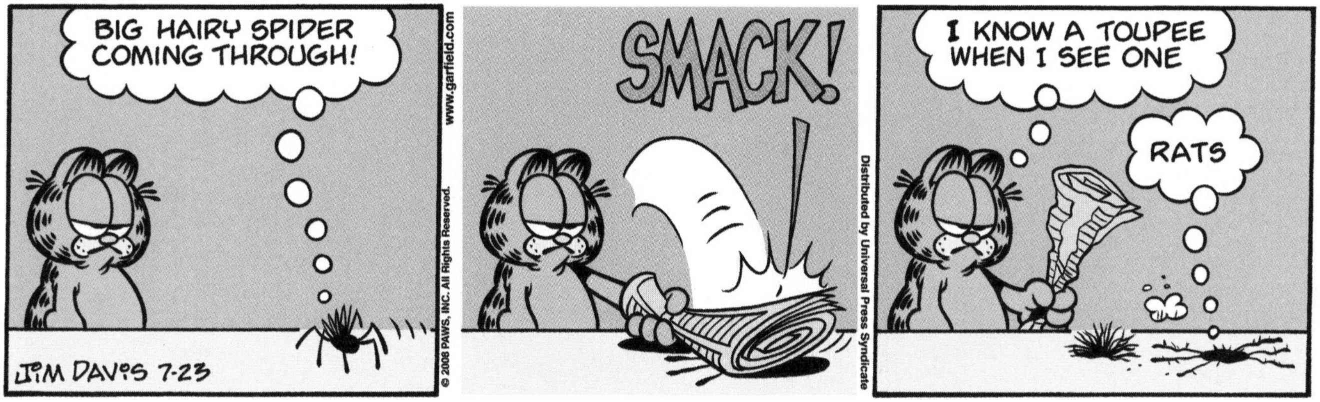
BIG HAIRY SPIDER COMING THROUGH!
JIM DAVIS 7-23
© 2008 PAWS, INC. All Rights Reserved.
www.garfield.com
SMACK!
Distributed by Universal Press Syndicate
I KNOW A TOUPEE WHEN I SEE ONE
RATS

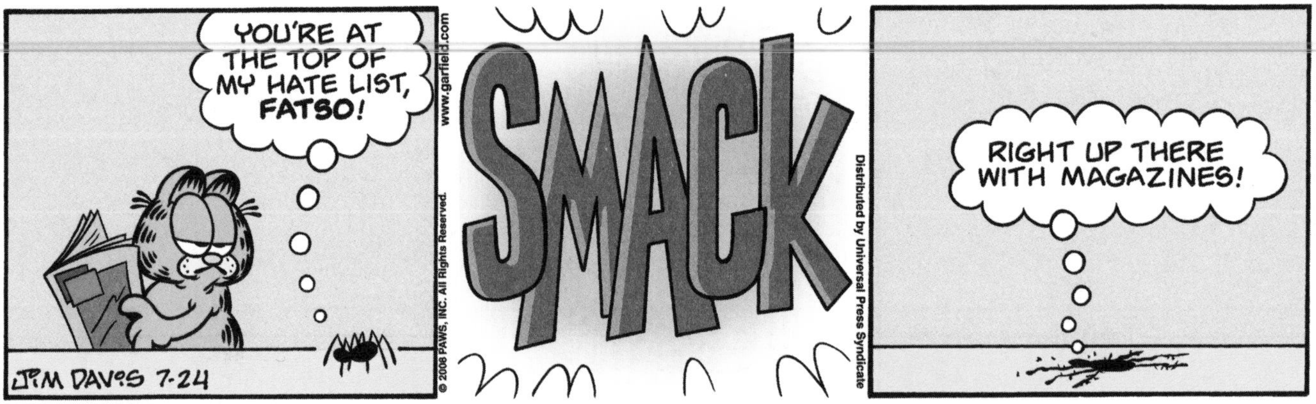
YOU'RE AT THE TOP OF MY HATE LIST, FATSO!
JIM DAVIS 7-24
www.garfield.com
© 2008 PAWS, INC. All Rights Reserved.
SMACK
Distributed by Universal Press Syndicate
RIGHT UP THERE WITH MAGAZINES!

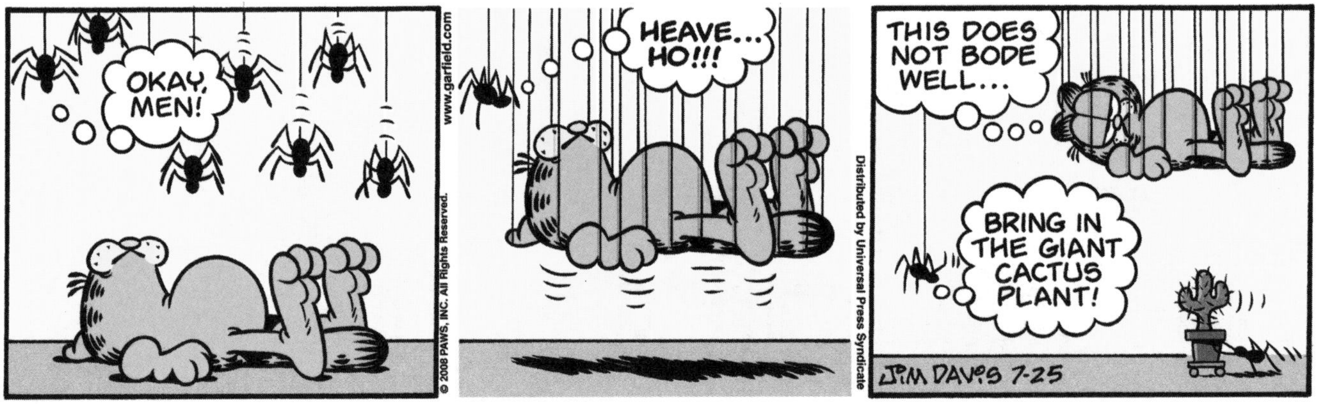
OKAY, MEN!
www.garfield.com
© 2008 PAWS, INC. All Rights Reserved.
HEAVE... HO!!!
Distributed by Universal Press Syndicate
THIS DOES NOT BODE WELL...
BRING IN THE GIANT CACTUS PLANT!
JIM DAVIS 7-25

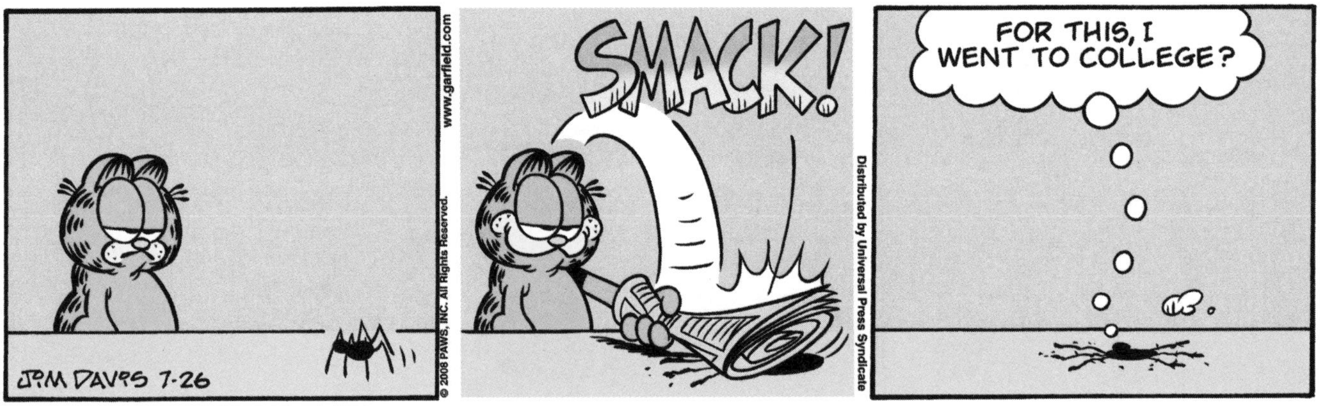
JIM DAVIS 7-26
www.garfield.com
© 2008 PAWS, INC. All Rights Reserved.
SMACK!
Distributed by Universal Press Syndicate
FOR THIS, I WENT TO COLLEGE?

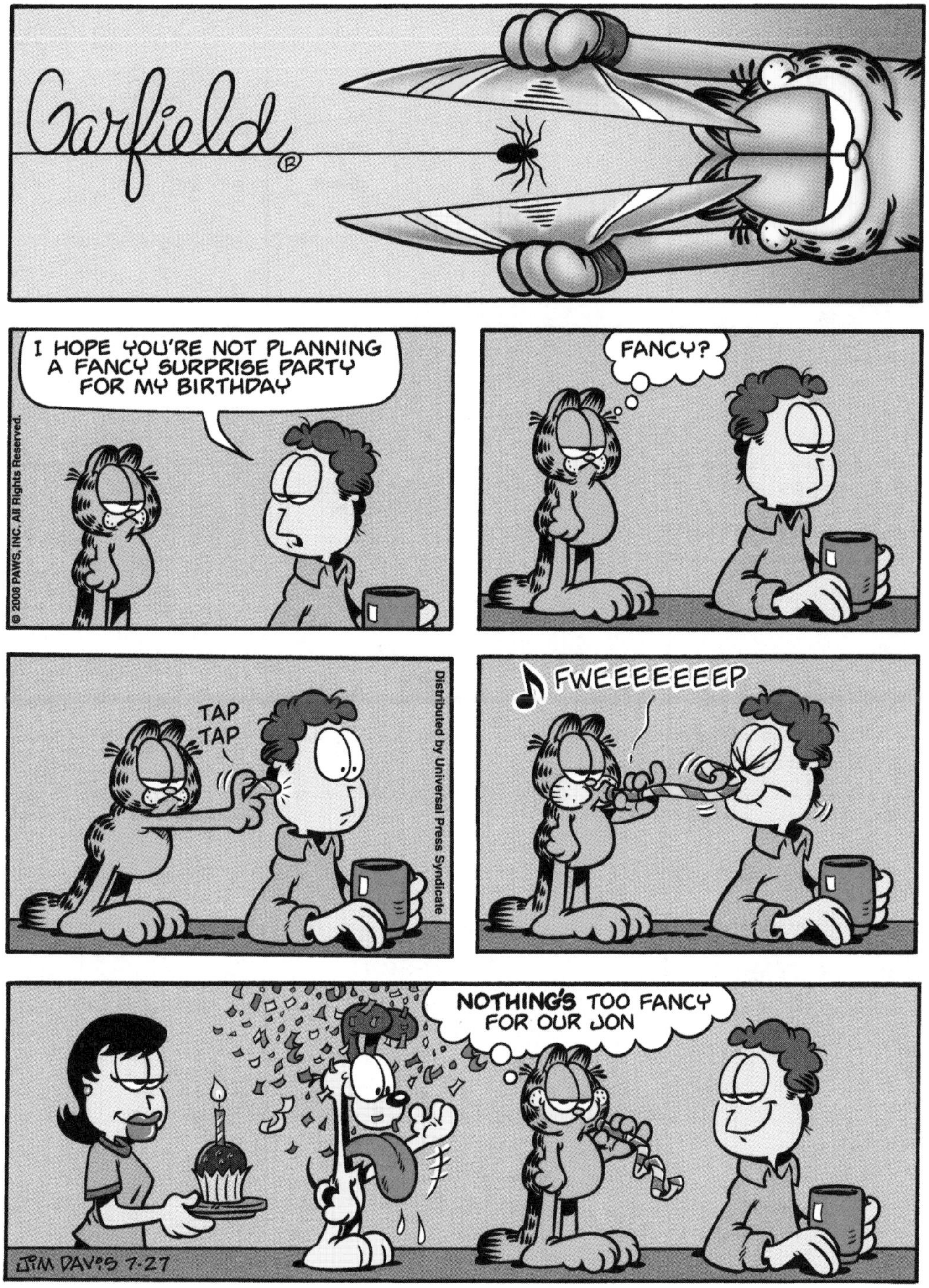
Garfield®
I HOPE YOU'RE NOT PLANNING A FANCY SURPRISE PARTY FOR MY BIRTHDAY
© 2008 PAWS, INC. All Rights Reserved.
FANCY?
TAP TAP
Distributed by Universal Press Syndicate
FWEEEEEEEP
NOTHING'S TOO FANCY FOR OUR JON
JIM DAVIS 7-27

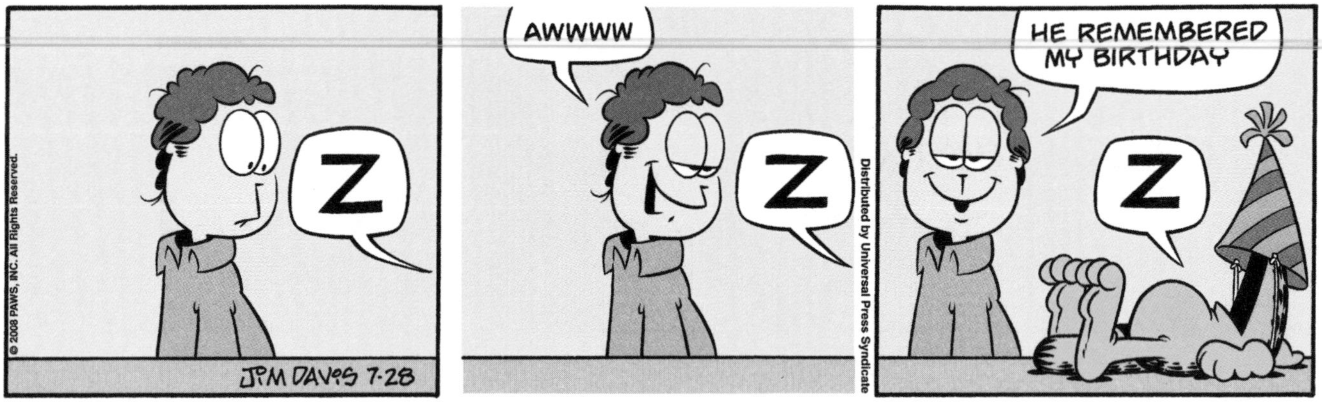
© 2008 PAWS, INC. All Rights Reserved.
Z
JIM DAVIS 7-28
AWWWW
Z
Distributed by Universal Press Syndicate
HE REMEMBERED MY BIRTHDAY
Z

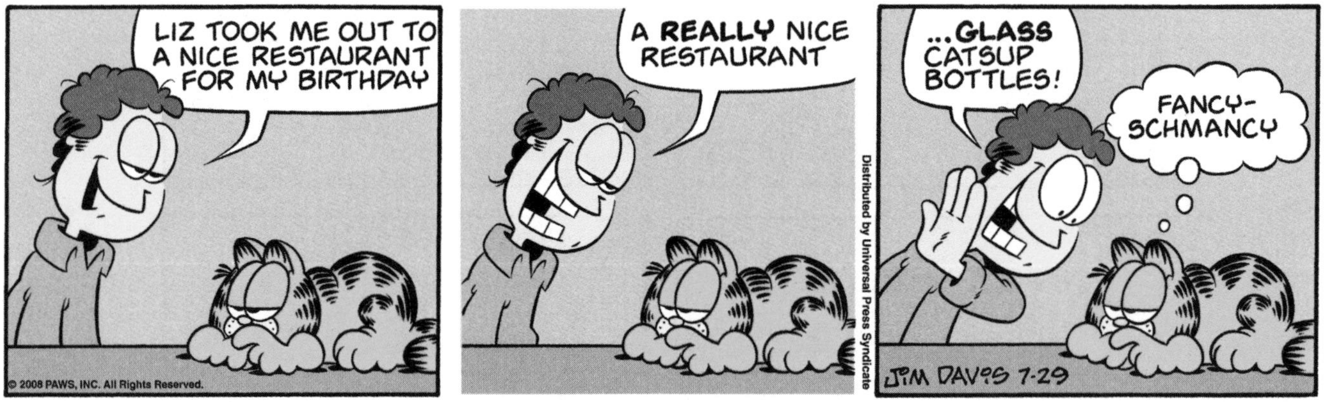
LIZ TOOK ME OUT TO A NICE RESTAURANT FOR MY BIRTHDAY
© 2008 PAWS, INC. All Rights Reserved.
A **REALLY** NICE RESTAURANT
Distributed by Universal Press Syndicate
...**GLASS** CATSUP BOTTLES!
FANCY-SCHMANCY
JIM DAVIS 7-29

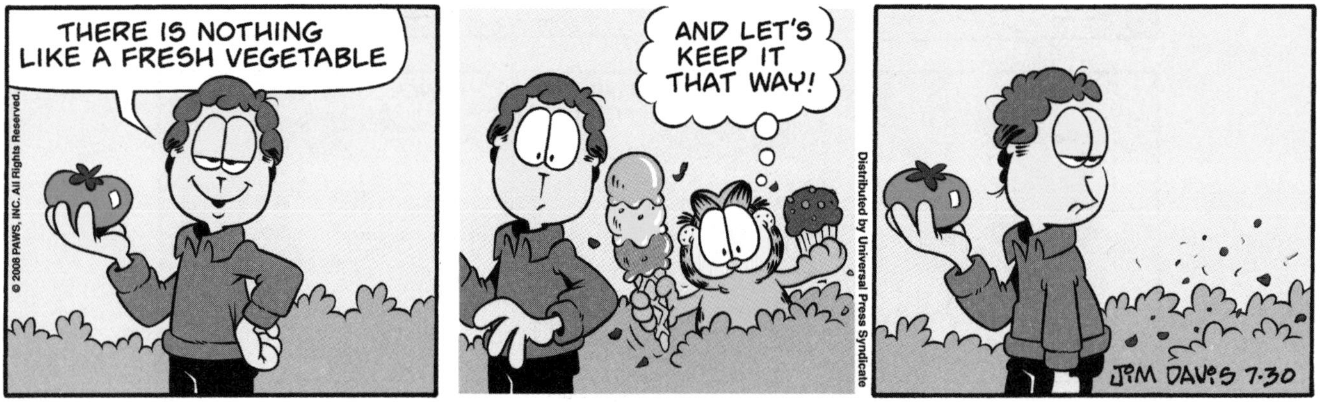
THERE IS NOTHING LIKE A FRESH VEGETABLE
© 2008 PAWS, INC. All Rights Reserved.
AND LET'S KEEP IT THAT WAY!
Distributed by Universal Press Syndicate
JIM DAVIS 7-30

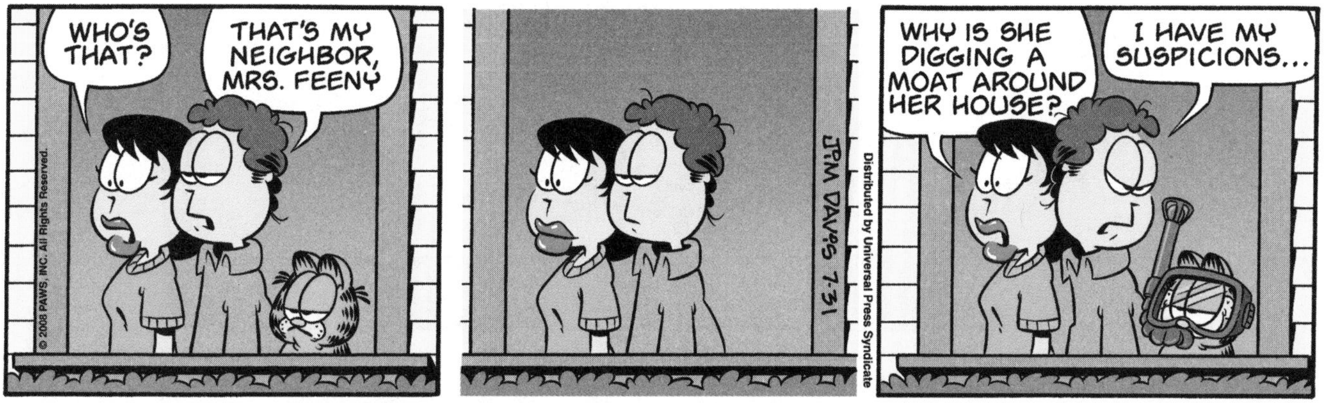
WHO'S THAT?
THAT'S MY NEIGHBOR, MRS. FEENY
WHY IS SHE DIGGING A MOAT AROUND HER HOUSE?
I HAVE MY SUSPICIONS...
JIM DAVIS 7-31
© 2008 PAWS, INC. All Rights Reserved.
Distributed by Universal Press Syndicate

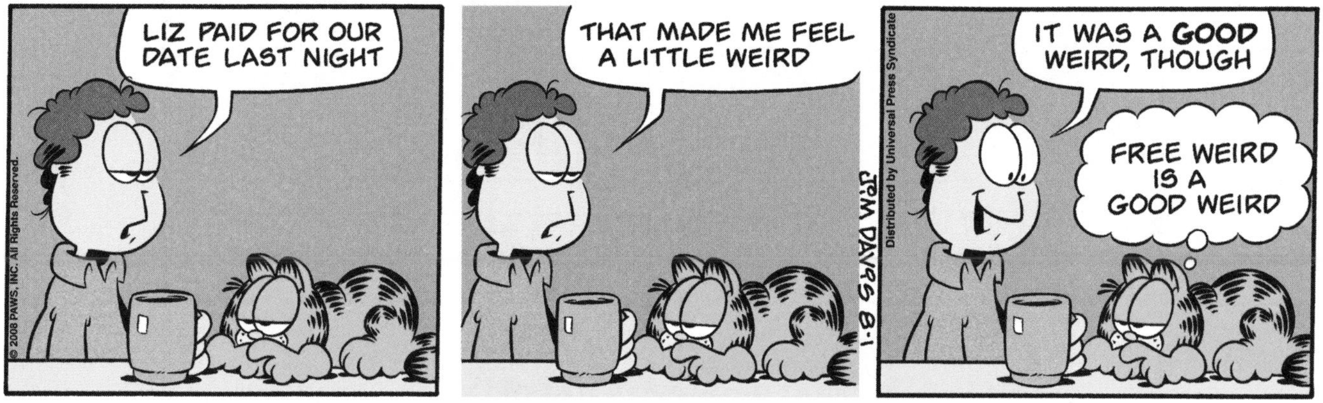
LIZ PAID FOR OUR DATE LAST NIGHT
THAT MADE ME FEEL A LITTLE WEIRD
IT WAS A **GOOD** WEIRD, THOUGH
FREE WEIRD IS A GOOD WEIRD
JIM DAVIS 8-1
© 2008 PAWS, INC. All Rights Reserved.
Distributed by Universal Press Syndicate

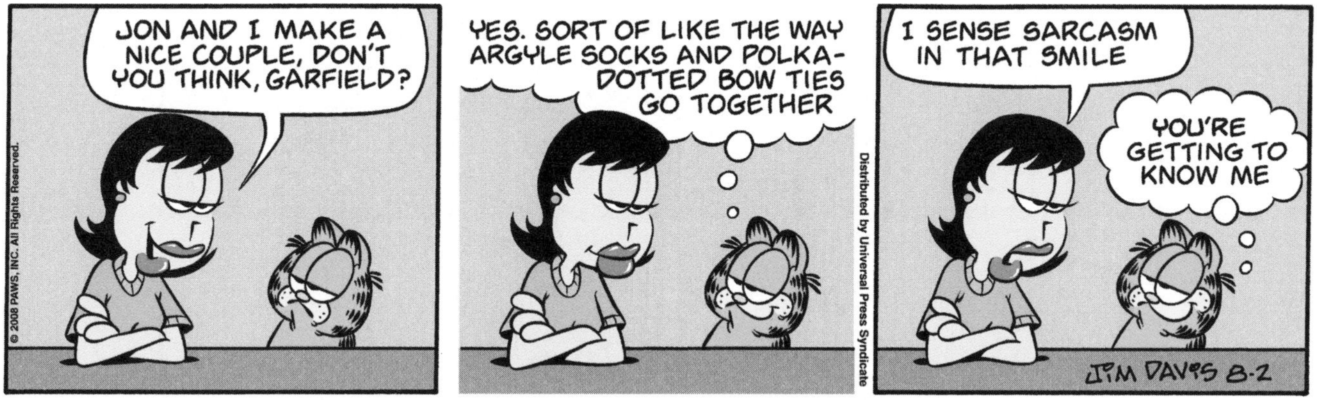
JON AND I MAKE A NICE COUPLE, DON'T YOU THINK, GARFIELD?
YES. SORT OF LIKE THE WAY ARGYLE SOCKS AND POLKA-DOTTED BOW TIES GO TOGETHER
I SENSE SARCASM IN THAT SMILE
YOU'RE GETTING TO KNOW ME
JIM DAVIS 8-2
© 2008 PAWS, INC. All Rights Reserved.
Distributed by Universal Press Syndicate

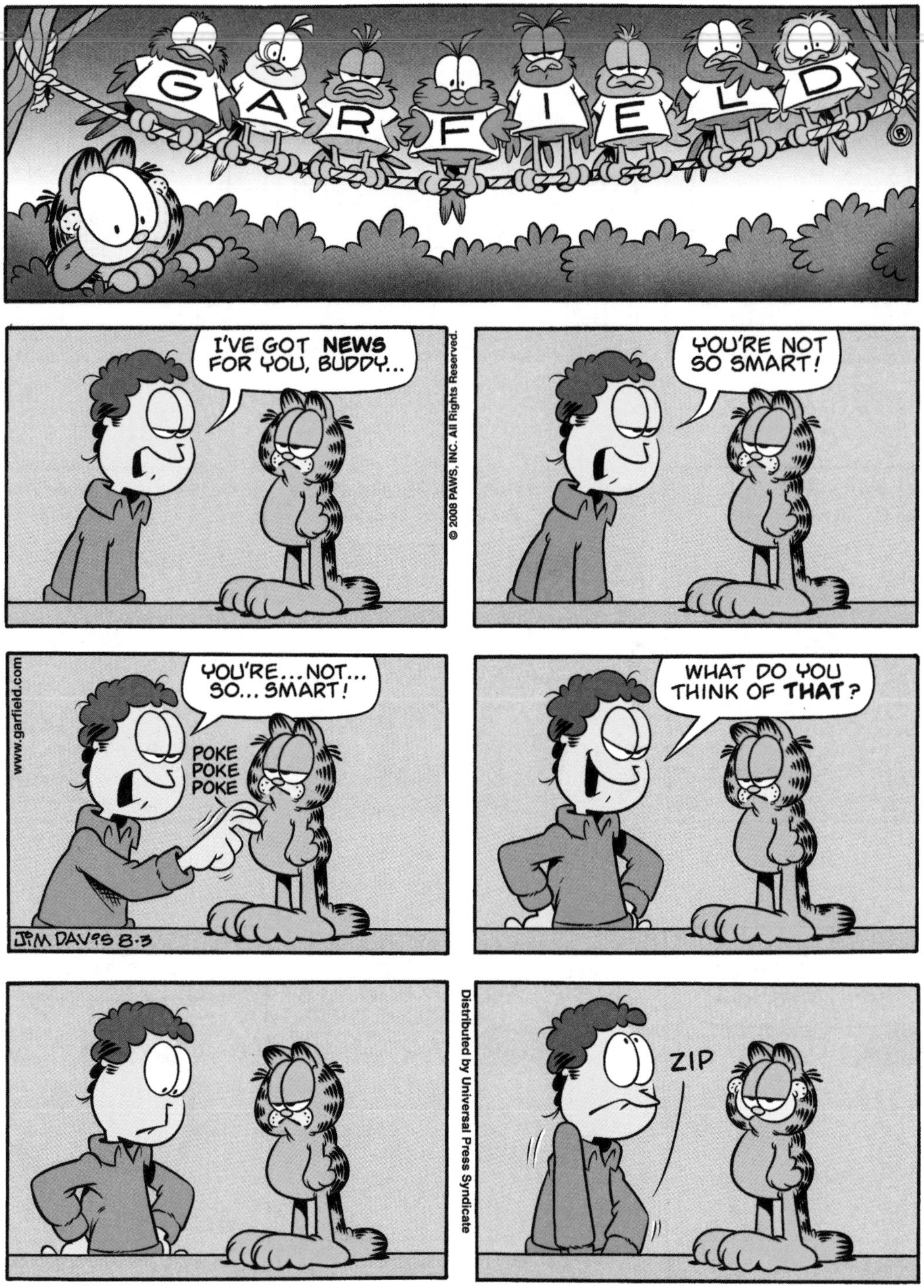
G A R F I E L D
I'VE GOT **NEWS** FOR YOU, BUDDY...
YOU'RE NOT SO SMART!
YOU'RE... NOT... SO... SMART!
POKE POKE POKE
WHAT DO YOU THINK OF **THAT**?
ZIP
JIM DAVIS 8-3
© 2008 PAWS, INC. All Rights Reserved.
www.garfield.com
Distributed by Universal Press Syndicate

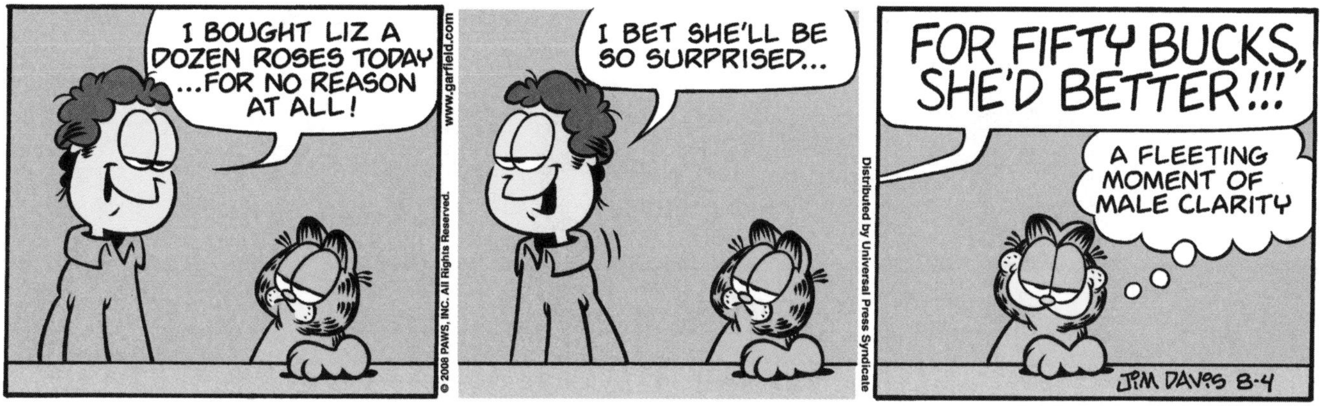
I BOUGHT LIZ A DOZEN ROSES TODAY ...FOR NO REASON AT ALL!
I BET SHE'LL BE SO SURPRISED...
FOR FIFTY BUCKS, SHE'D BETTER!!!
A FLEETING MOMENT OF MALE CLARITY
JIM DAVIS 8-4
www.garfield.com
© 2008 PAWS, INC. All Rights Reserved.
Distributed by Universal Press Syndicate

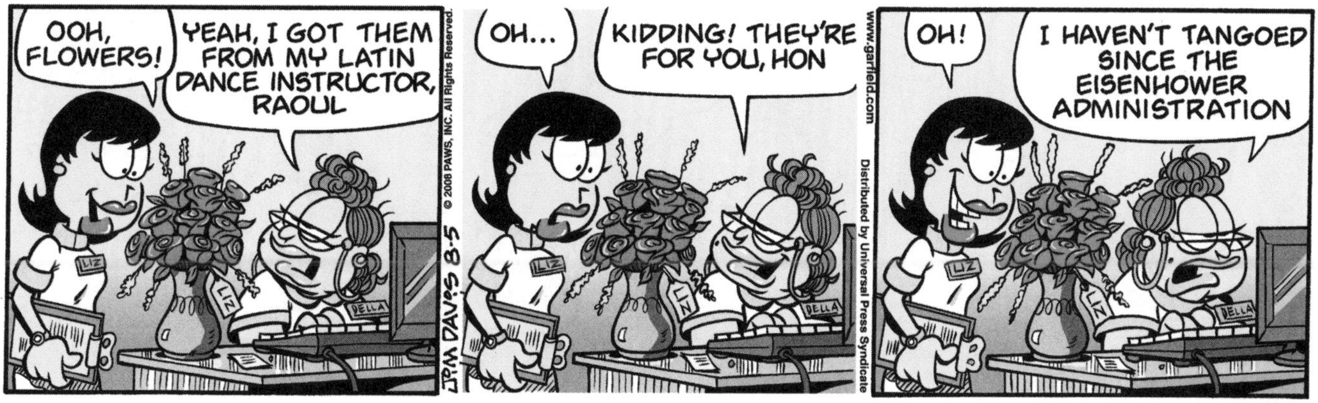
OOH, FLOWERS!
YEAH, I GOT THEM FROM MY LATIN DANCE INSTRUCTOR, RAOUL
OH...
KIDDING! THEY'RE FOR YOU, HON
OH!
I HAVEN'T TANGOED SINCE THE EISENHOWER ADMINISTRATION
LIZ
DELLA
JIM DAVIS 8-5
© 2008 PAWS, INC. All Rights Reserved.
www.garfield.com
Distributed by Universal Press Syndicate

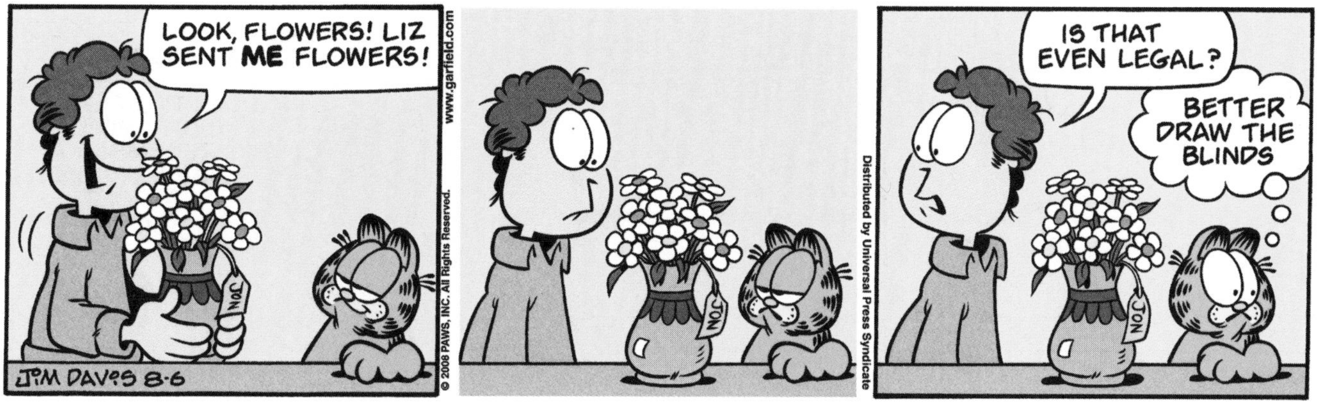
LOOK, FLOWERS! LIZ SENT **ME** FLOWERS!
IS THAT EVEN LEGAL?
BETTER DRAW THE BLINDS
JON
JIM DAVIS 8-6
www.garfield.com
© 2008 PAWS, INC. All Rights Reserved.
Distributed by Universal Press Syndicate

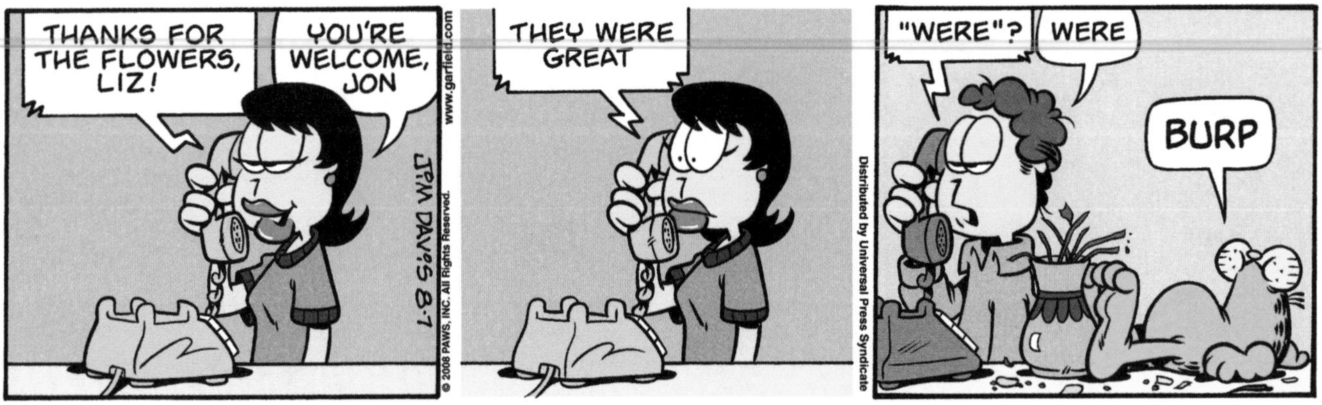
THANKS FOR THE FLOWERS, LIZ!
YOU'RE WELCOME, JON
JIM DAVIS 8-7
www.garfield.com
© 2008 PAWS, INC. All Rights Reserved.
THEY WERE GREAT
Distributed by Universal Press Syndicate
"WERE"?
WERE
BURP

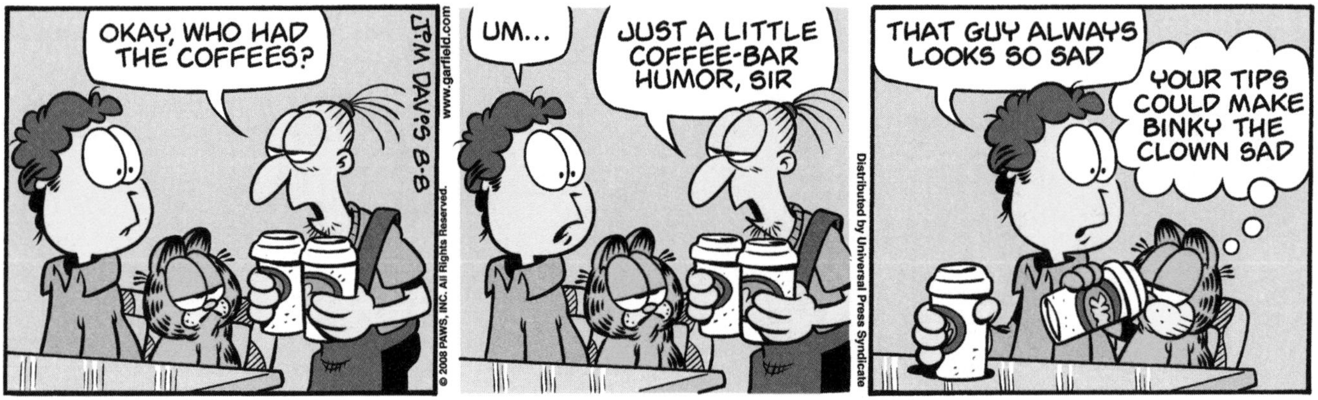
OKAY, WHO HAD THE COFFEES?
JIM DAVIS 8-8
www.garfield.com
© 2008 PAWS, INC. All Rights Reserved.
UM...
JUST A LITTLE COFFEE-BAR HUMOR, SIR
Distributed by Universal Press Syndicate
THAT GUY ALWAYS LOOKS SO SAD
YOUR TIPS COULD MAKE BINKY THE CLOWN SAD

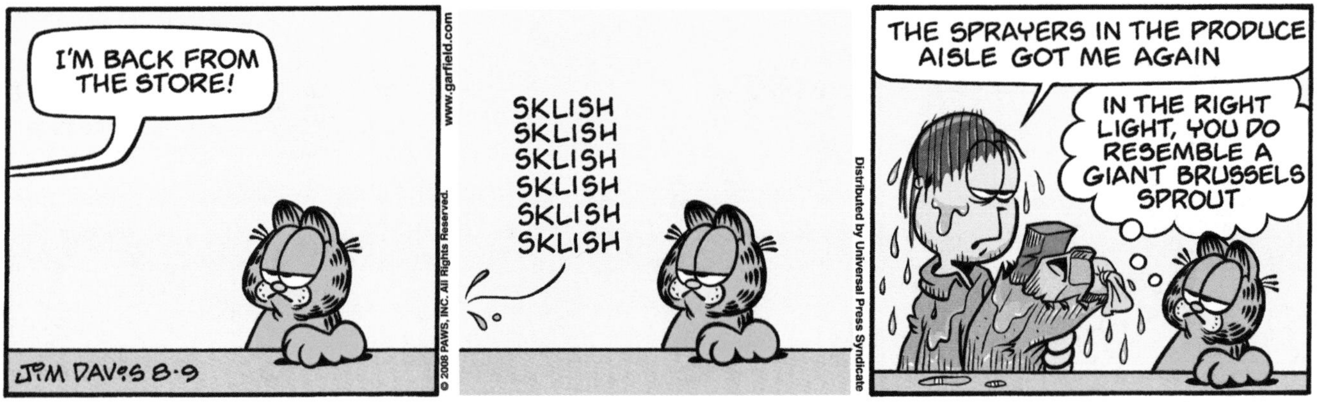
I'M BACK FROM THE STORE!
JIM DAVIS 8-9
www.garfield.com
© 2008 PAWS, INC. All Rights Reserved.
SKLISH SKLISH SKLISH SKLISH SKLISH SKLISH
Distributed by Universal Press Syndicate
THE SPRAYERS IN THE PRODUCE AISLE GOT ME AGAIN
IN THE RIGHT LIGHT, YOU DO RESEMBLE A GIANT BRUSSELS SPROUT

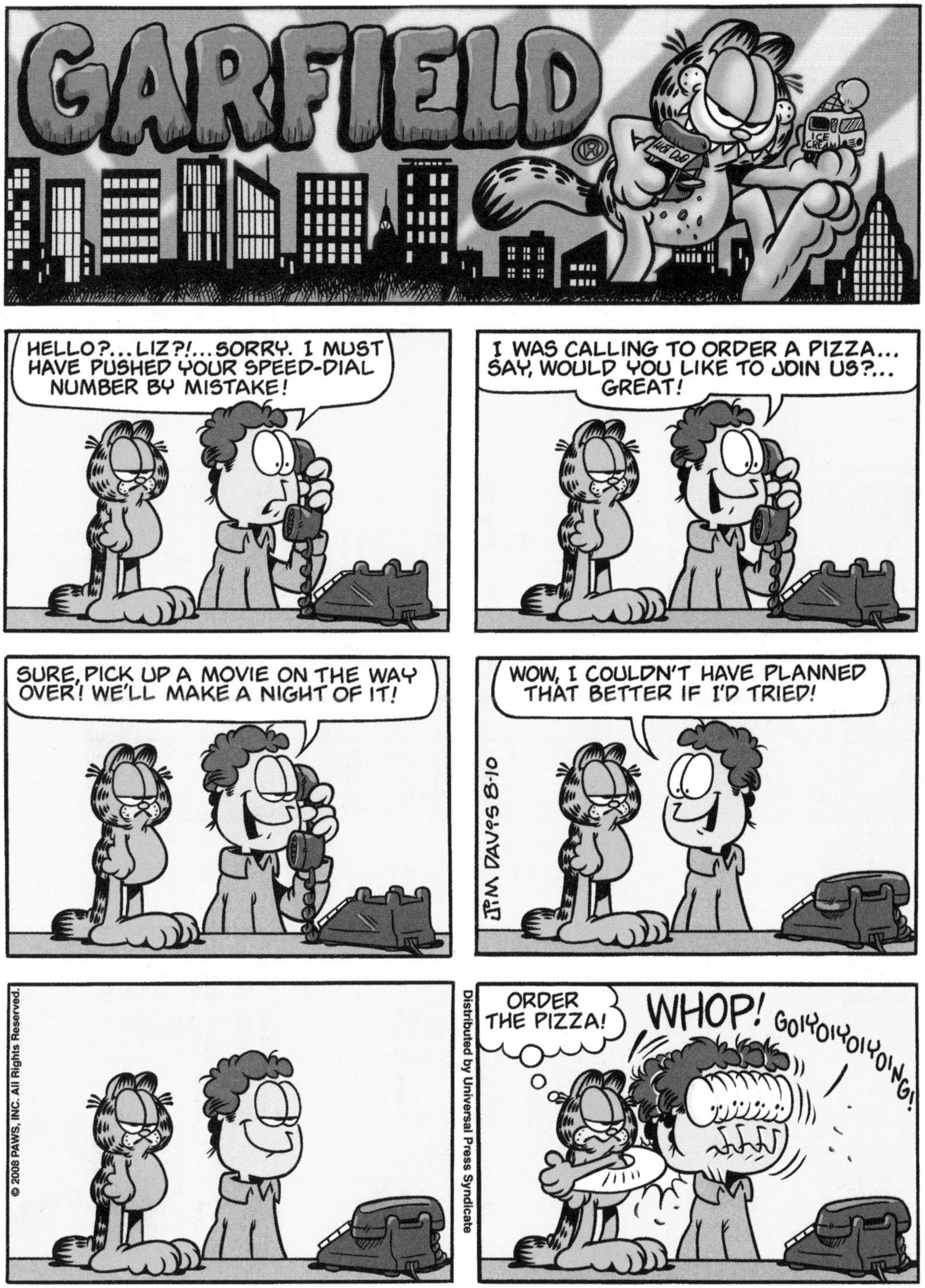
GARFIELD
HOT DOG
ICE CREAM
HELLO?...LIZ?!...SORRY. I MUST HAVE PUSHED YOUR SPEED-DIAL NUMBER BY MISTAKE!
I WAS CALLING TO ORDER A PIZZA... SAY, WOULD YOU LIKE TO JOIN US?... GREAT!
SURE, PICK UP A MOVIE ON THE WAY OVER! WE'LL MAKE A NIGHT OF IT!
WOW, I COULDN'T HAVE PLANNED THAT BETTER IF I'D TRIED!
JIM DAVIS 8-10
© 2008 PAWS, INC. All Rights Reserved.
Distributed by Universal Press Syndicate
ORDER THE PIZZA!
WHOP!
GOIYOIYOIYOIYOING!

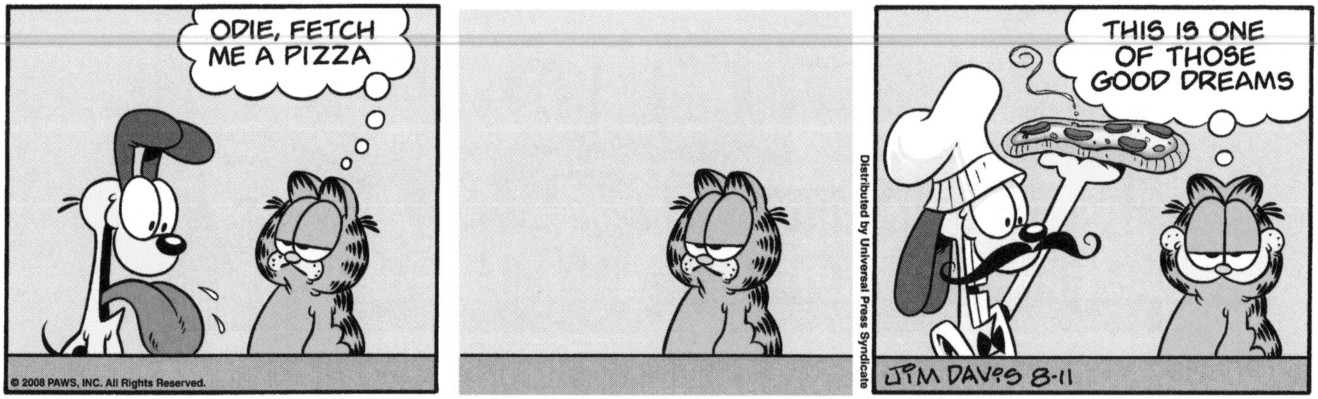
ODIE, FETCH ME A PIZZA
THIS IS ONE OF THOSE GOOD DREAMS
© 2008 PAWS, INC. All Rights Reserved.
Distributed by Universal Press Syndicate
JIM DAVIS 8-11

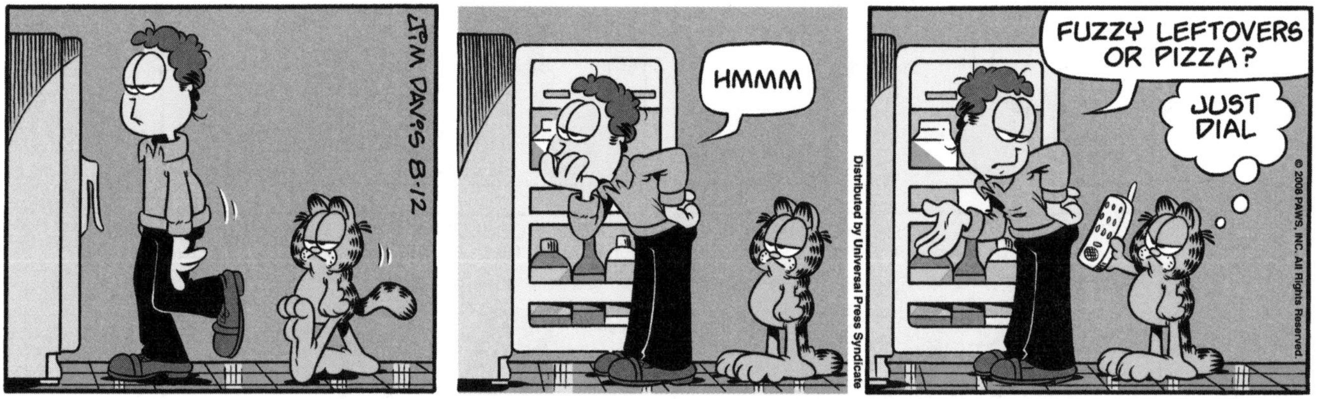
JIM DAVIS 8-12
HMMM
Distributed by Universal Press Syndicate
FUZZY LEFTOVERS OR PIZZA?
JUST DIAL
© 2008 PAWS, INC. All Rights Reserved.

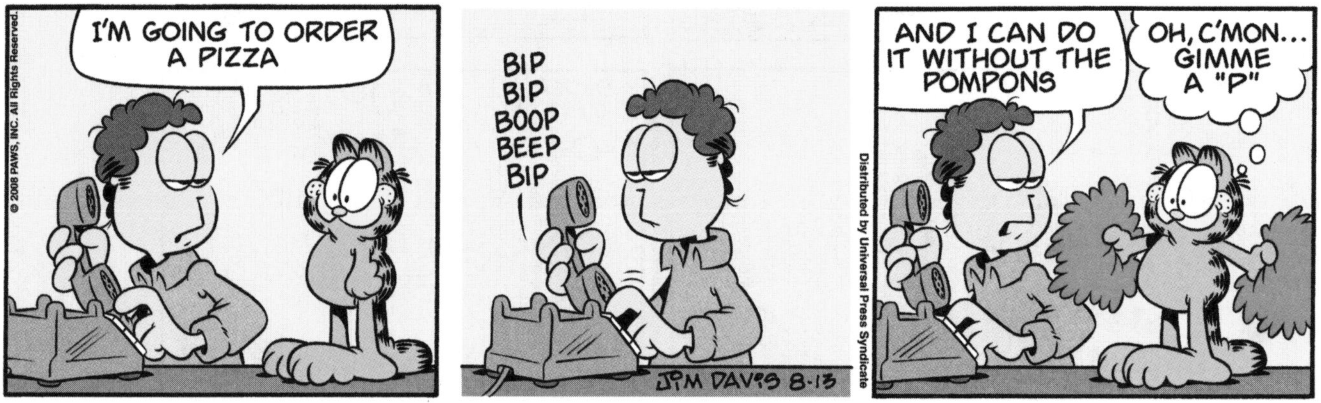
© 2008 PAWS, INC. All Rights Reserved.
I'M GOING TO ORDER A PIZZA
BIP BIP BOOP BEEP BIP
JIM DAVIS 8-13
Distributed by Universal Press Syndicate
AND I CAN DO IT WITHOUT THE POMPONS
OH, C'MON... GIMME A "P"

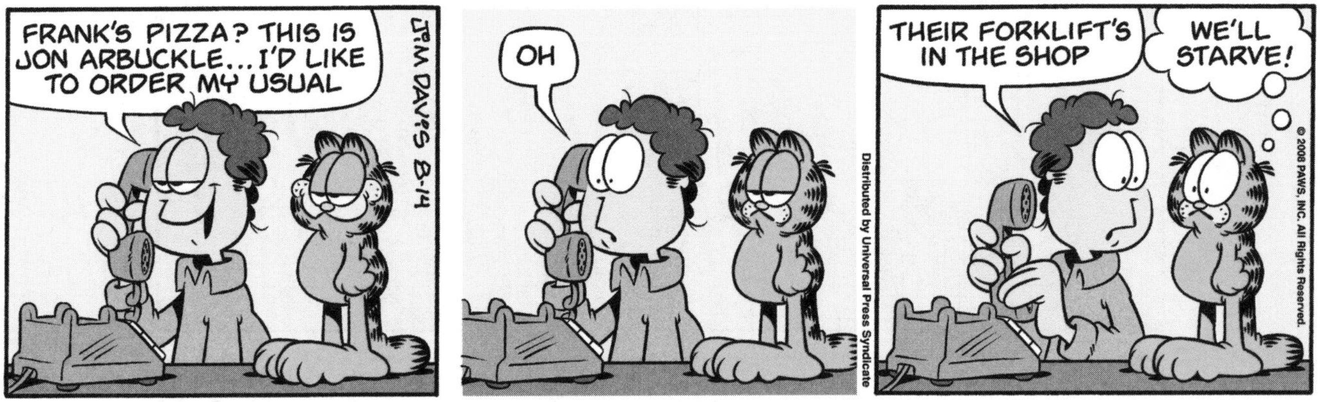
FRANK'S PIZZA? THIS IS JON ARBUCKLE...I'D LIKE TO ORDER MY USUAL
JIM DAVIS 8-14
OH
Distributed by Universal Press Syndicate
THEIR FORKLIFT'S IN THE SHOP
WE'LL STARVE!
© 2008 PAWS, INC. All Rights Reserved.

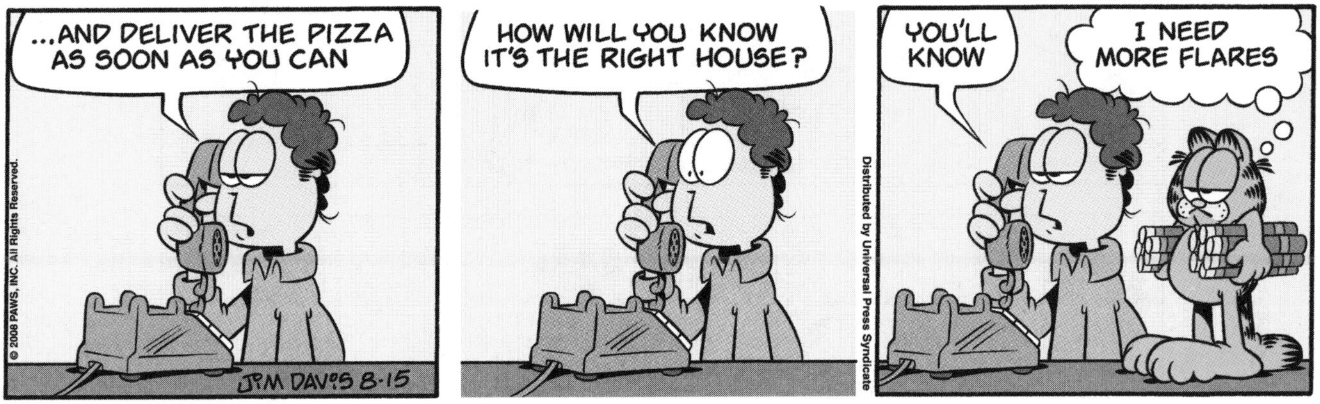
...AND DELIVER THE PIZZA AS SOON AS YOU CAN
© 2008 PAWS, INC. All Rights Reserved.
JIM DAVIS 8-15
HOW WILL YOU KNOW IT'S THE RIGHT HOUSE?
Distributed by Universal Press Syndicate
YOU'LL KNOW
I NEED MORE FLARES

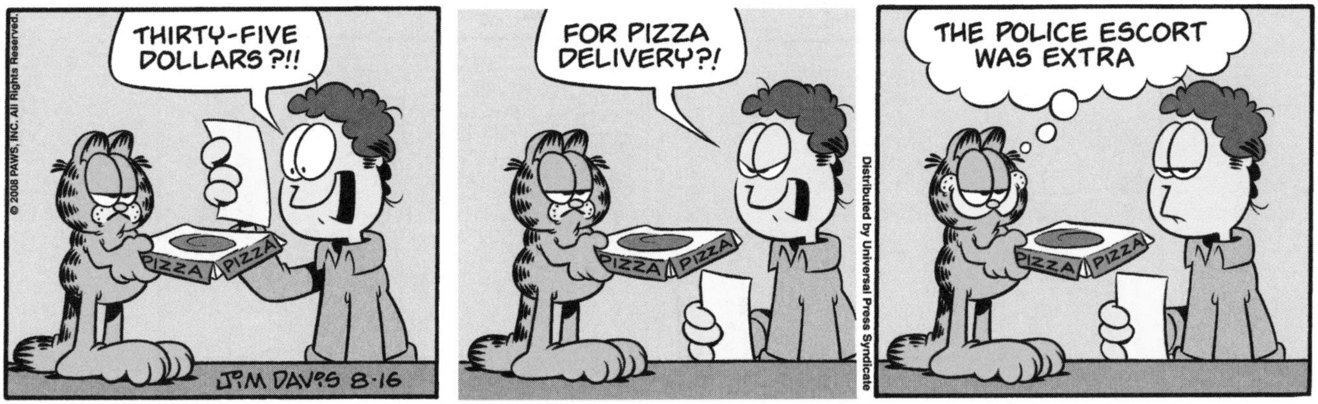
THIRTY-FIVE DOLLARS?!!
PIZZA
PIZZA
© 2008 PAWS, INC. All Rights Reserved.
JIM DAVIS 8-16
FOR PIZZA DELIVERY?!
Distributed by Universal Press Syndicate
THE POLICE ESCORT WAS EXTRA

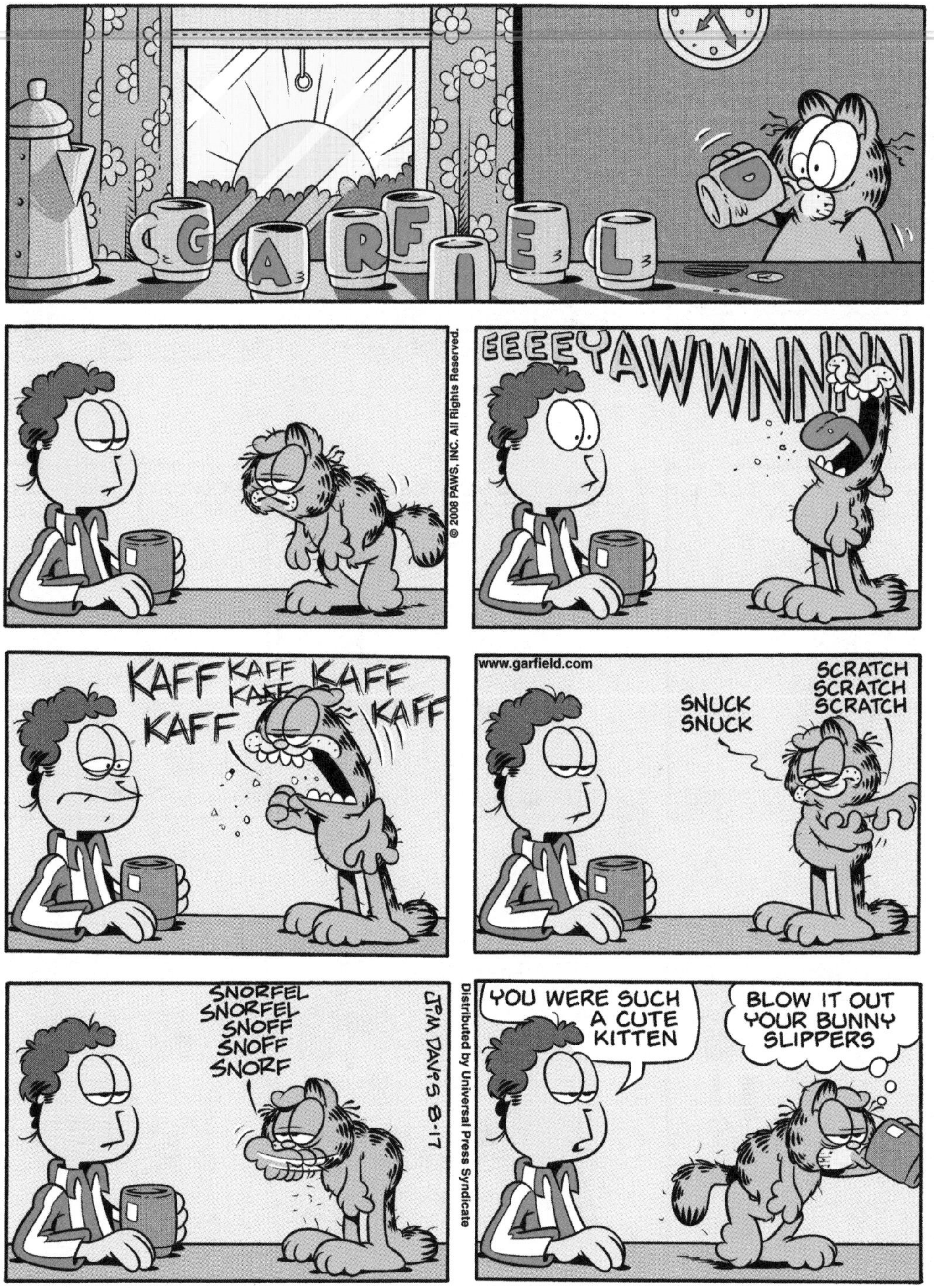

GARFIELD
D
EEEEYAWWNNNN
KAFF KAFF KAFF KAFF KAFF KAFF
www.garfield.com
SNUCK SNUCK
SCRATCH SCRATCH SCRATCH
SNORFEL SNORFEL SNOFF SNOFF SNORF
YOU WERE SUCH A CUTE KITTEN
BLOW IT OUT YOUR BUNNY SLIPPERS
JPM DAVIS 8-17

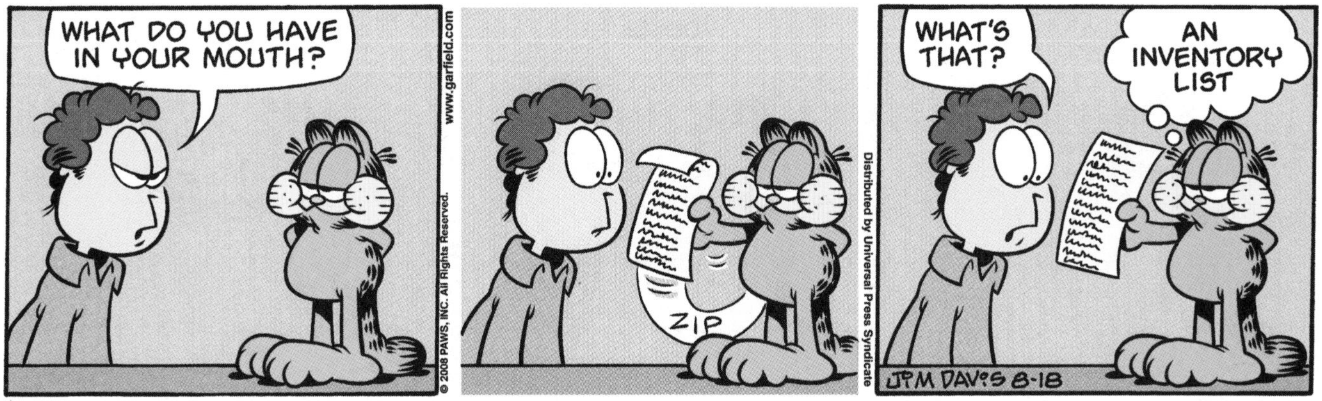
WHAT DO YOU HAVE IN YOUR MOUTH?
ZIP
WHAT'S THAT?
AN INVENTORY LIST
JIM DAVIS 8-18
© 2008 PAWS, INC. All Rights Reserved. www.garfield.com
Distributed by Universal Press Syndicate

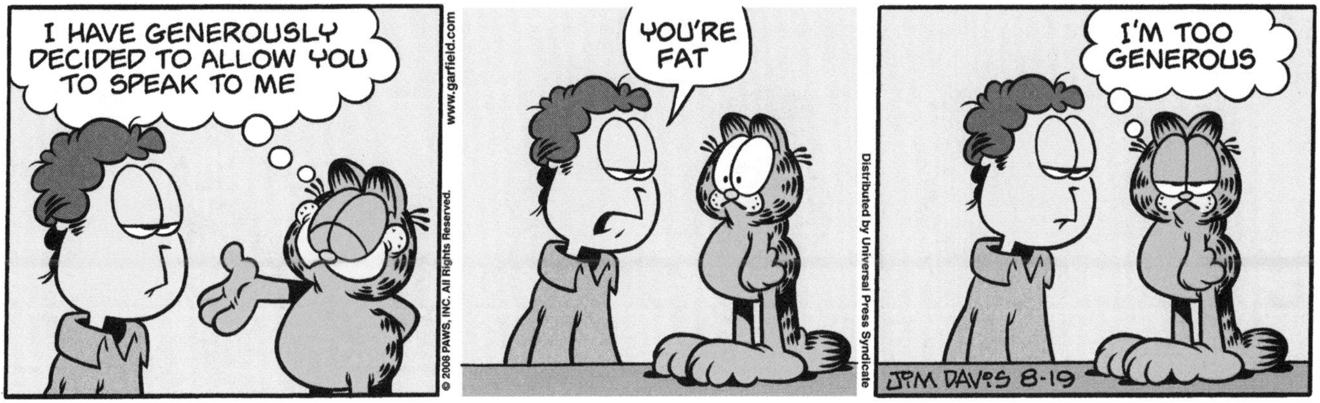
I HAVE GENEROUSLY DECIDED TO ALLOW YOU TO SPEAK TO ME
YOU'RE FAT
I'M TOO GENEROUS
JIM DAVIS 8-19
© 2008 PAWS, INC. All Rights Reserved. www.garfield.com
Distributed by Universal Press Syndicate

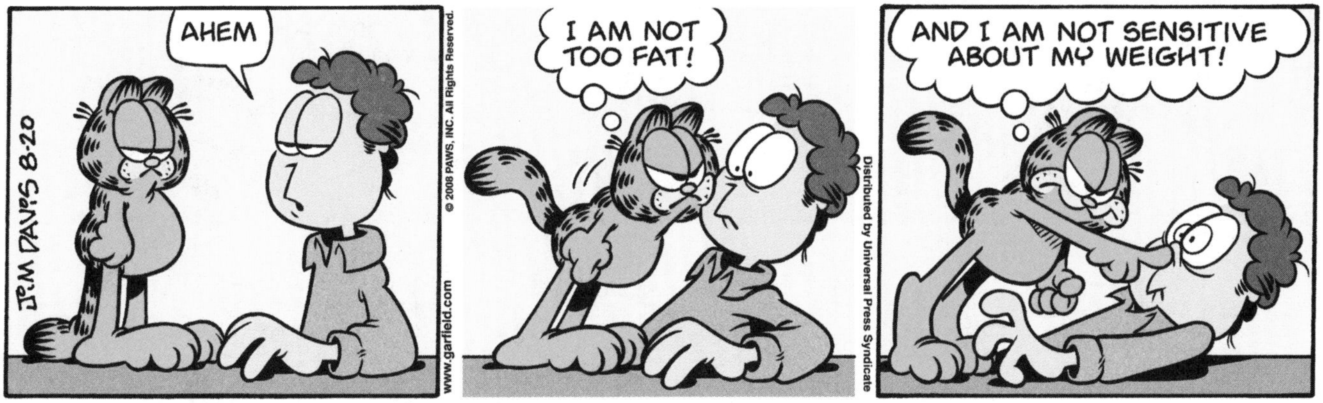
JIM DAVIS 8-20
AHEM
I AM NOT TOO FAT!
AND I AM NOT SENSITIVE ABOUT MY WEIGHT!
© 2008 PAWS, INC. All Rights Reserved. www.garfield.com
Distributed by Universal Press Syndicate

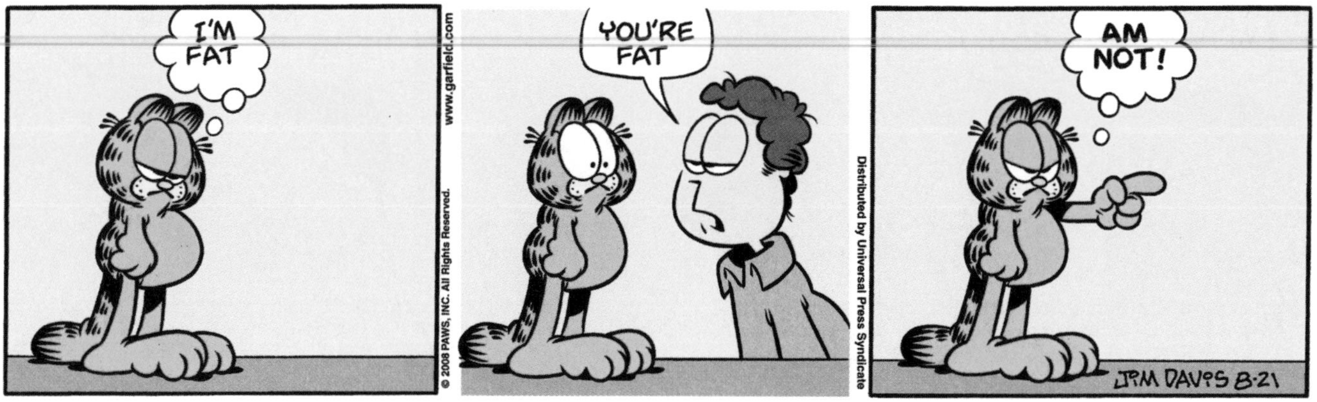
I'M FAT
YOU'RE FAT
AM NOT!
JIM DAVIS 8-21
© 2008 PAWS, INC. All Rights Reserved.
www.garfield.com
Distributed by Universal Press Syndicate

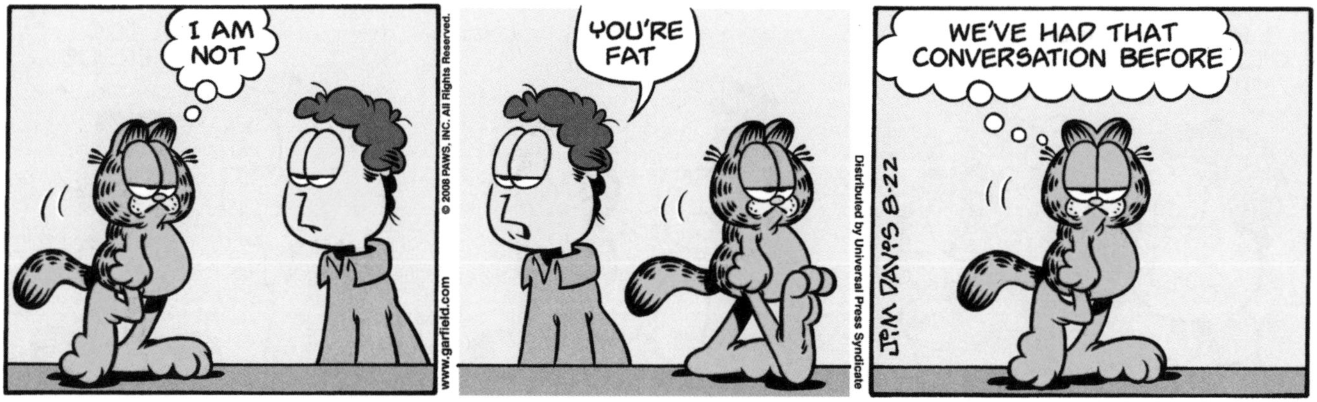
I AM NOT
YOU'RE FAT
WE'VE HAD THAT CONVERSATION BEFORE
JIM DAVIS 8-22
© 2008 PAWS, INC. All Rights Reserved.
www.garfield.com
Distributed by Universal Press Syndicate

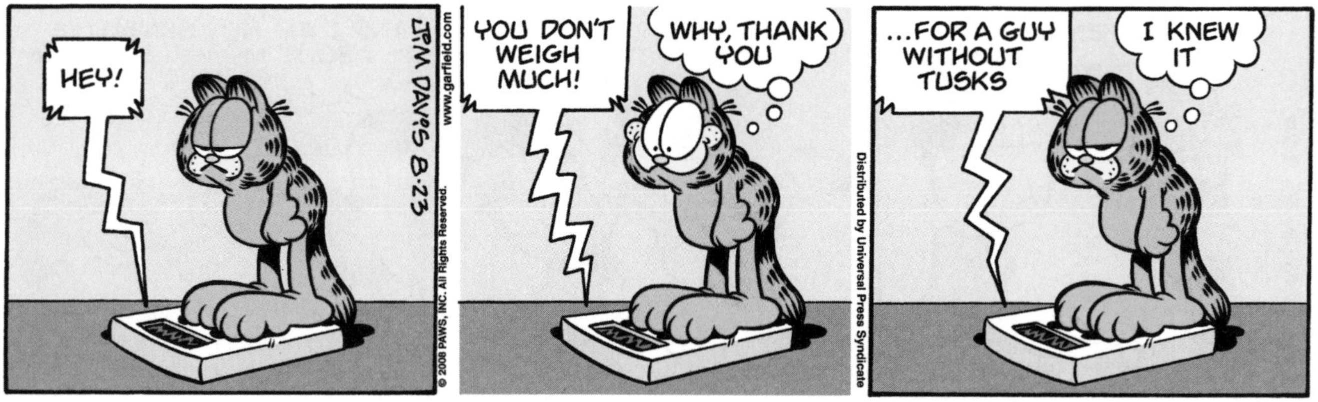
HEY!
YOU DON'T WEIGH MUCH!
WHY, THANK YOU
...FOR A GUY WITHOUT TUSKS
I KNEW IT
JIM DAVIS 8-23
© 2008 PAWS, INC. All Rights Reserved.
www.garfield.com
Distributed by Universal Press Syndicate

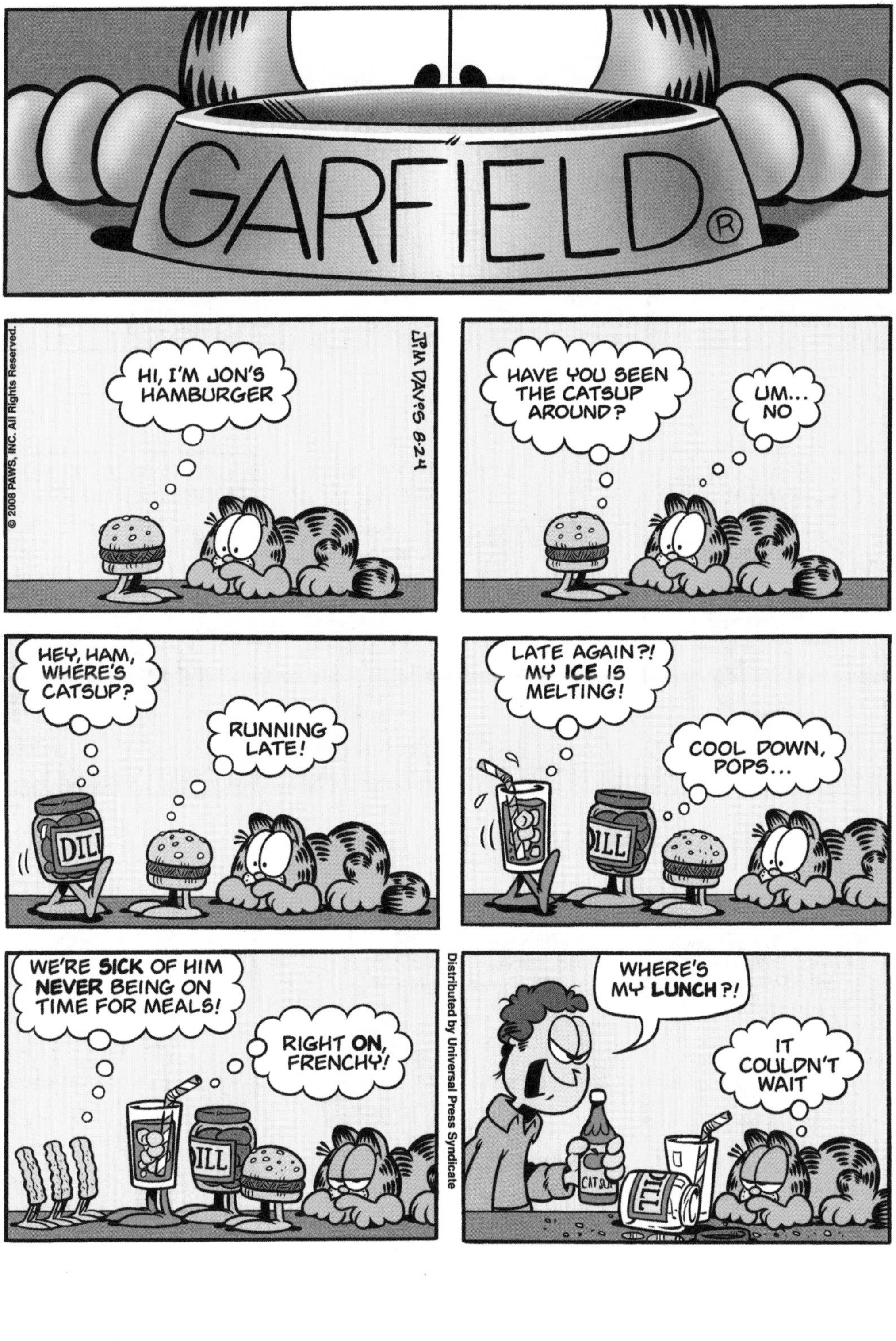
GARFIELD®
© 2008 PAWS, INC. All Rights Reserved.
JPM DAVPS 8-24
HI, I'M JON'S HAMBURGER
HAVE YOU SEEN THE CATSUP AROUND?
UM... NO
HEY, HAM, WHERE'S CATSUP?
RUNNING LATE!
DILL
LATE AGAIN?! MY ICE IS MELTING!
COOL DOWN, POPS...
WE'RE SICK OF HIM NEVER BEING ON TIME FOR MEALS!
RIGHT ON, FRENCHY!
Distributed by Universal Press Syndicate
WHERE'S MY LUNCH?!
IT COULDN'T WAIT
CATSUP

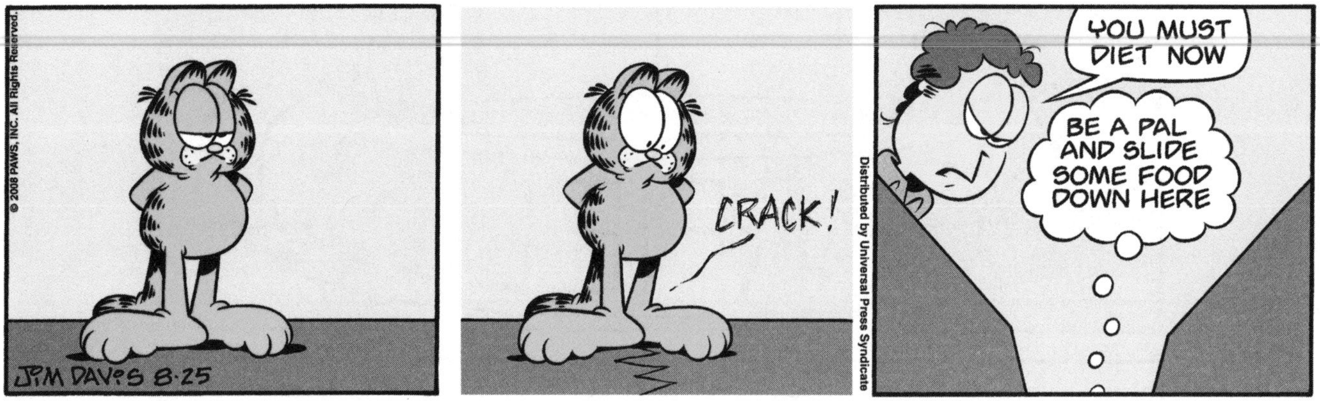
© 2008 PAWS, INC. All Rights Reserved.
JIM DAVIS 8-25
CRACK!
Distributed by Universal Press Syndicate
YOU MUST DIET NOW
BE A PAL AND SLIDE SOME FOOD DOWN HERE

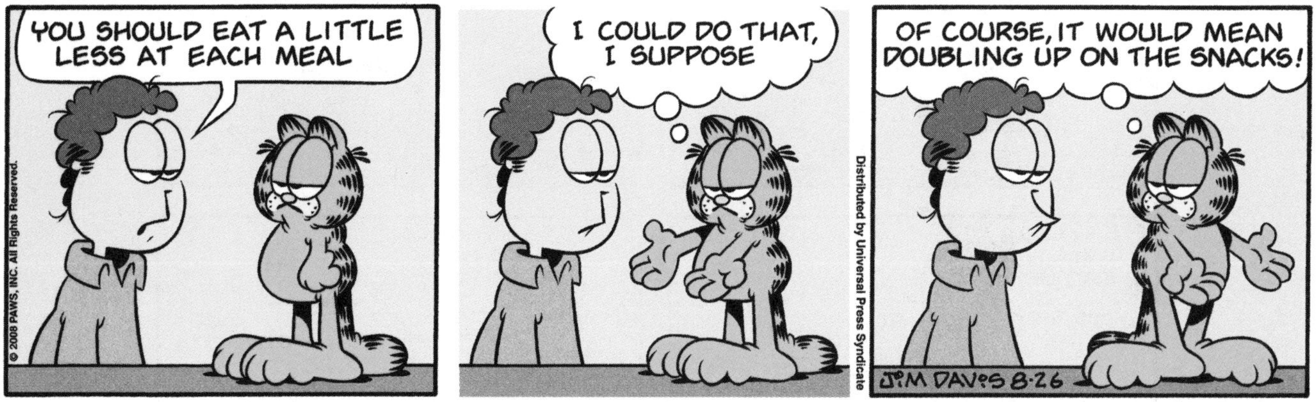
YOU SHOULD EAT A LITTLE LESS AT EACH MEAL
© 2008 PAWS, INC. All Rights Reserved.
I COULD DO THAT, I SUPPOSE
Distributed by Universal Press Syndicate
OF COURSE, IT WOULD MEAN DOUBLING UP ON THE SNACKS!
JIM DAVIS 8-26

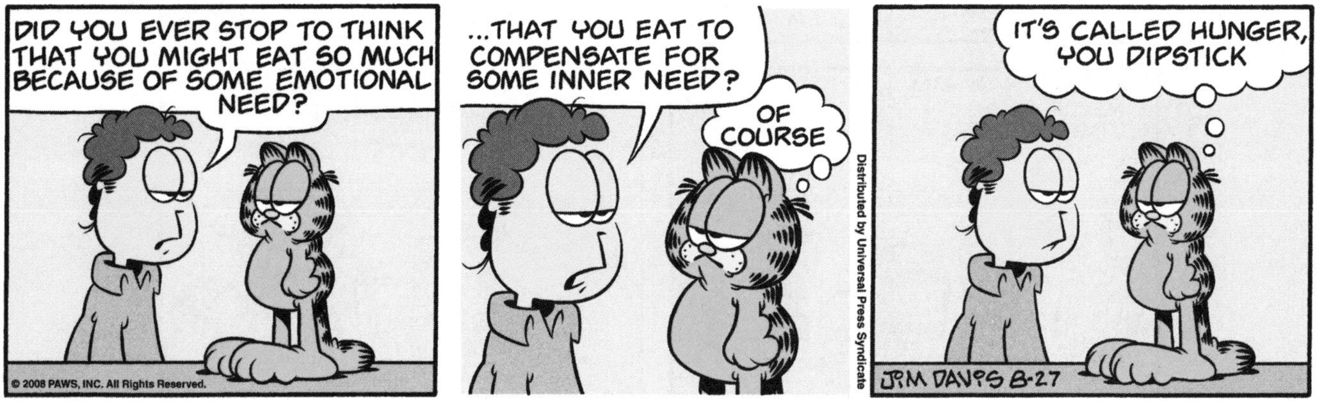
DID YOU EVER STOP TO THINK THAT YOU MIGHT EAT SO MUCH BECAUSE OF SOME EMOTIONAL NEED?
© 2008 PAWS, INC. All Rights Reserved.
...THAT YOU EAT TO COMPENSATE FOR SOME INNER NEED?
OF COURSE
Distributed by Universal Press Syndicate
IT'S CALLED HUNGER, YOU DIPSTICK
JIM DAVIS 8-27

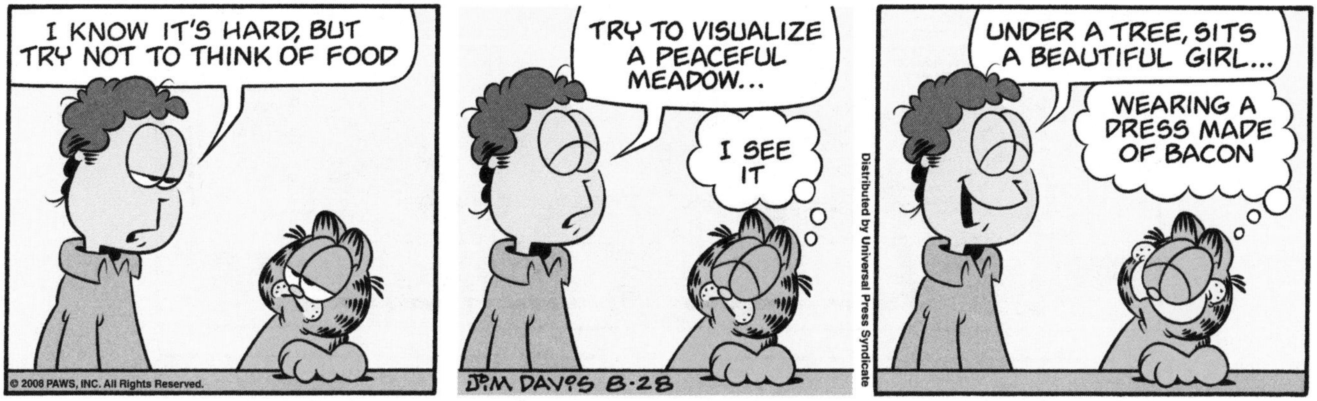
I KNOW IT'S HARD, BUT TRY NOT TO THINK OF FOOD
TRY TO VISUALIZE A PEACEFUL MEADOW...
I SEE IT
UNDER A TREE, SITS A BEAUTIFUL GIRL...
WEARING A DRESS MADE OF BACON
© 2008 PAWS, INC. All Rights Reserved.
JIM DAVIS 8-28
Distributed by Universal Press Syndicate

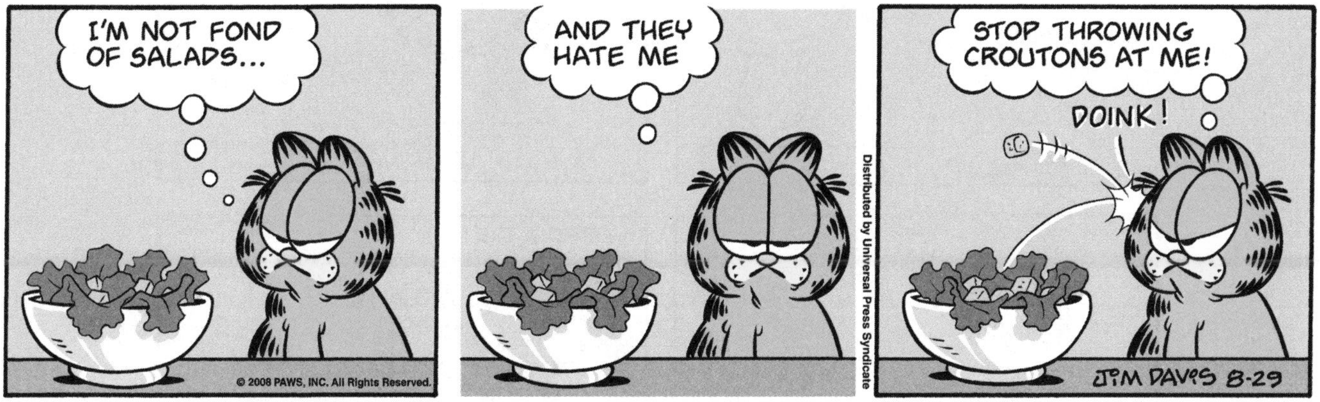
I'M NOT FOND OF SALADS...
AND THEY HATE ME
STOP THROWING CROUTONS AT ME!
DOINK!
© 2008 PAWS, INC. All Rights Reserved.
JIM DAVIS 8-29
Distributed by Universal Press Syndicate

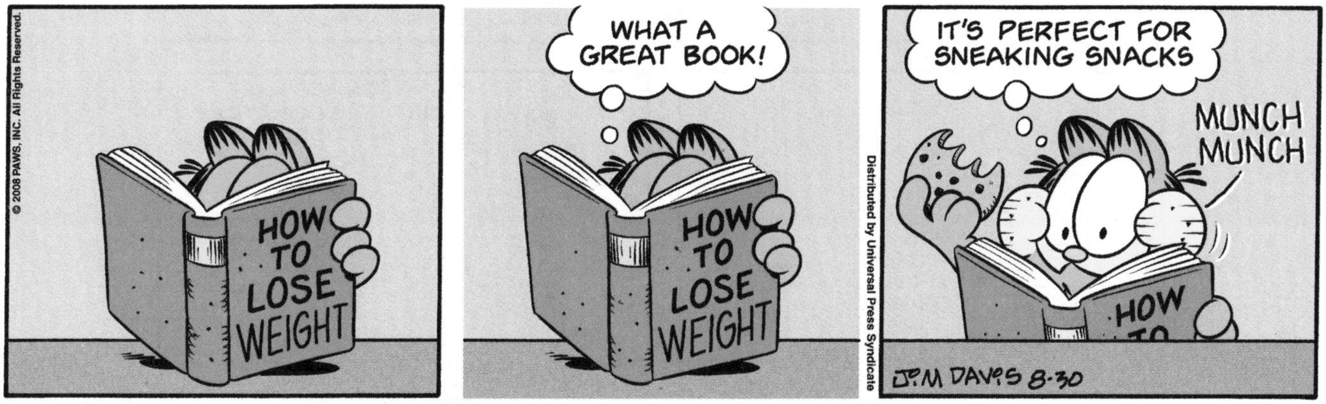
© 2008 PAWS, INC. All Rights Reserved.
HOW TO LOSE WEIGHT
WHAT A GREAT BOOK!
HOW TO LOSE WEIGHT
IT'S PERFECT FOR SNEAKING SNACKS
MUNCH MUNCH
HOW
JIM DAVIS 8-30
Distributed by Universal Press Syndicate

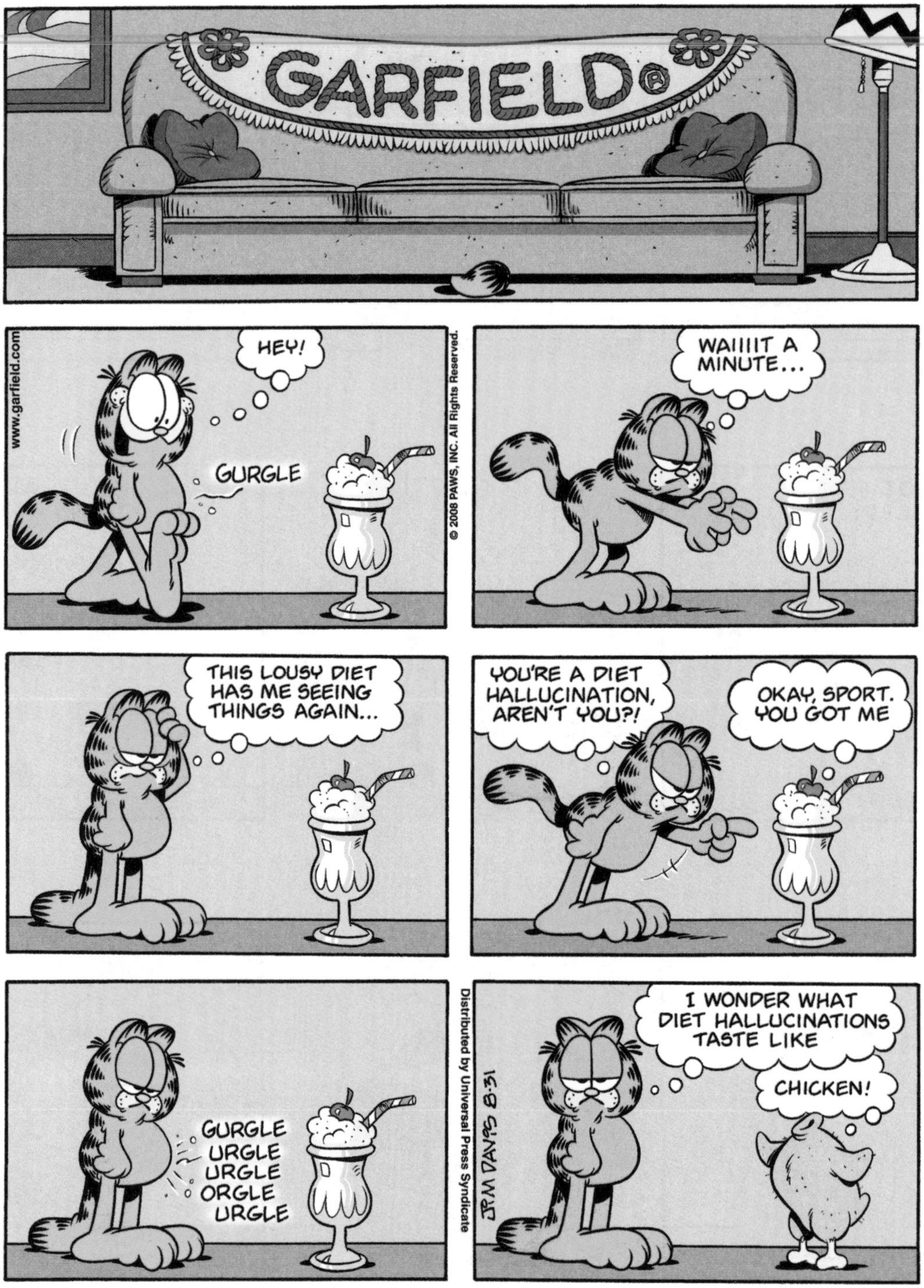
GARFIELD®
www.garfield.com
HEY!
GURGLE
© 2008 PAWS, INC. All Rights Reserved.
WAIIIIT A MINUTE...
THIS LOUSY DIET HAS ME SEEING THINGS AGAIN...
YOU'RE A DIET HALLUCINATION, AREN'T YOU?!
OKAY, SPORT. YOU GOT ME
GURGLE
URGLE
URGLE
ORGLE
URGLE
Distributed by Universal Press Syndicate
JPM DAVPS 8-31
I WONDER WHAT DIET HALLUCINATIONS TASTE LIKE
CHICKEN!

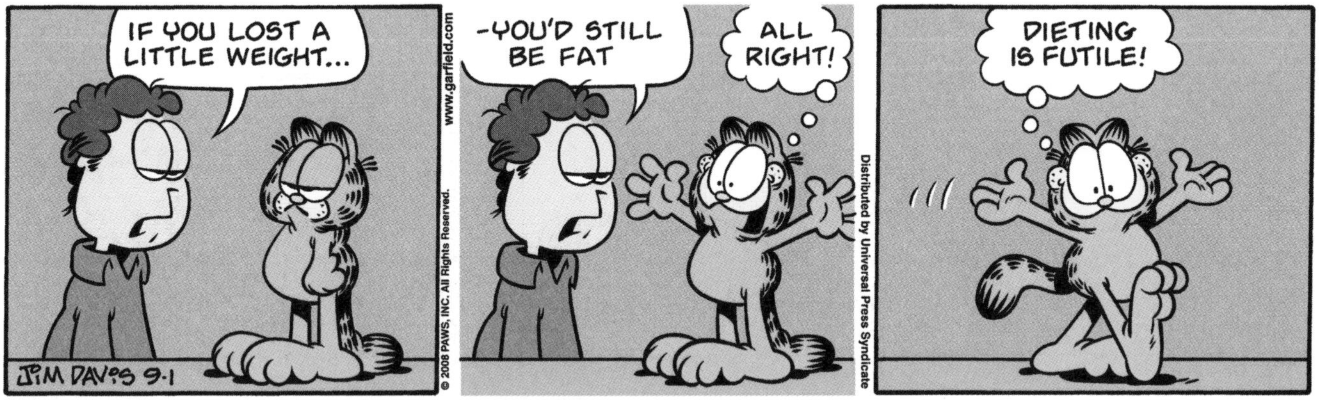
IF YOU LOST A LITTLE WEIGHT...
-YOU'D STILL BE FAT
ALL RIGHT!
DIETING IS FUTILE!
JIM DAVIS 9-1
© 2008 PAWS, INC. All Rights Reserved.
www.garfield.com
Distributed by Universal Press Syndicate

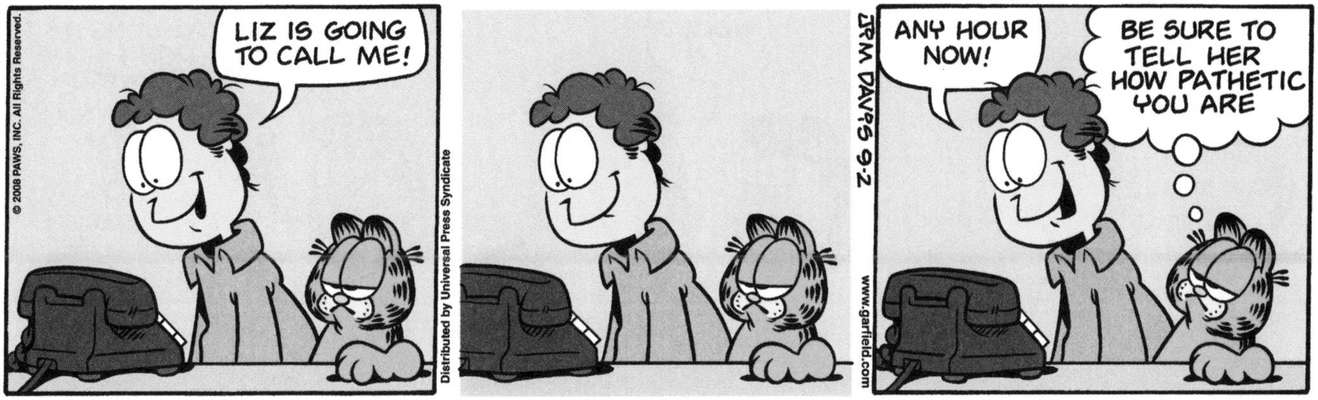
LIZ IS GOING TO CALL ME!
ANY HOUR NOW!
BE SURE TO TELL HER HOW PATHETIC YOU ARE
JIM DAVIS 9-2
© 2008 PAWS, INC. All Rights Reserved.
Distributed by Universal Press Syndicate
www.garfield.com

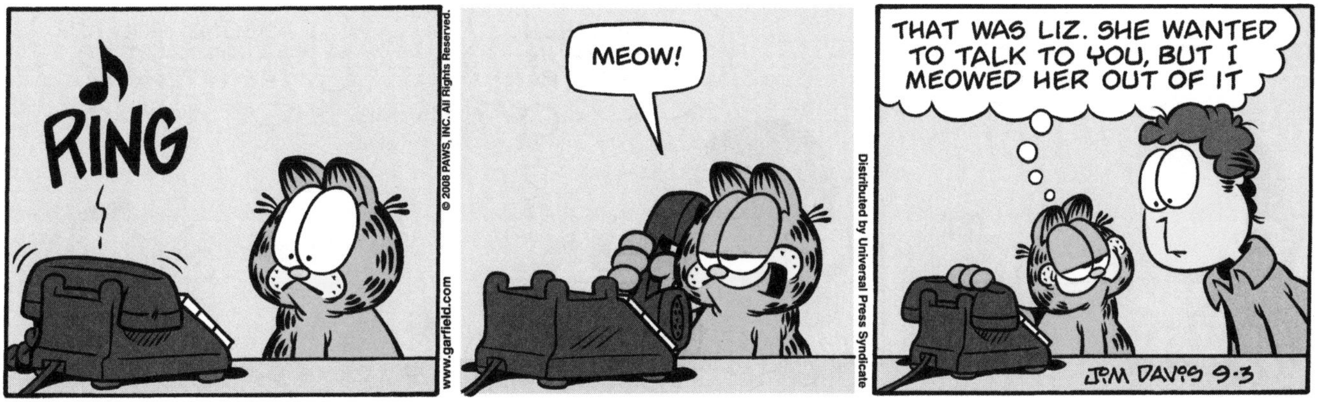
RING
MEOW!
THAT WAS LIZ. SHE WANTED TO TALK TO YOU, BUT I MEOWED HER OUT OF IT
JIM DAVIS 9-3
© 2008 PAWS, INC. All Rights Reserved.
www.garfield.com
Distributed by Universal Press Syndicate

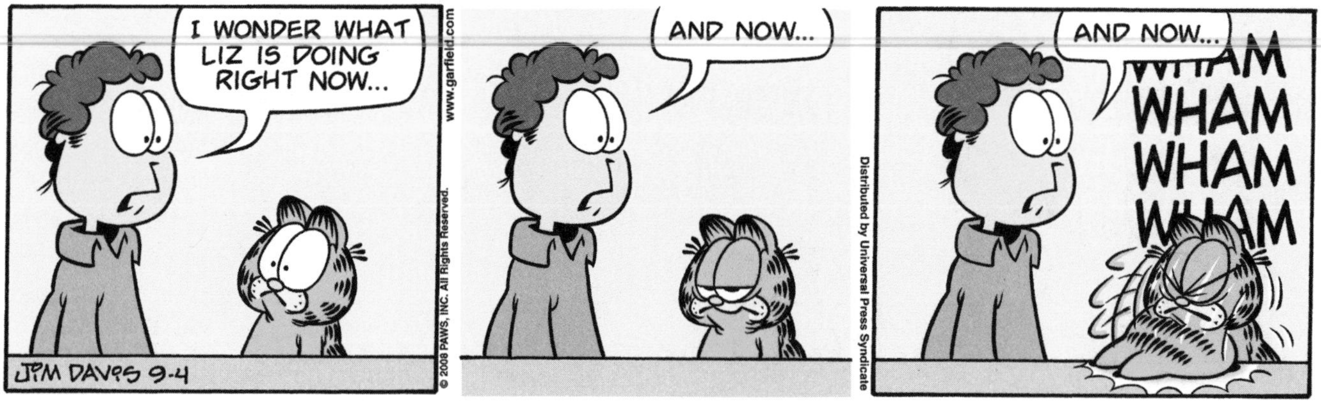
I WONDER WHAT LIZ IS DOING RIGHT NOW...
JIM DAVIS 9-4
© 2008 PAWS, INC. All Rights Reserved. www.garfield.com
AND NOW...
Distributed by Universal Press Syndicate
AND NOW...
WHAM
WHAM

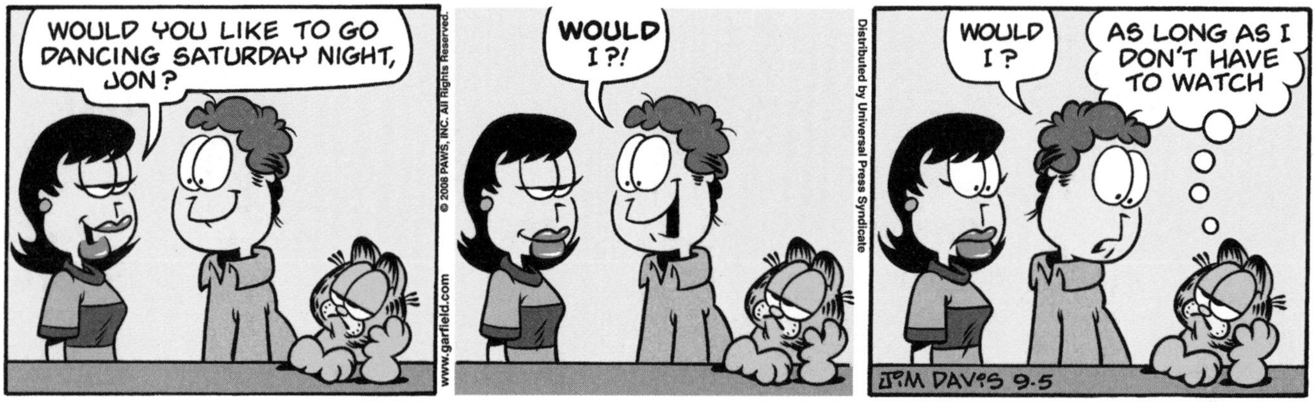
WOULD YOU LIKE TO GO DANCING SATURDAY NIGHT, JON?
www.garfield.com © 2008 PAWS, INC. All Rights Reserved.
WOULD I?!
Distributed by Universal Press Syndicate
WOULD I?
AS LONG AS I DON'T HAVE TO WATCH
JIM DAVIS 9-5

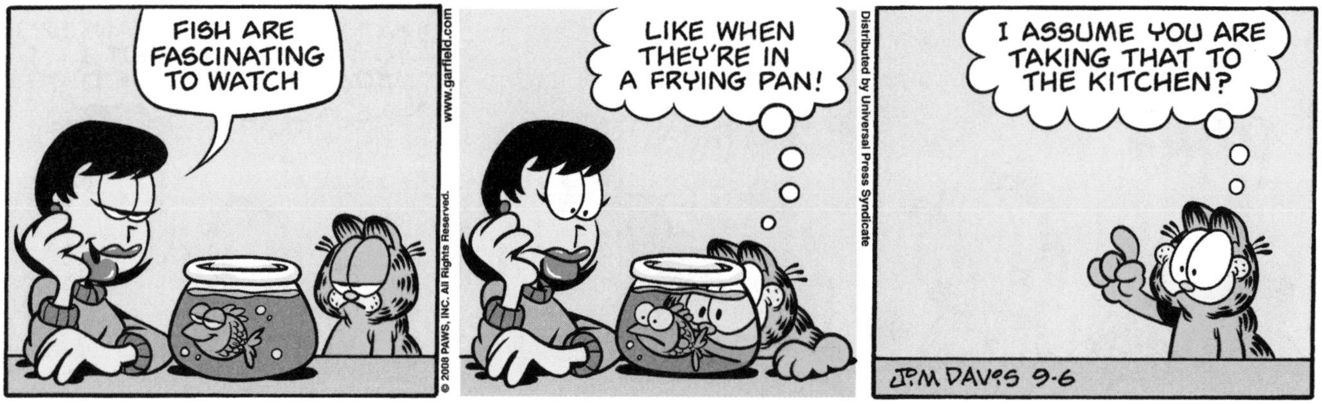
FISH ARE FASCINATING TO WATCH
© 2008 PAWS, INC. All Rights Reserved. www.garfield.com
LIKE WHEN THEY'RE IN A FRYING PAN!
Distributed by Universal Press Syndicate
I ASSUME YOU ARE TAKING THAT TO THE KITCHEN?
JIM DAVIS 9-6

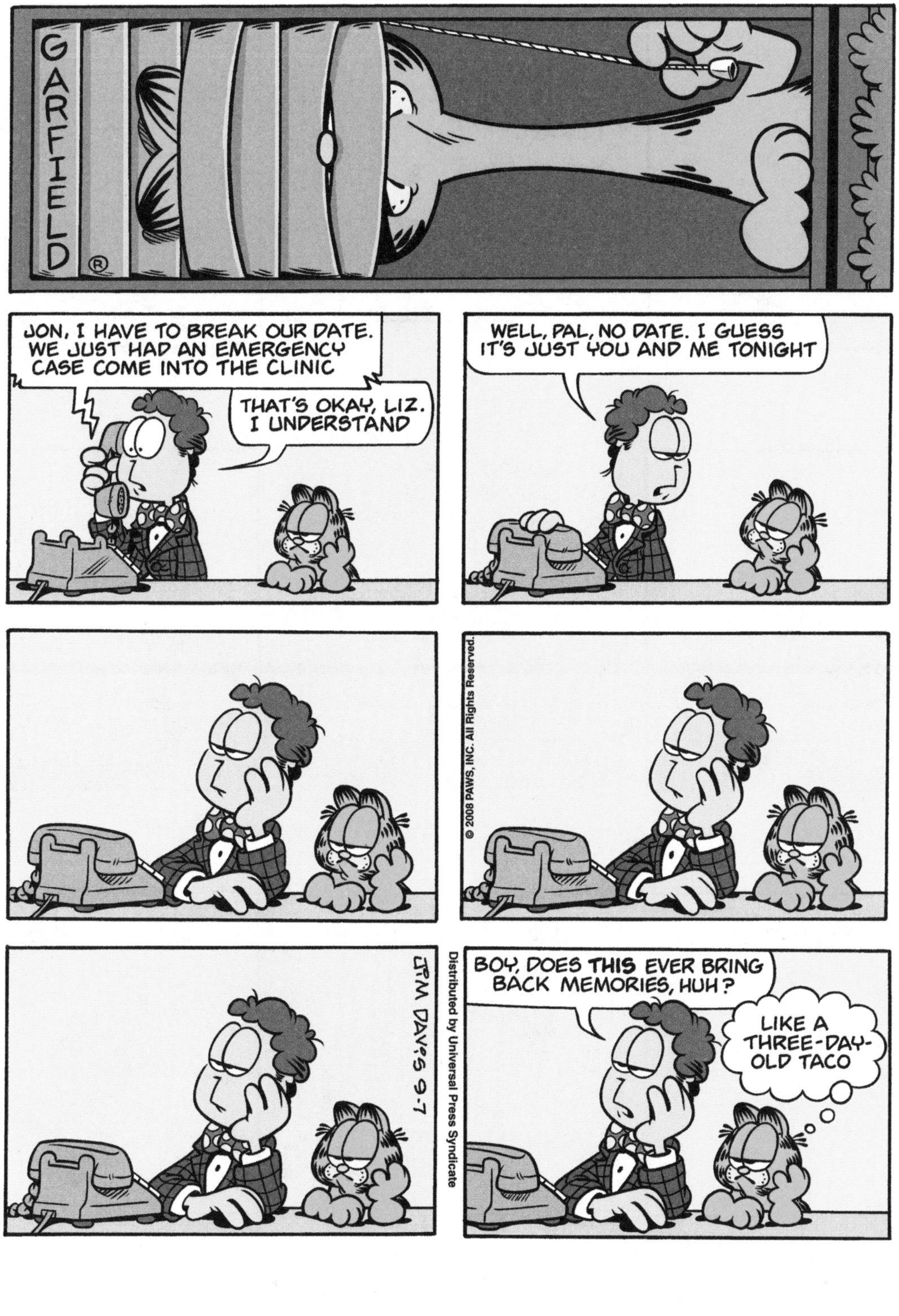
GARFIELD ®
JON, I HAVE TO BREAK OUR DATE. WE JUST HAD AN EMERGENCY CASE COME INTO THE CLINIC
THAT'S OKAY, LIZ. I UNDERSTAND
WELL, PAL, NO DATE. I GUESS IT'S JUST YOU AND ME TONIGHT
© 2008 PAWS, INC. All Rights Reserved.
JIM DAVIS 9-7
Distributed by Universal Press Syndicate
BOY, DOES **THIS** EVER BRING BACK MEMORIES, HUH?
LIKE A THREE-DAY-OLD TACO

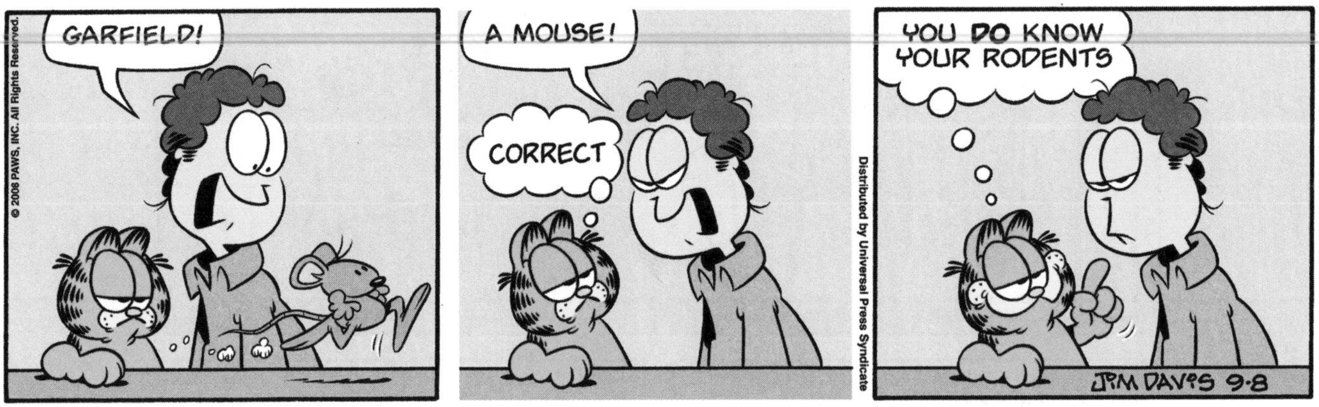
GARFIELD!
A MOUSE!
CORRECT
YOU DO KNOW YOUR RODENTS
JIM DAVIS 9-8
© 2008 PAWS, INC. All Rights Reserved.
Distributed by Universal Press Syndicate

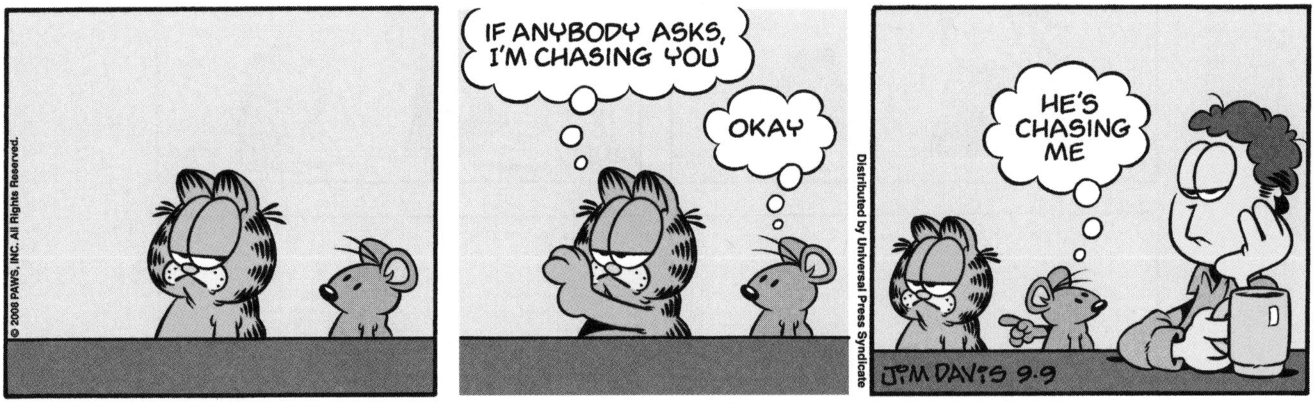
IF ANYBODY ASKS, I'M CHASING YOU
OKAY
HE'S CHASING ME
JIM DAVIS 9-9
© 2008 PAWS, INC. All Rights Reserved.
Distributed by Universal Press Syndicate

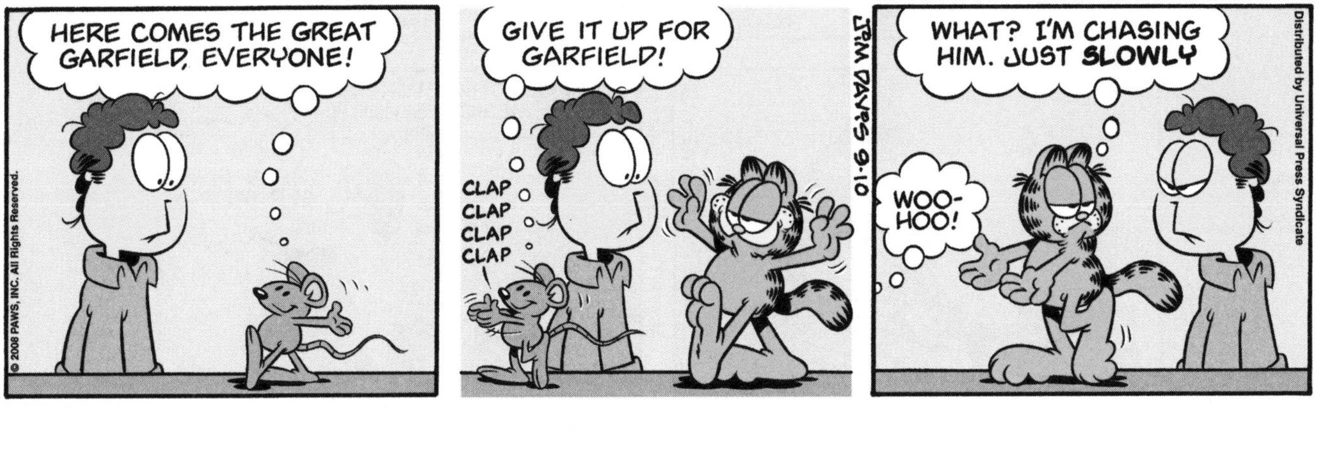
HERE COMES THE GREAT GARFIELD, EVERYONE!
GIVE IT UP FOR GARFIELD!
CLAP CLAP CLAP CLAP
WHAT? I'M CHASING HIM. JUST SLOWLY
WOO-HOO!
JIM DAVIS 9-10
© 2008 PAWS, INC. All Rights Reserved.
Distributed by Universal Press Syndicate

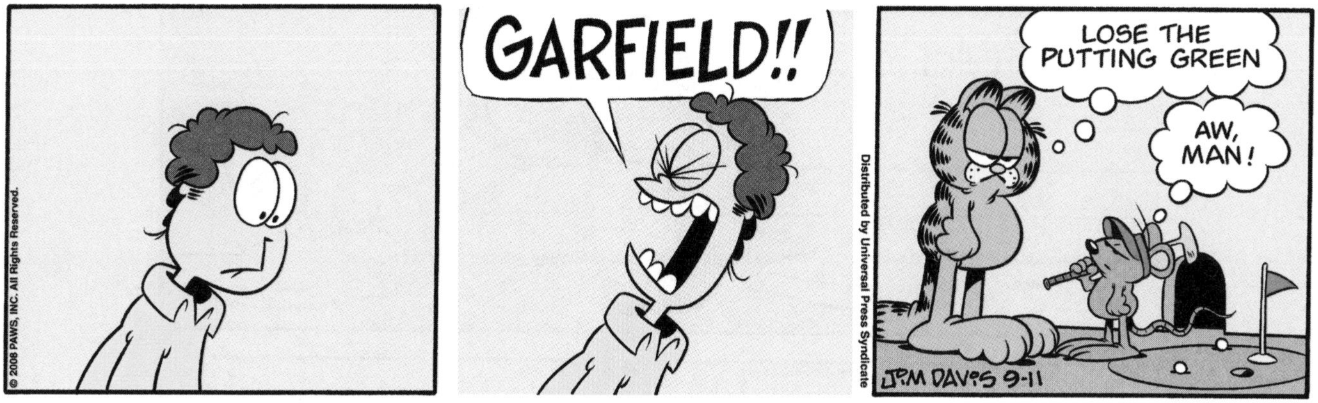
© 2008 PAWS, INC. All Rights Reserved.
GARFIELD!!
Distributed by Universal Press Syndicate
LOSE THE PUTTING GREEN
AW, MAN!
JIM DAVIS 9-11

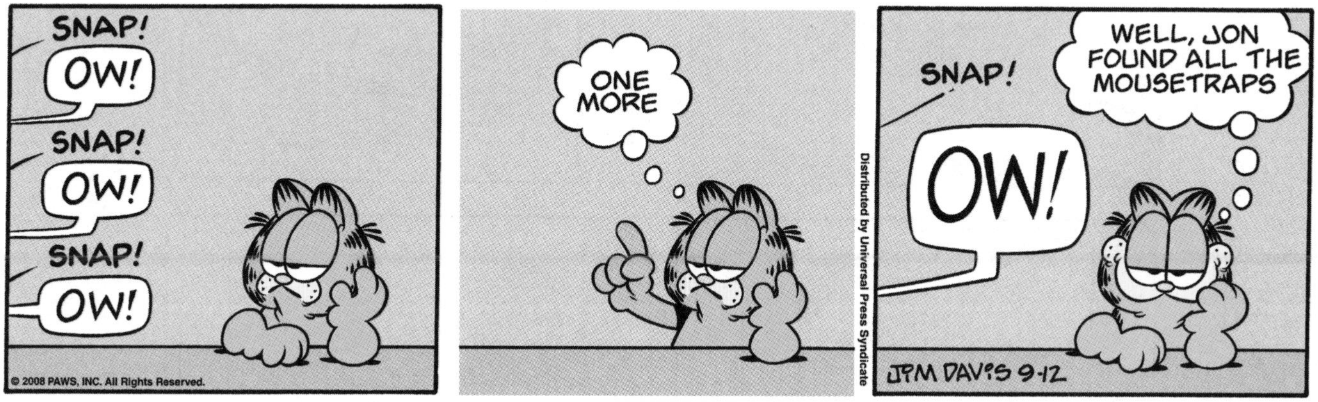
SNAP!
OW!
SNAP!
OW!
SNAP!
OW!
© 2008 PAWS, INC. All Rights Reserved.
ONE MORE
Distributed by Universal Press Syndicate
SNAP!
OW!
WELL, JON FOUND ALL THE MOUSETRAPS
JIM DAVIS 9-12

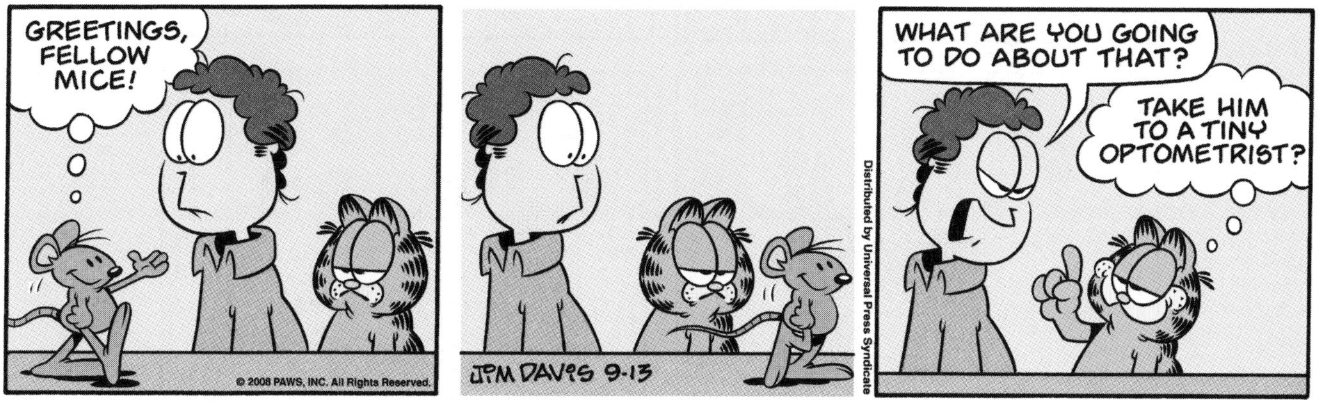
GREETINGS, FELLOW MICE!
© 2008 PAWS, INC. All Rights Reserved.
JIM DAVIS 9-13
Distributed by Universal Press Syndicate
WHAT ARE YOU GOING TO DO ABOUT THAT?
TAKE HIM TO A TINY OPTOMETRIST?

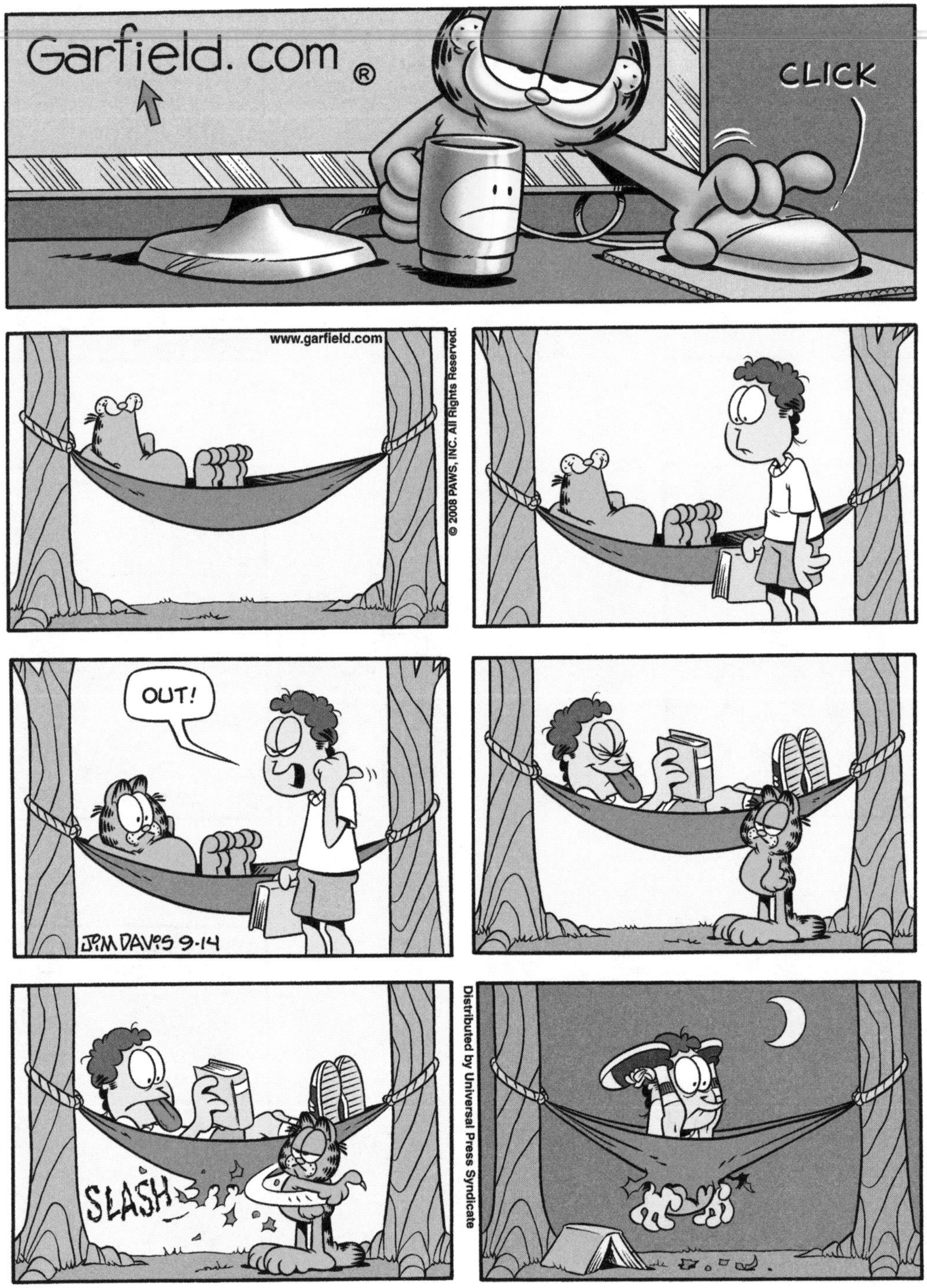
Garfield.com ®
CLICK
www.garfield.com
© 2008 PAWS, INC. All Rights Reserved.
OUT!
JIM DAVIS 9-14
Distributed by Universal Press Syndicate
SLASH

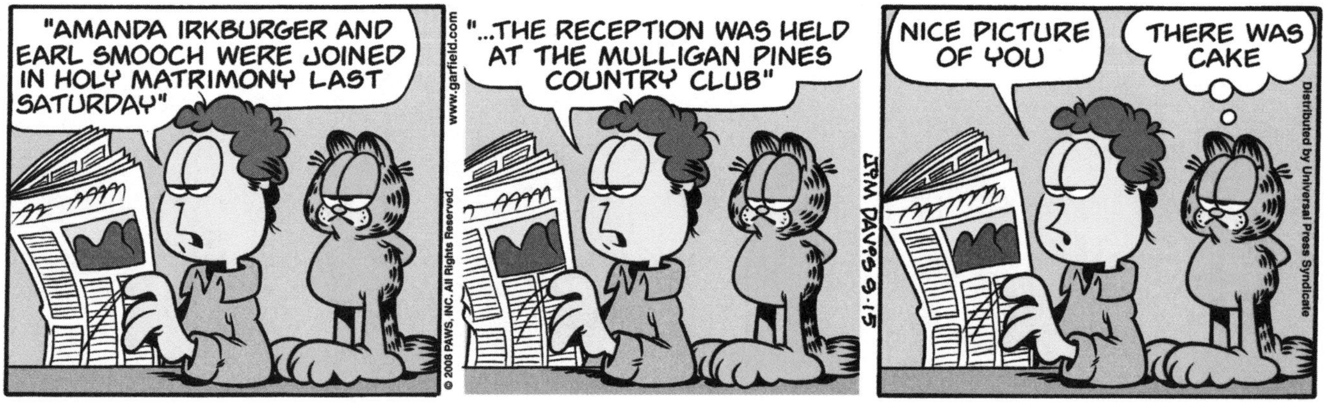
"AMANDA IRKBURGER AND EARL SMOOCH WERE JOINED IN HOLY MATRIMONY LAST SATURDAY"
"...THE RECEPTION WAS HELD AT THE MULLIGAN PINES COUNTRY CLUB"
NICE PICTURE OF YOU
THERE WAS CAKE
© 2008 PAWS, INC. All Rights Reserved.
www.garfield.com
Distributed by Universal Press Syndicate

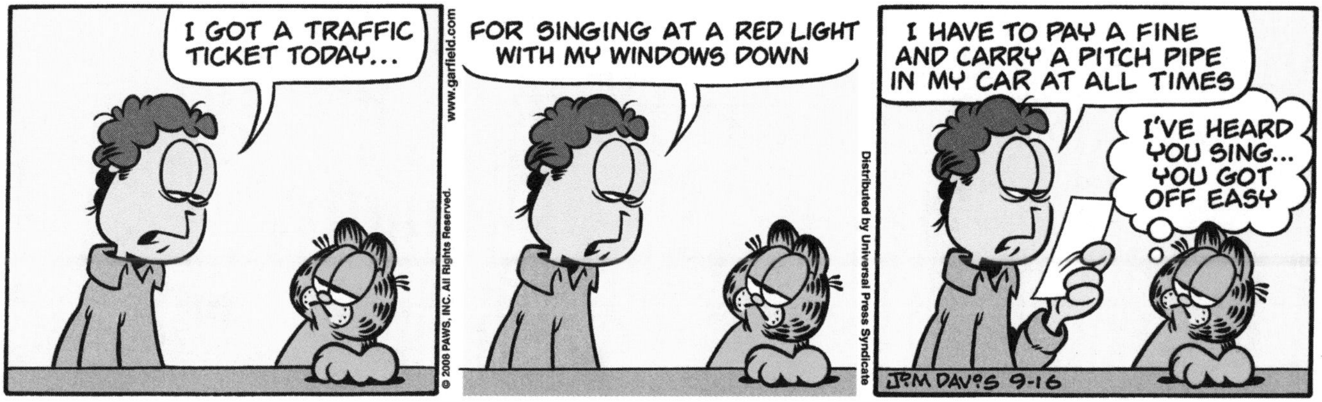
I GOT A TRAFFIC TICKET TODAY...
FOR SINGING AT A RED LIGHT WITH MY WINDOWS DOWN
I HAVE TO PAY A FINE AND CARRY A PITCH PIPE IN MY CAR AT ALL TIMES
I'VE HEARD YOU SING... YOU GOT OFF EASY
© 2008 PAWS, INC. All Rights Reserved.
www.garfield.com
Distributed by Universal Press Syndicate

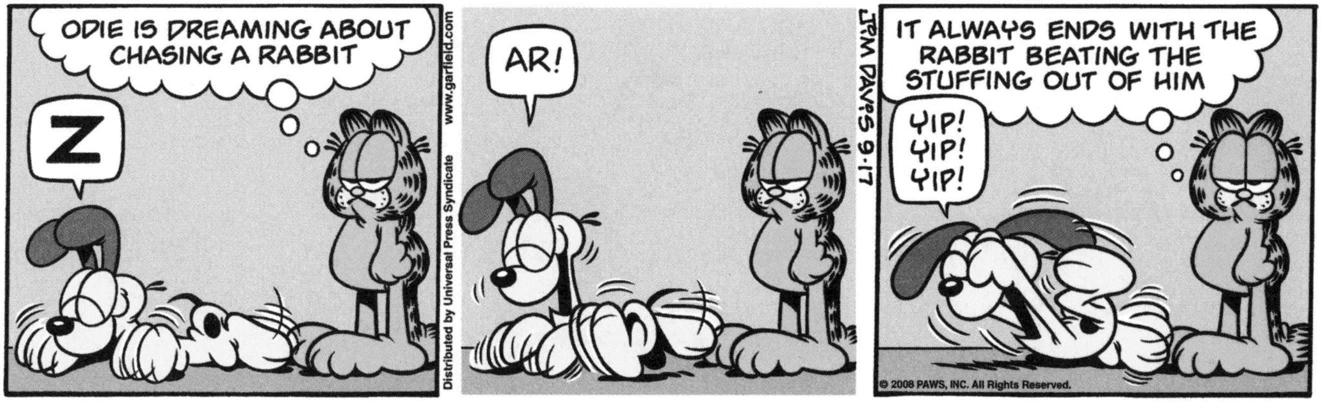
ODIE IS DREAMING ABOUT CHASING A RABBIT
Z
AR!
IT ALWAYS ENDS WITH THE RABBIT BEATING THE STUFFING OUT OF HIM
YIP! YIP! YIP!
www.garfield.com
Distributed by Universal Press Syndicate
© 2008 PAWS, INC. All Rights Reserved.

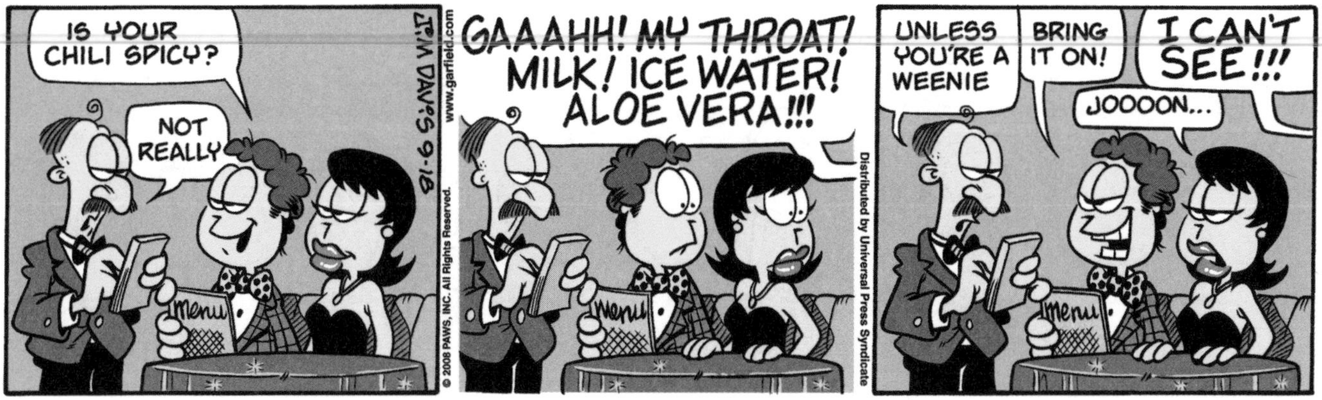

IS YOUR CHILI SPICY?
NOT REALLY
JIM DAVIS 9-18
www.garfield.com
© 2008 PAWS, INC. All Rights Reserved.
GAAAHH! MY THROAT! MILK! ICE WATER! ALOE VERA!!!
Distributed by Universal Press Syndicate
UNLESS YOU'RE A WEENIE
BRING IT ON!
I CAN'T SEE!!!
JOOOON...

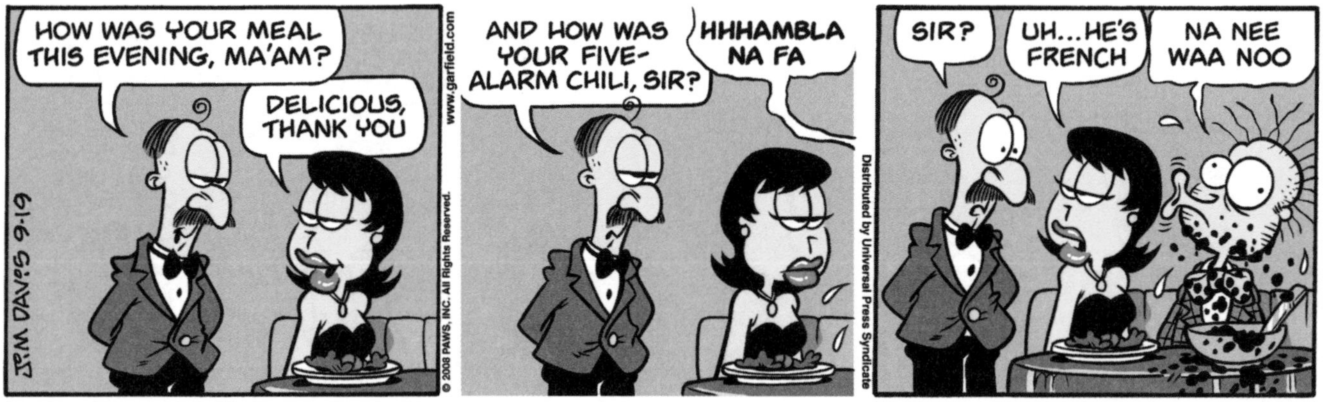

HOW WAS YOUR MEAL THIS EVENING, MA'AM?
DELICIOUS, THANK YOU
JIM DAVIS 9-19
www.garfield.com
© 2008 PAWS, INC. All Rights Reserved.
AND HOW WAS YOUR FIVE-ALARM CHILI, SIR?
HHHAMBLA NA FA
Distributed by Universal Press Syndicate
SIR?
UH...HE'S FRENCH
NA NEE WAA NOO

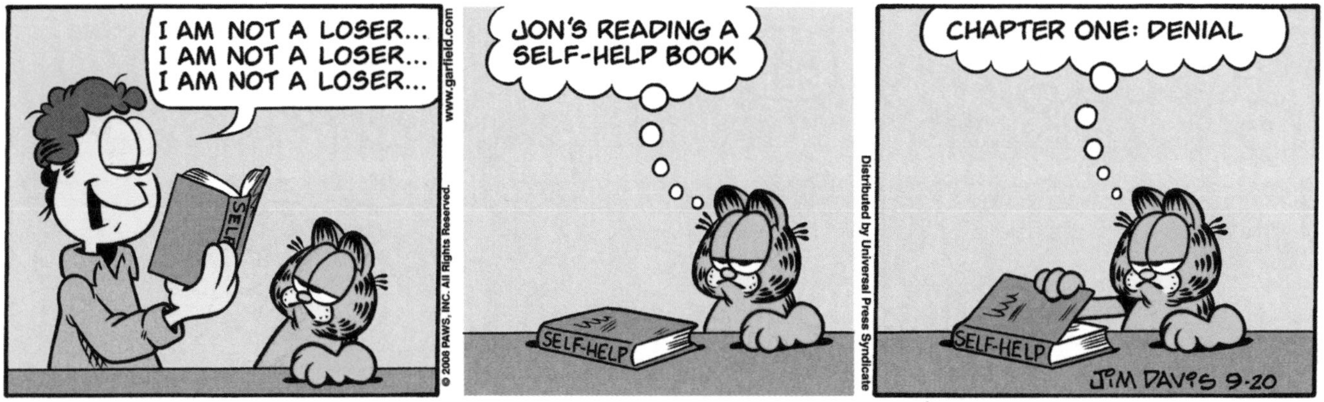

I AM NOT A LOSER... I AM NOT A LOSER... I AM NOT A LOSER...
www.garfield.com
© 2008 PAWS, INC. All Rights Reserved.
JON'S READING A SELF-HELP BOOK
SELF-HELP
Distributed by Universal Press Syndicate
CHAPTER ONE: DENIAL
SELF-HELP
JIM DAVIS 9-20

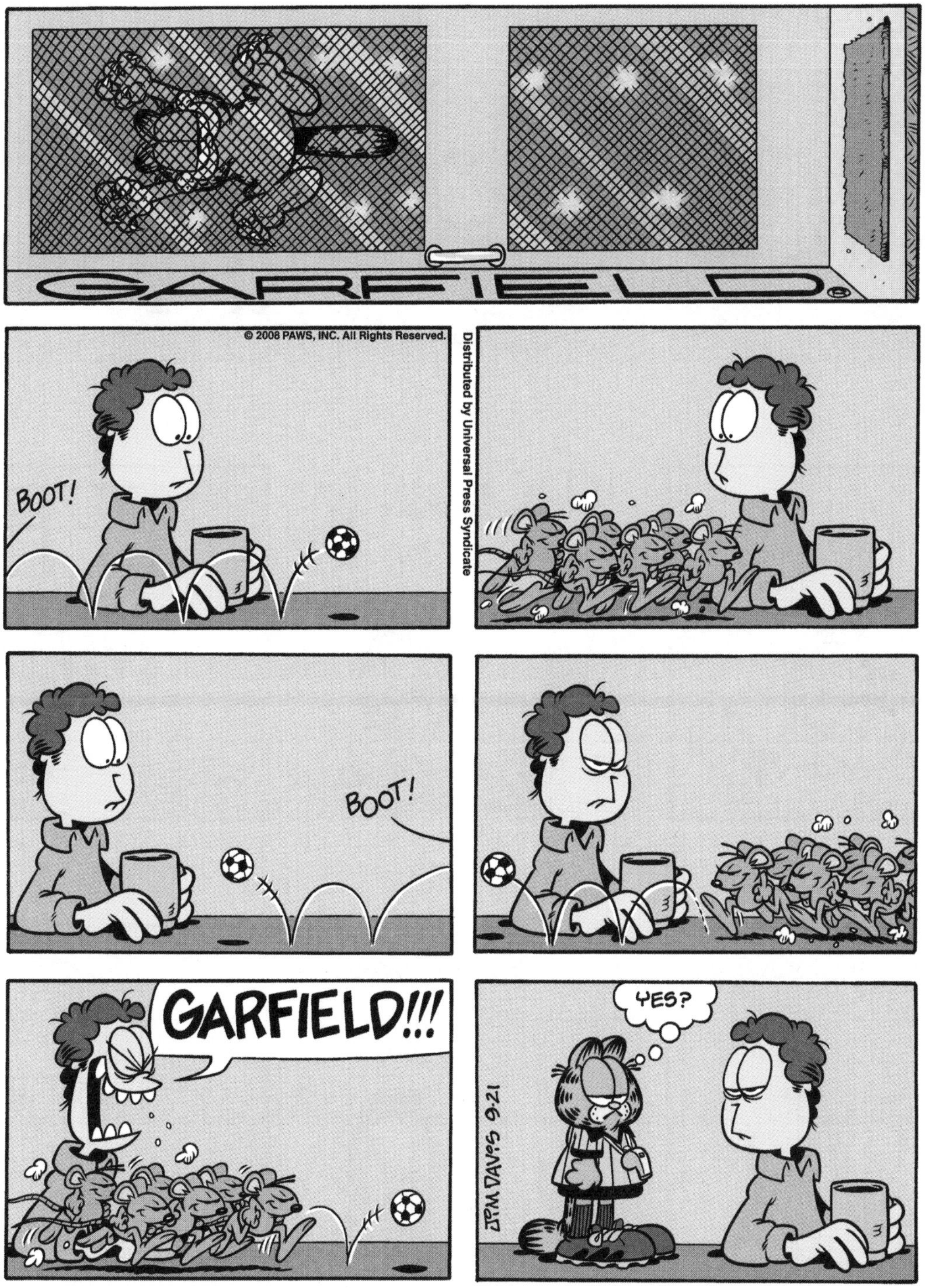
GARFIELD®
© 2008 PAWS, INC. All Rights Reserved.
Distributed by Universal Press Syndicate
BOOT!
BOOT!
GARFIELD!!!
JPM DAVIS 9-21
YES?

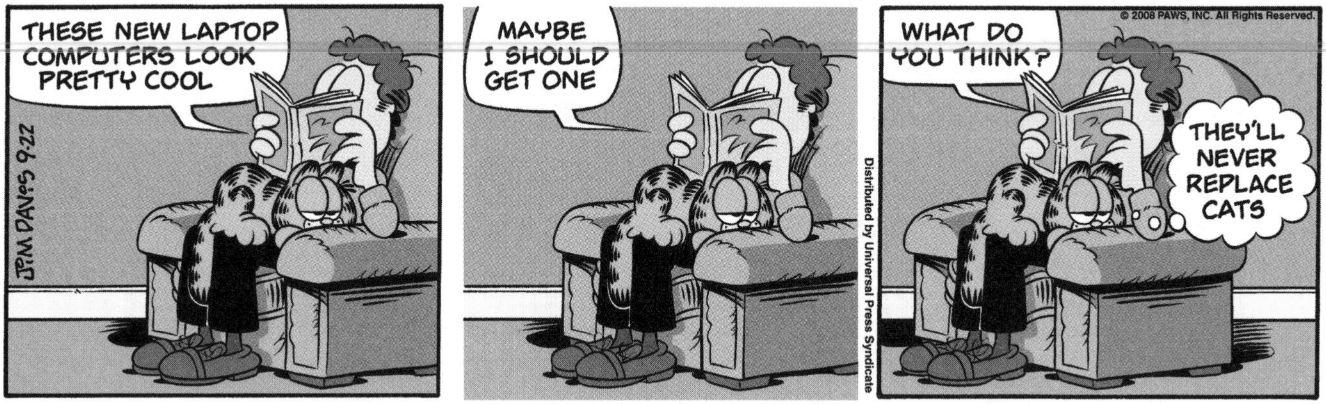
THESE NEW LAPTOP COMPUTERS LOOK PRETTY COOL
JIM DAVIS 9-22
MAYBE I SHOULD GET ONE
Distributed by Universal Press Syndicate
© 2008 PAWS, INC. All Rights Reserved.
WHAT DO YOU THINK?
THEY'LL NEVER REPLACE CATS

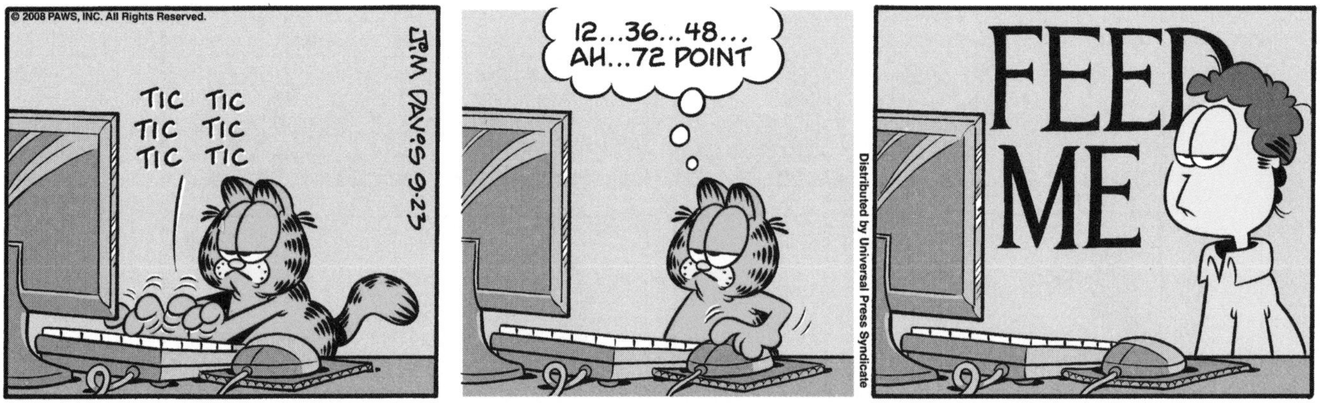
© 2008 PAWS, INC. All Rights Reserved.
JIM DAVIS 9-23
TIC TIC TIC TIC TIC TIC
12...36...48..., AH...72 POINT
Distributed by Universal Press Syndicate
FEED ME

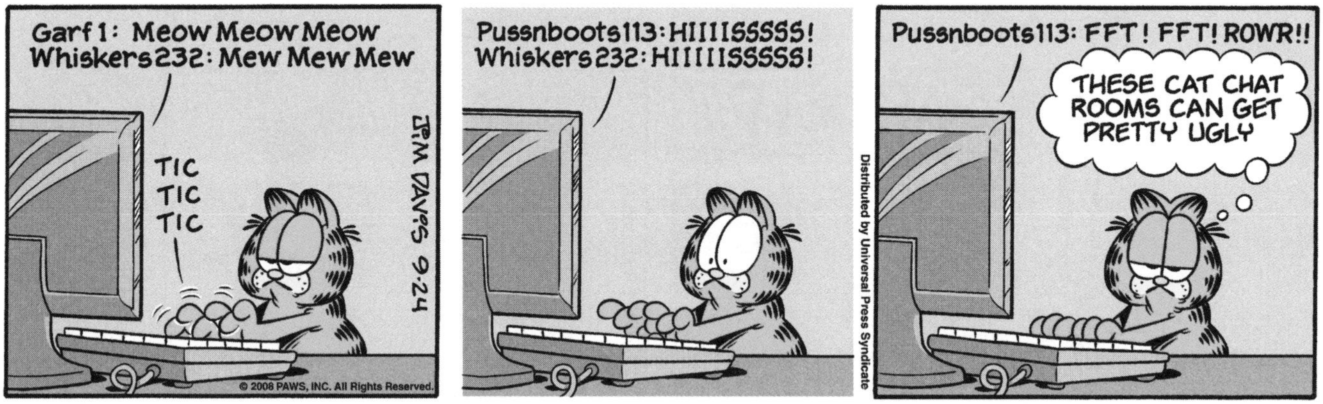
Garf1: Meow Meow Meow
Whiskers232: Mew Mew Mew
TIC TIC TIC
JIM DAVIS 9-24
© 2008 PAWS, INC. All Rights Reserved.
Pussnboots113: HIIIISSSSS!
Whiskers232: HIIIISSSSS!
Distributed by Universal Press Syndicate
Pussnboots113: FFT! FFT! ROWR!!
THESE CAT CHAT ROOMS CAN GET PRETTY UGLY

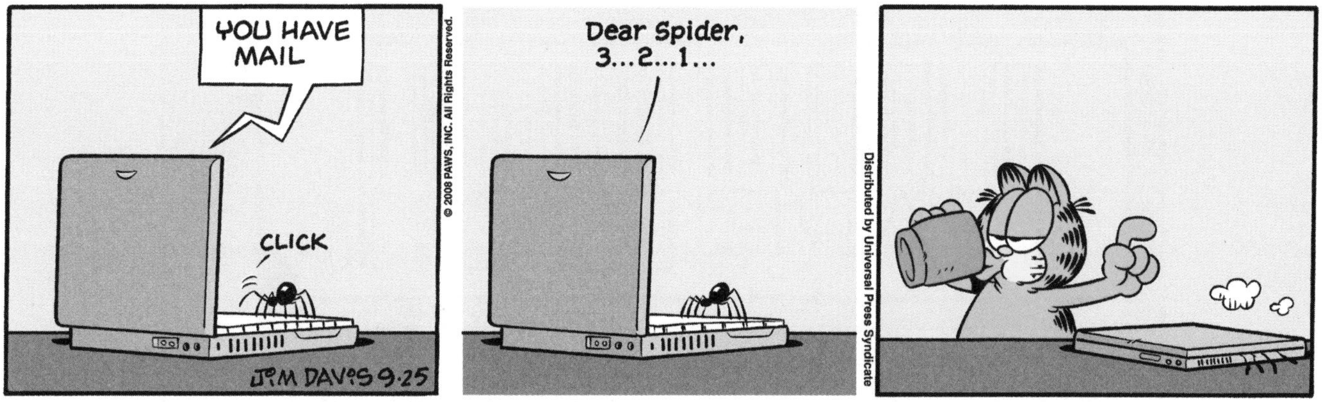
YOU HAVE MAIL
CLICK
JIM DAVIS 9·25
© 2008 PAWS, INC. All Rights Reserved.
Dear Spider,
3...2...1...
Distributed by Universal Press Syndicate

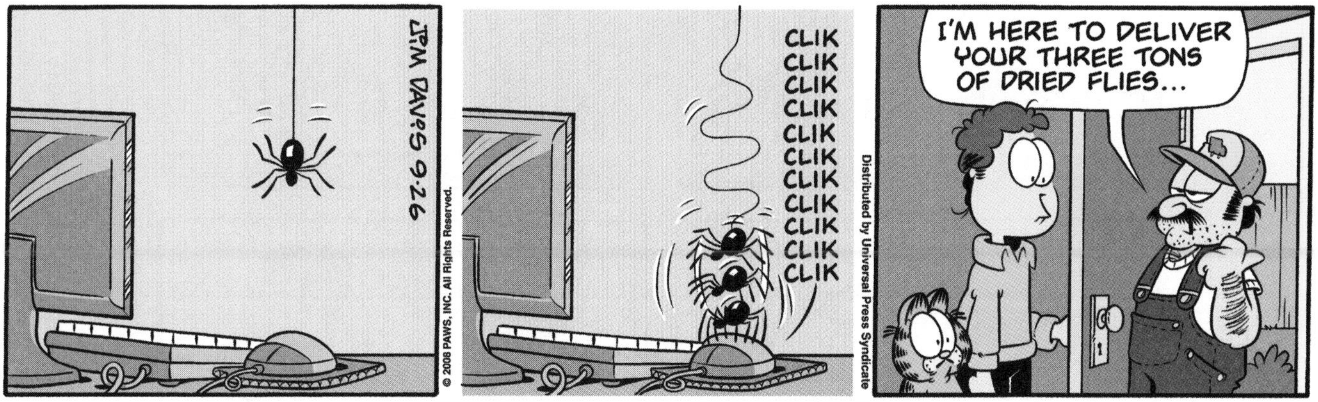
JIM DAVIS 9·26
© 2008 PAWS, INC. All Rights Reserved.
CLIK CLIK CLIK CLIK CLIK CLIK CLIK CLIK CLIK CLIK CLIK
Distributed by Universal Press Syndicate
I'M HERE TO DELIVER YOUR THREE TONS OF DRIED FLIES...

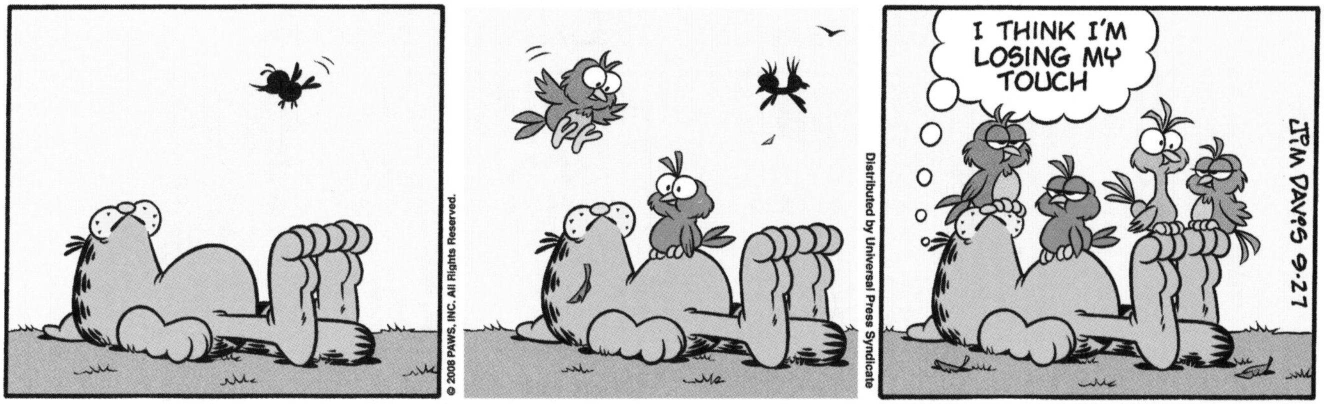
© 2008 PAWS, INC. All Rights Reserved.
Distributed by Universal Press Syndicate
I THINK I'M LOSING MY TOUCH
JIM DAVIS 9·27

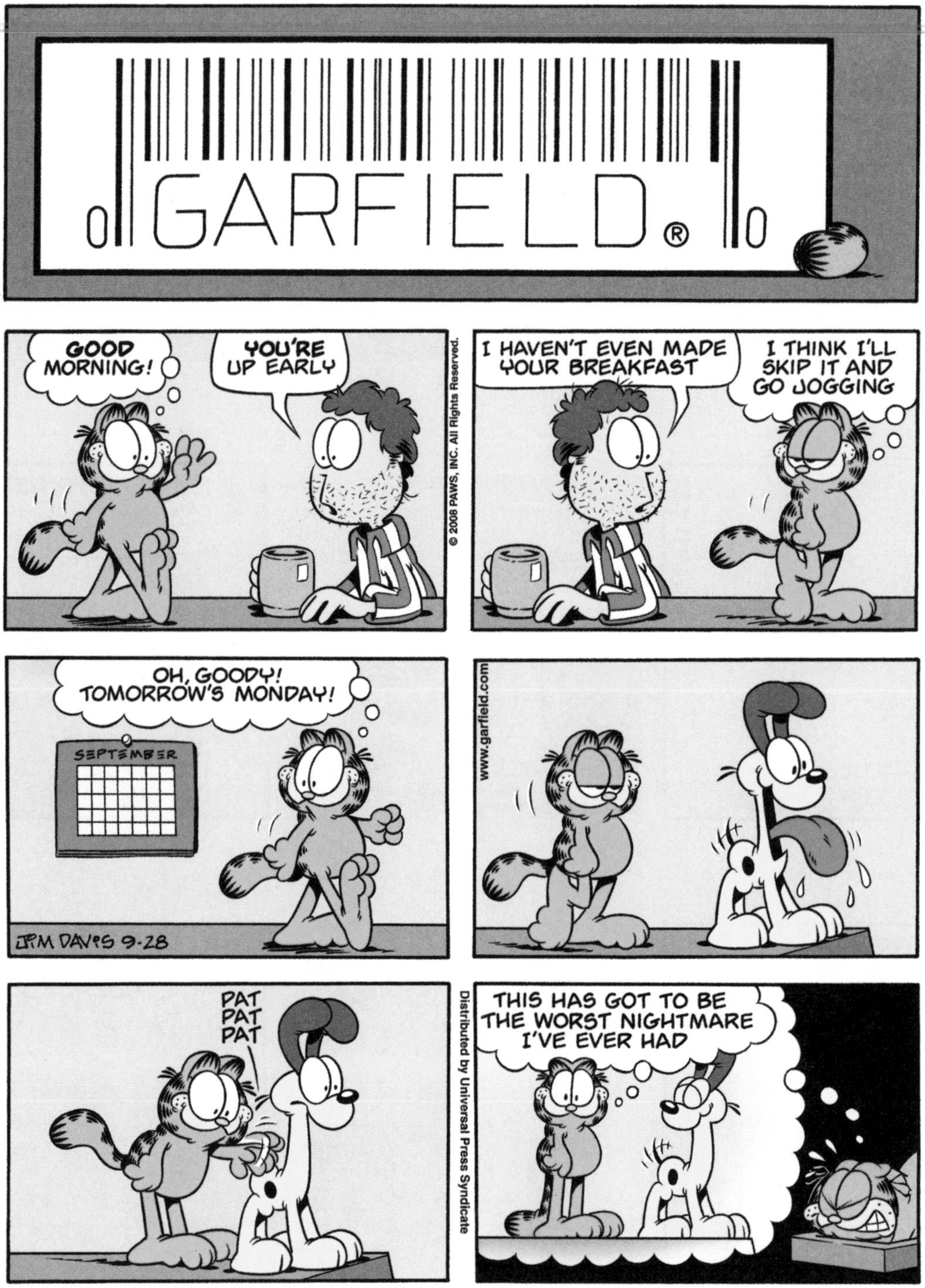
GARFIELD®
GOOD MORNING!
YOU'RE UP EARLY
© 2008 PAWS, INC. All Rights Reserved.
I HAVEN'T EVEN MADE YOUR BREAKFAST
I THINK I'LL SKIP IT AND GO JOGGING
OH, GOODY! TOMORROW'S MONDAY!
SEPTEMBER
JIM DAVIS 9-28
www.garfield.com
PAT PAT PAT
Distributed by Universal Press Syndicate
THIS HAS GOT TO BE THE WORST NIGHTMARE I'VE EVER HAD

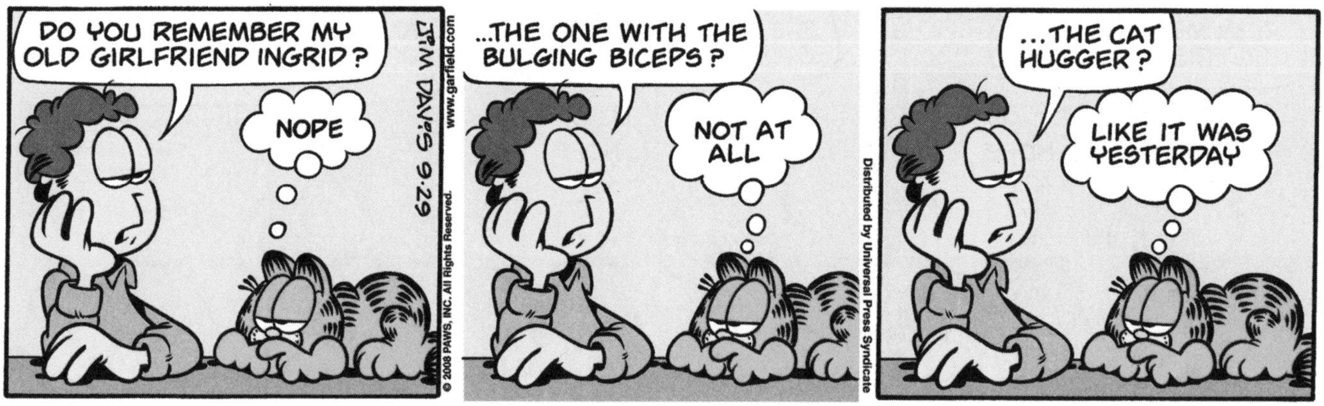
DO YOU REMEMBER MY OLD GIRLFRIEND INGRID?
NOPE
JIM DAVIS 9-29
www.garfield.com
© 2008 PAWS, INC. All Rights Reserved.
...THE ONE WITH THE BULGING BICEPS?
NOT AT ALL
Distributed by Universal Press Syndicate
...THE CAT HUGGER?
LIKE IT WAS YESTERDAY

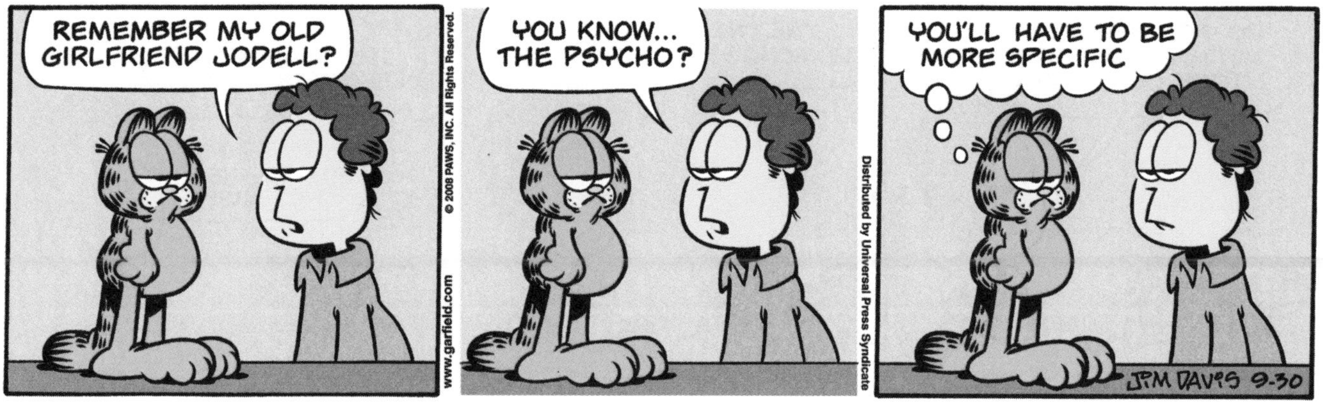
REMEMBER MY OLD GIRLFRIEND JODELL?
© 2008 PAWS, INC. All Rights Reserved.
www.garfield.com
YOU KNOW... THE PSYCHO?
Distributed by Universal Press Syndicate
YOU'LL HAVE TO BE MORE SPECIFIC
JIM DAVIS 9-30

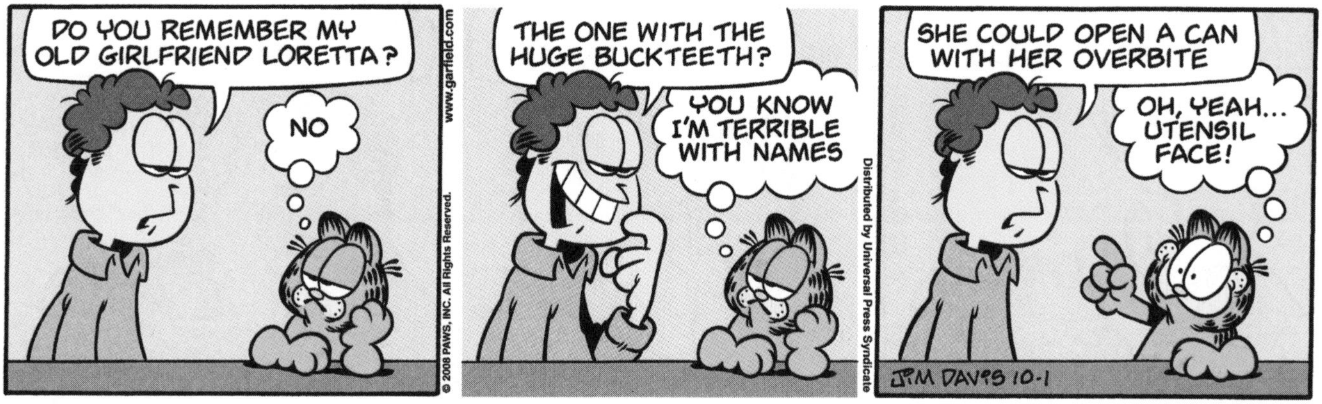
DO YOU REMEMBER MY OLD GIRLFRIEND LORETTA?
NO
www.garfield.com
© 2008 PAWS, INC. All Rights Reserved.
THE ONE WITH THE HUGE BUCKTEETH?
YOU KNOW I'M TERRIBLE WITH NAMES
Distributed by Universal Press Syndicate
SHE COULD OPEN A CAN WITH HER OVERBITE
OH, YEAH... UTENSIL FACE!
JIM DAVIS 10-1

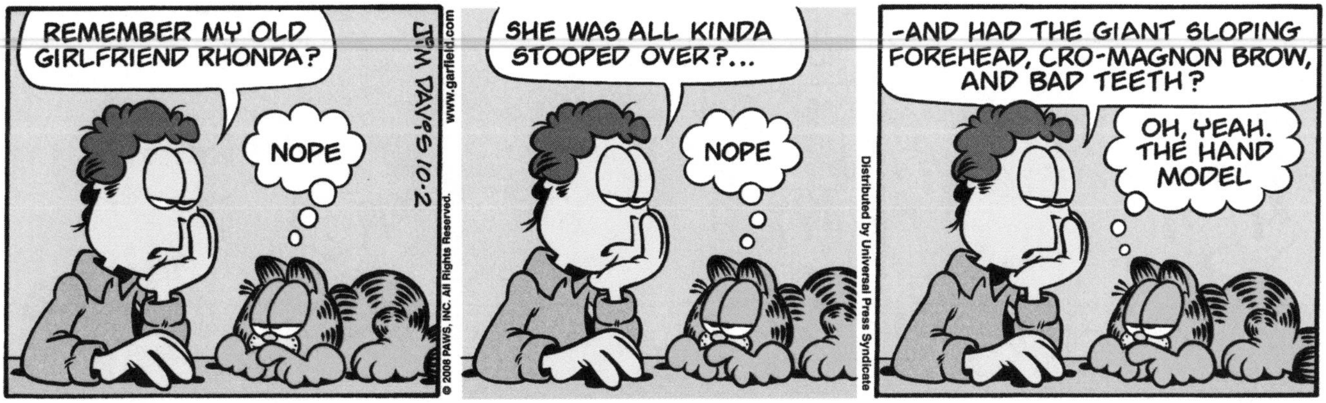
REMEMBER MY OLD GIRLFRIEND RHONDA?
NOPE
JPM DAVPS 10-2
SHE WAS ALL KINDA STOOPED OVER?...
NOPE
-AND HAD THE GIANT SLOPING FOREHEAD, CRO-MAGNON BROW, AND BAD TEETH?
OH, YEAH. THE HAND MODEL

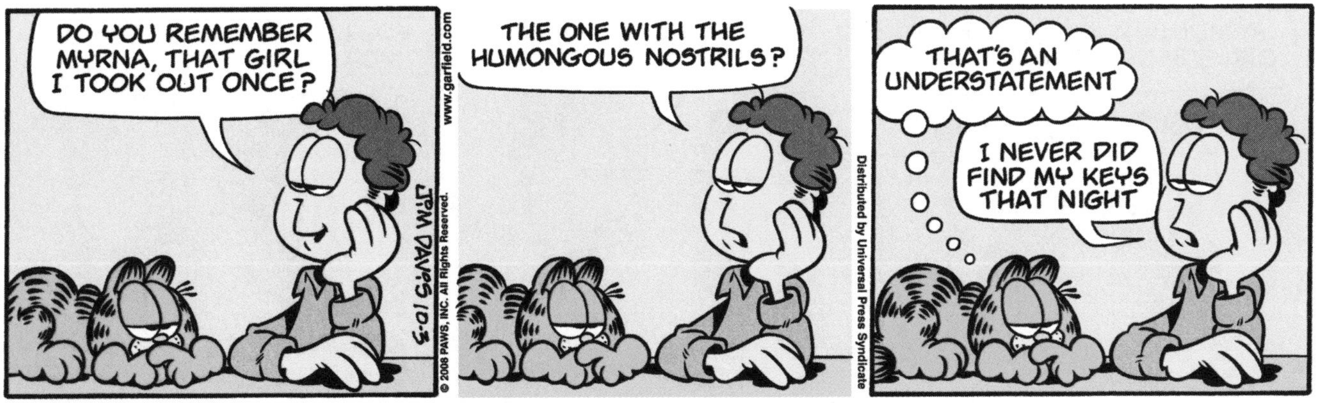
DO YOU REMEMBER MYRNA, THAT GIRL I TOOK OUT ONCE?
JPM DAVPS 10-3
THE ONE WITH THE HUMONGOUS NOSTRILS?
THAT'S AN UNDERSTATEMENT
I NEVER DID FIND MY KEYS THAT NIGHT

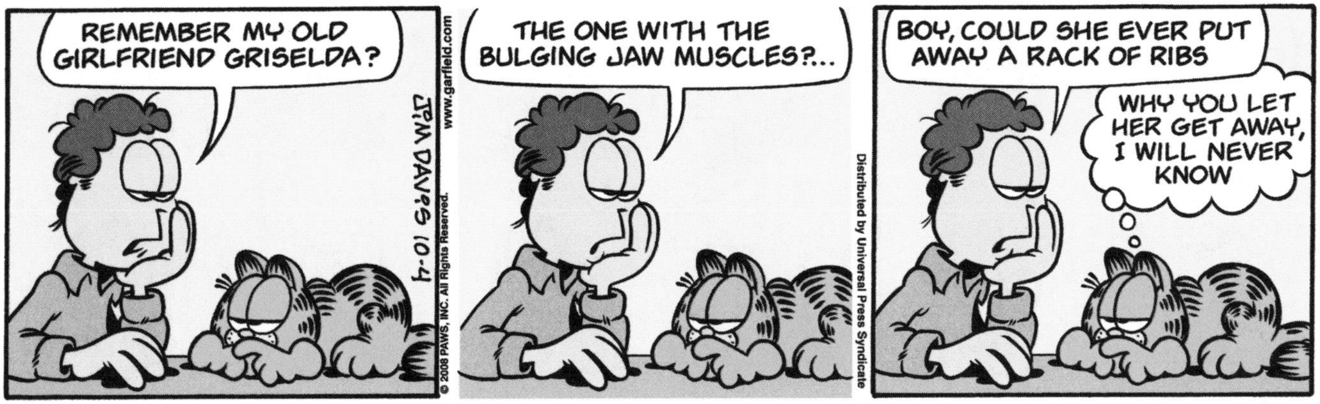
REMEMBER MY OLD GIRLFRIEND GRISELDA?
JPM DAVPS 10-4
THE ONE WITH THE BULGING JAW MUSCLES?...
BOY, COULD SHE EVER PUT AWAY A RACK OF RIBS
WHY YOU LET HER GET AWAY, I WILL NEVER KNOW

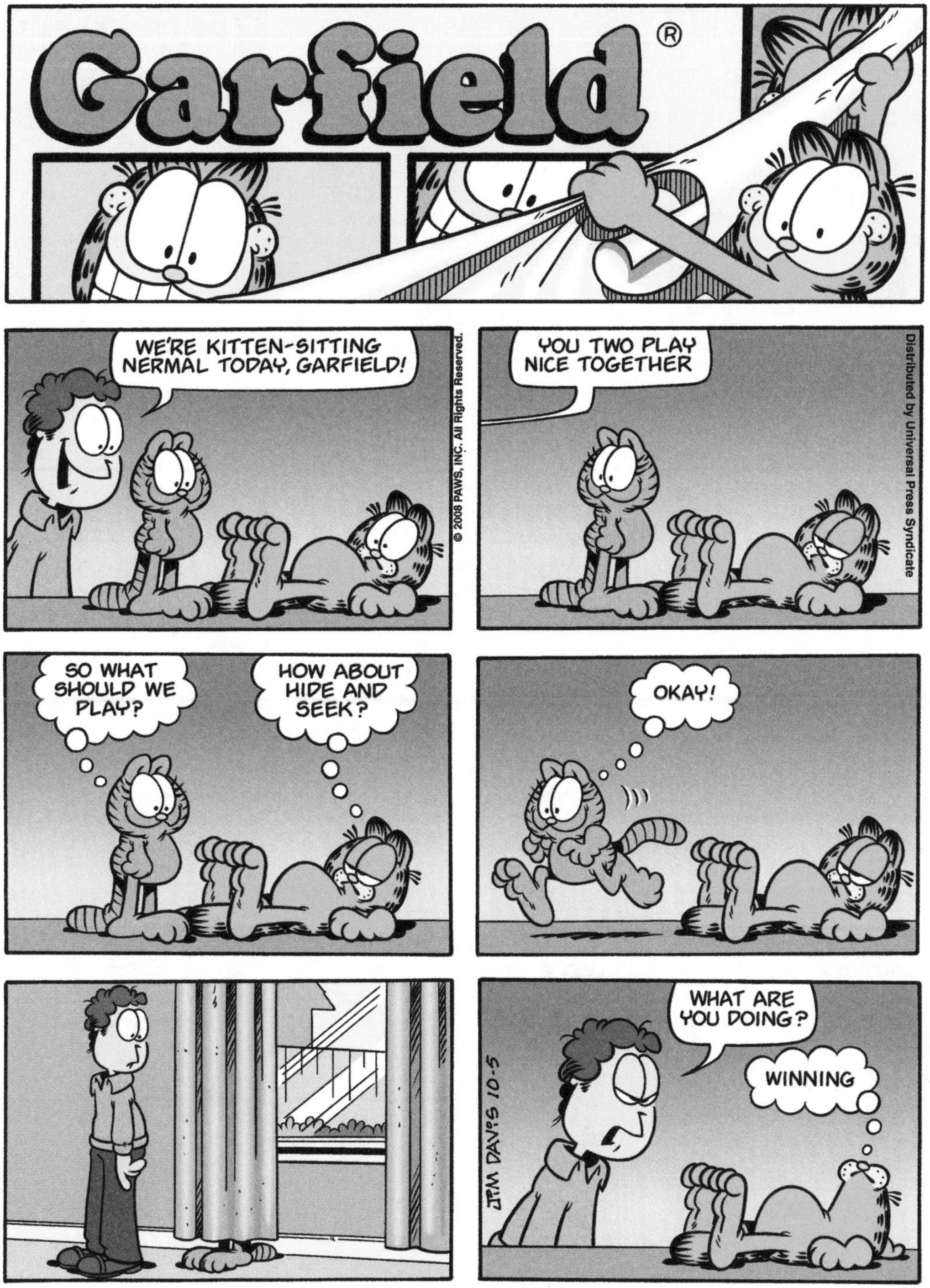
Garfield®
WE'RE KITTEN-SITTING NERMAL TODAY, GARFIELD!
© 2008 PAWS, INC. All Rights Reserved.
YOU TWO PLAY NICE TOGETHER
Distributed by Universal Press Syndicate
SO WHAT SHOULD WE PLAY?
HOW ABOUT HIDE AND SEEK?
OKAY!
JIM DAVIS 10-5
WHAT ARE YOU DOING?
WINNING

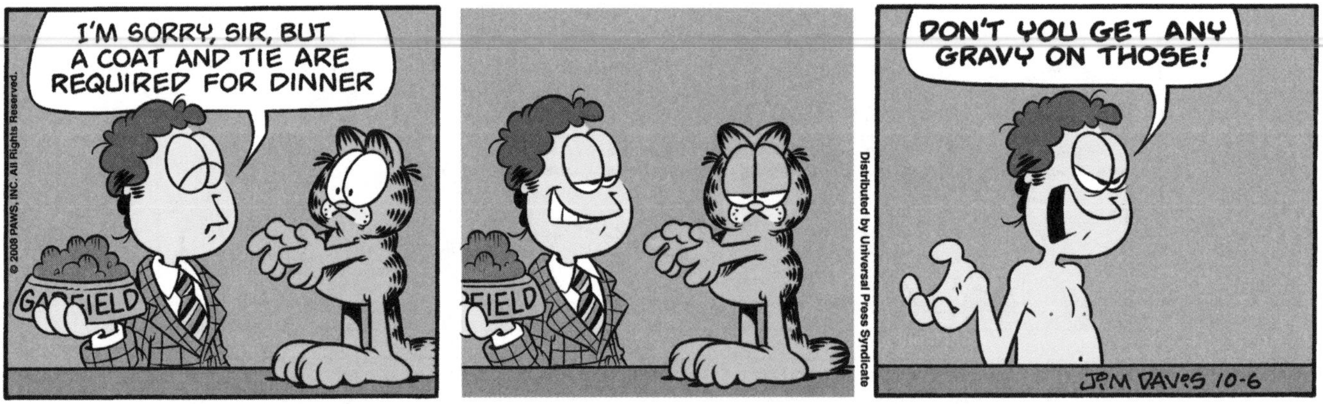
I'M SORRY, SIR, BUT A COAT AND TIE ARE REQUIRED FOR DINNER
DON'T YOU GET ANY GRAVY ON THOSE!
JIM DAVIS 10-6
© 2008 PAWS, INC. All Rights Reserved.
Distributed by Universal Press Syndicate

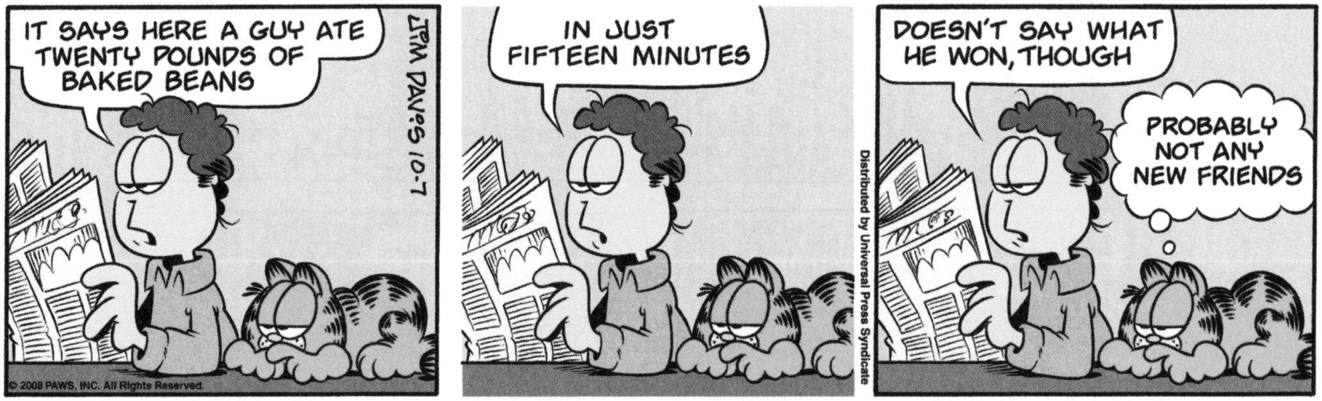
IT SAYS HERE A GUY ATE TWENTY POUNDS OF BAKED BEANS
JIM DAVIS 10-7
IN JUST FIFTEEN MINUTES
DOESN'T SAY WHAT HE WON, THOUGH
PROBABLY NOT ANY NEW FRIENDS
© 2008 PAWS, INC. All Rights Reserved.
Distributed by Universal Press Syndicate

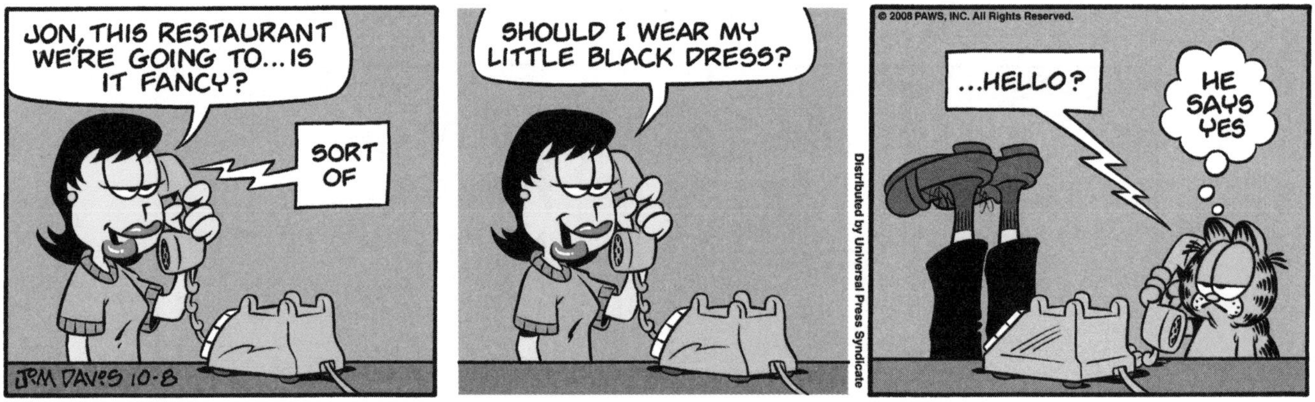
JON, THIS RESTAURANT WE'RE GOING TO... IS IT FANCY?
SORT OF
SHOULD I WEAR MY LITTLE BLACK DRESS?
...HELLO?
HE SAYS YES
JIM DAVIS 10-8
© 2008 PAWS, INC. All Rights Reserved.
Distributed by Universal Press Syndicate

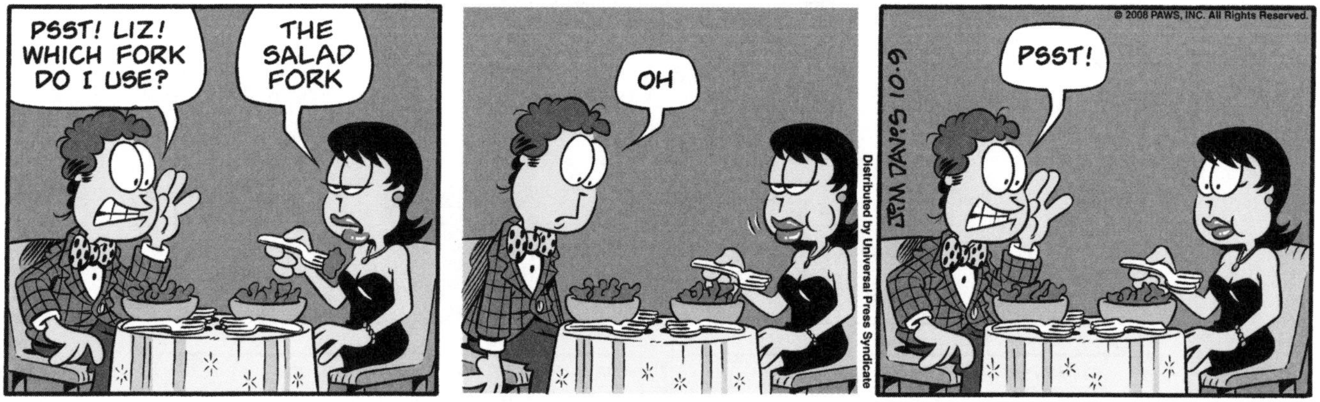
PSST! LIZ! WHICH FORK DO I USE?
THE SALAD FORK
OH
PSST!
JIM DAVIS 10-9
© 2008 PAWS, INC. All Rights Reserved.
Distributed by Universal Press Syndicate

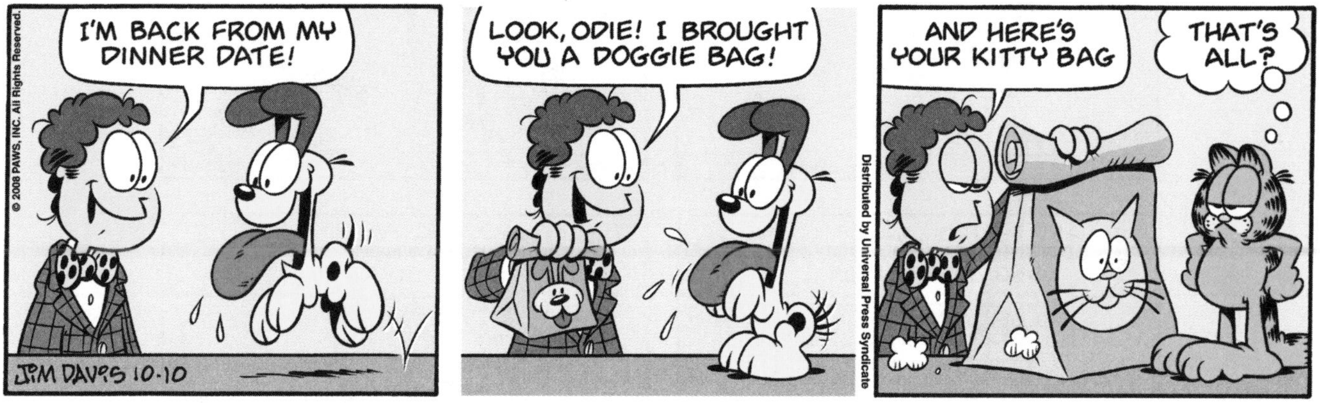
I'M BACK FROM MY DINNER DATE!
LOOK, ODIE! I BROUGHT YOU A DOGGIE BAG!
AND HERE'S YOUR KITTY BAG
THAT'S ALL?
JIM DAVIS 10-10
© 2008 PAWS, INC. All Rights Reserved.
Distributed by Universal Press Syndicate

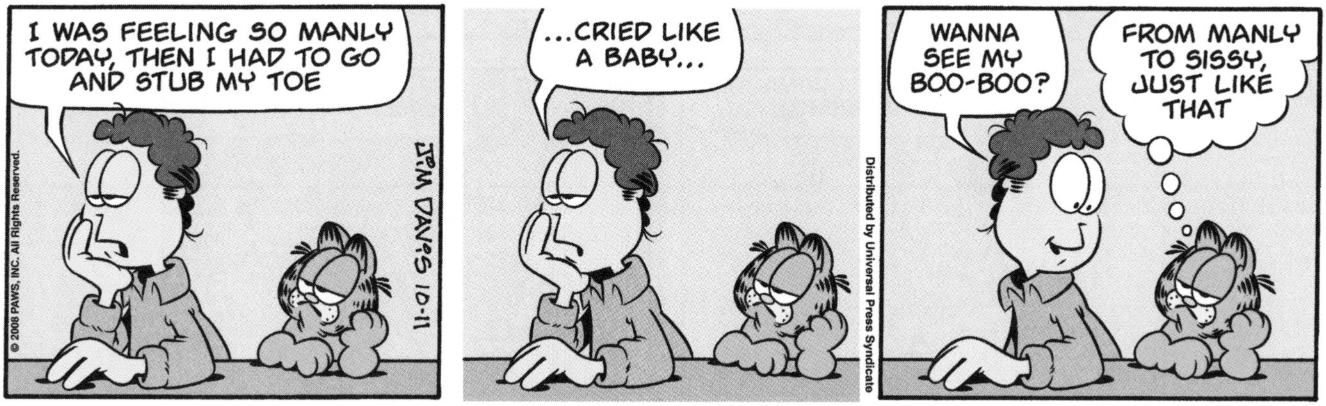
I WAS FEELING SO MANLY TODAY, THEN I HAD TO GO AND STUB MY TOE
...CRIED LIKE A BABY...
WANNA SEE MY BOO-BOO?
FROM MANLY TO SISSY, JUST LIKE THAT
JIM DAVIS 10-11
© 2008 PAWS, INC. All Rights Reserved.
Distributed by Universal Press Syndicate

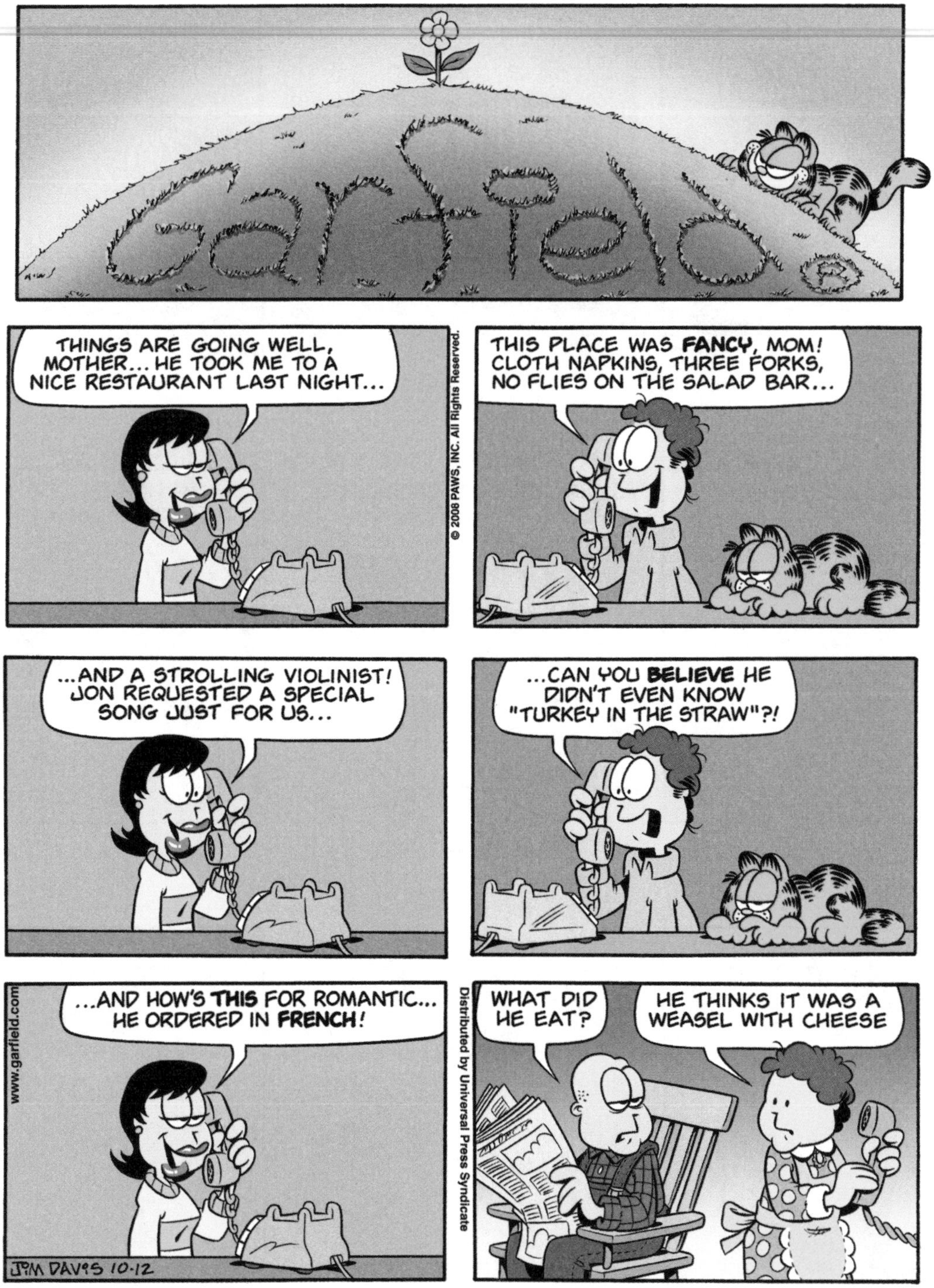
Garfield®
THINGS ARE GOING WELL, MOTHER... HE TOOK ME TO A NICE RESTAURANT LAST NIGHT...
THIS PLACE WAS FANCY, MOM! CLOTH NAPKINS, THREE FORKS, NO FLIES ON THE SALAD BAR...
...AND A STROLLING VIOLINIST! JON REQUESTED A SPECIAL SONG JUST FOR US...
...CAN YOU BELIEVE HE DIDN'T EVEN KNOW "TURKEY IN THE STRAW"?!
...AND HOW'S THIS FOR ROMANTIC... HE ORDERED IN FRENCH!
WHAT DID HE EAT?
HE THINKS IT WAS A WEASEL WITH CHEESE
JIM DAVIS 10-12
www.garfield.com
© 2008 PAWS, INC. All Rights Reserved.
Distributed by Universal Press Syndicate

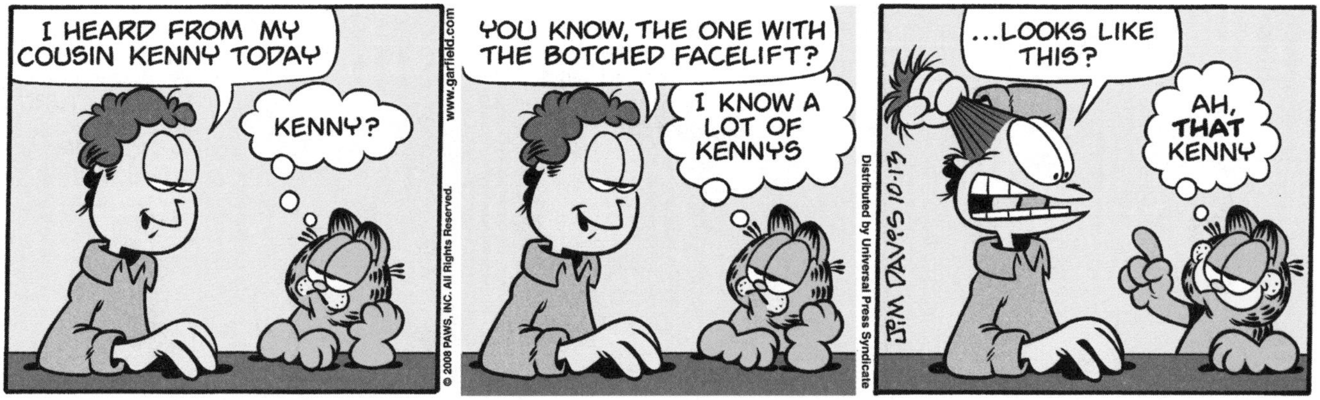
I HEARD FROM MY COUSIN KENNY TODAY
KENNY?
© 2008 PAWS, INC. All Rights Reserved.
www.garfield.com
YOU KNOW, THE ONE WITH THE BOTCHED FACELIFT?
I KNOW A LOT OF KENNYS
Distributed by Universal Press Syndicate
JPM DAVPS 10-13
...LOOKS LIKE THIS?
AH, **THAT** KENNY

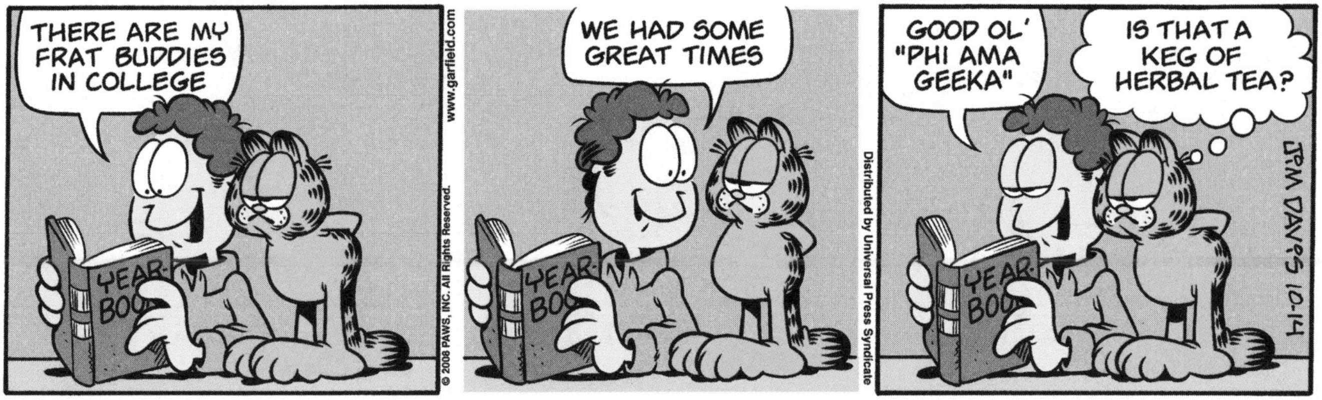
THERE ARE MY FRAT BUDDIES IN COLLEGE
YEAR BOOK
© 2008 PAWS, INC. All Rights Reserved.
www.garfield.com
WE HAD SOME GREAT TIMES
Distributed by Universal Press Syndicate
GOOD OL' "PHI AMA GEEKA"
IS THAT A KEG OF HERBAL TEA?
JPM DAVPS 10-14

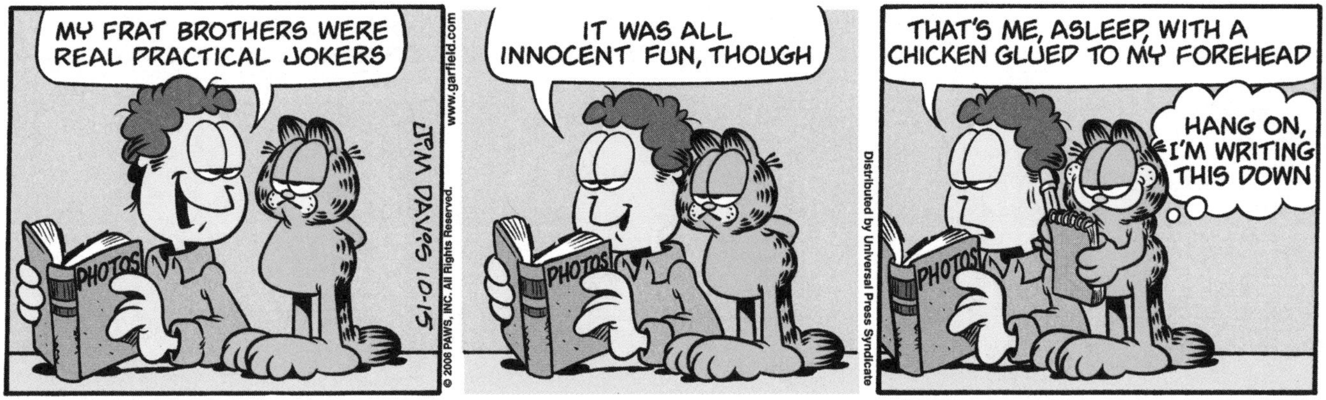
MY FRAT BROTHERS WERE REAL PRACTICAL JOKERS
PHOTOS
JPM DAVPS 10-15
© 2008 PAWS, INC. All Rights Reserved.
www.garfield.com
IT WAS ALL INNOCENT FUN, THOUGH
PHOTOS
Distributed by Universal Press Syndicate
THAT'S ME, ASLEEP, WITH A CHICKEN GLUED TO MY FOREHEAD
PHOTOS
HANG ON, I'M WRITING THIS DOWN

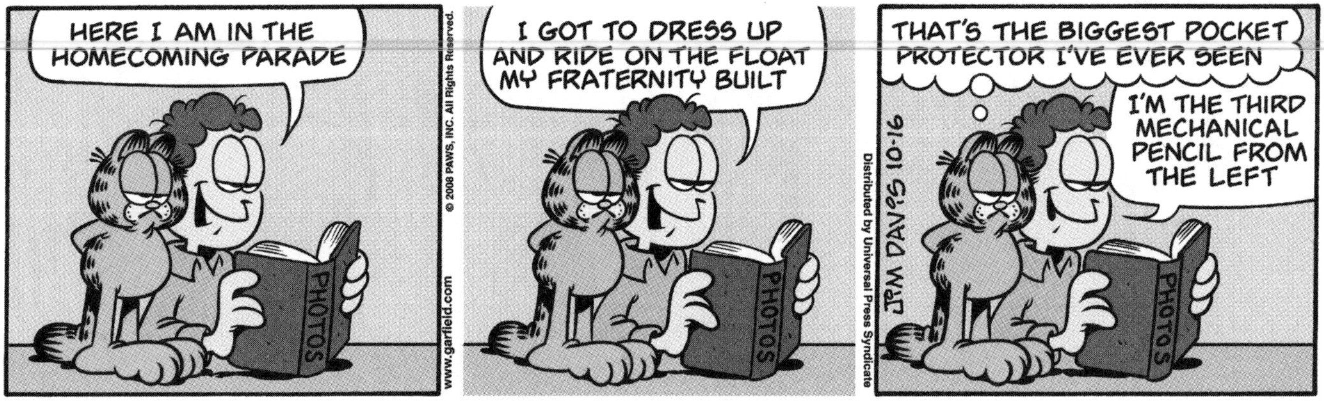
HERE I AM IN THE HOMECOMING PARADE
PHOTOS
© 2008 PAWS, INC. All Rights Reserved.
www.garfield.com
I GOT TO DRESS UP AND RIDE ON THE FLOAT MY FRATERNITY BUILT
PHOTOS
Distributed by Universal Press Syndicate
JIM DAVIS 10-16
THAT'S THE BIGGEST POCKET PROTECTOR I'VE EVER SEEN
I'M THE THIRD MECHANICAL PENCIL FROM THE LEFT
PHOTOS

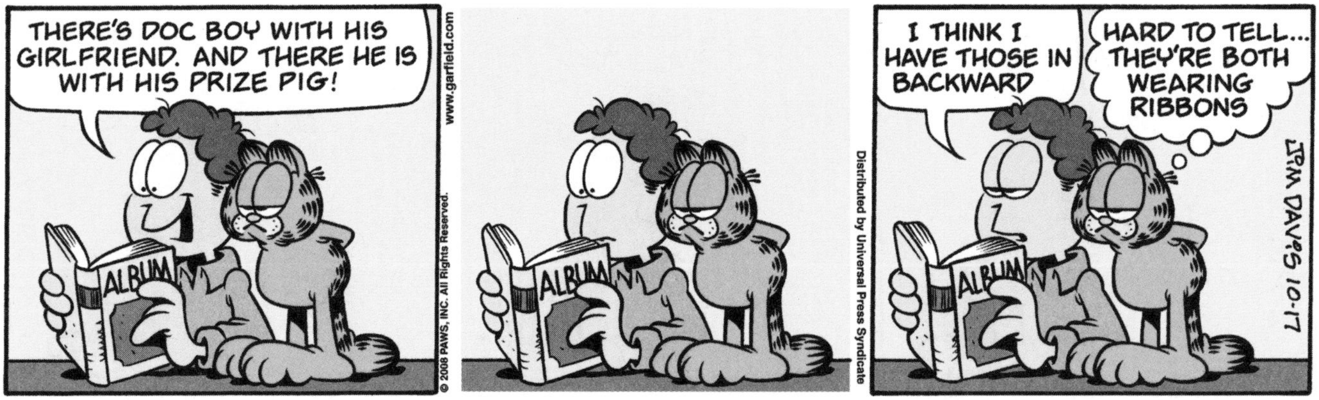
THERE'S DOC BOY WITH HIS GIRLFRIEND. AND THERE HE IS WITH HIS PRIZE PIG!
ALBUM
www.garfield.com
© 2008 PAWS, INC. All Rights Reserved.
ALBUM
Distributed by Universal Press Syndicate
I THINK I HAVE THOSE IN BACKWARD
HARD TO TELL... THEY'RE BOTH WEARING RIBBONS
ALBUM
JIM DAVIS 10-17

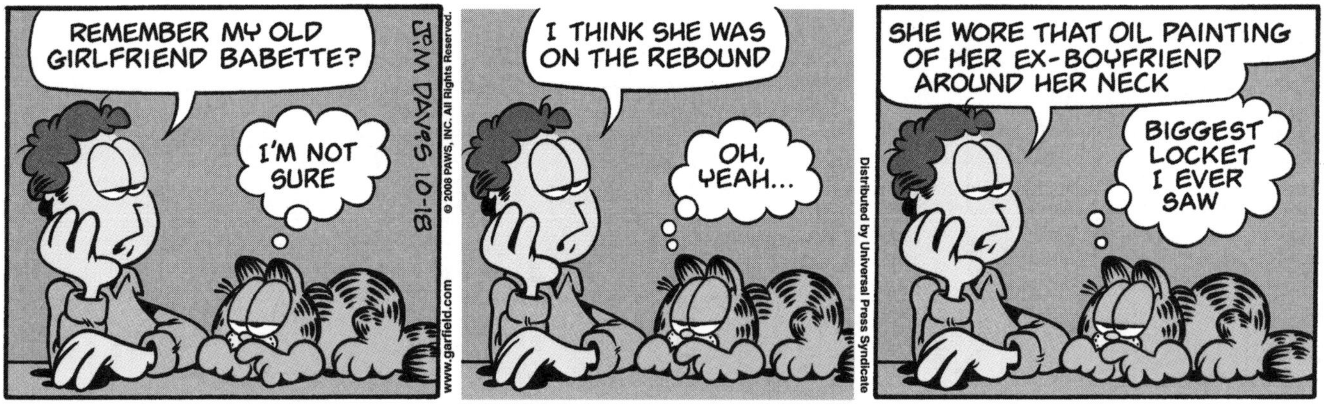
REMEMBER MY OLD GIRLFRIEND BABETTE?
I'M NOT SURE
JIM DAVIS 10-18
© 2008 PAWS, INC. All Rights Reserved.
www.garfield.com
I THINK SHE WAS ON THE REBOUND
OH, YEAH...
Distributed by Universal Press Syndicate
SHE WORE THAT OIL PAINTING OF HER EX-BOYFRIEND AROUND HER NECK
BIGGEST LOCKET I EVER SAW

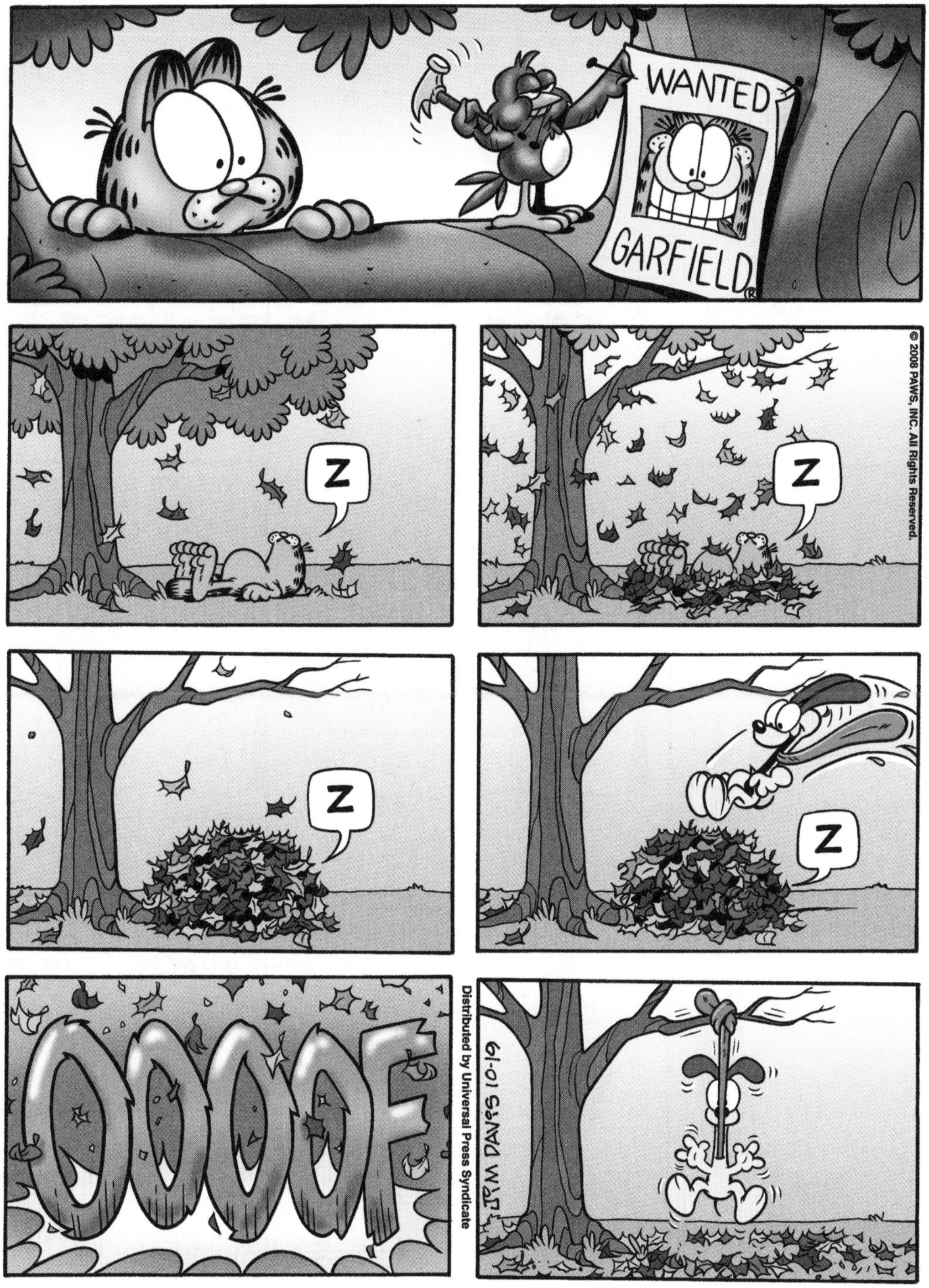

WANTED
GARFIELD
Z
Z
Z
Z
OOOOF
JPM DAVPS 10-19
Distributed by Universal Press Syndicate
© 2008 PAWS, INC. All Rights Reserved.

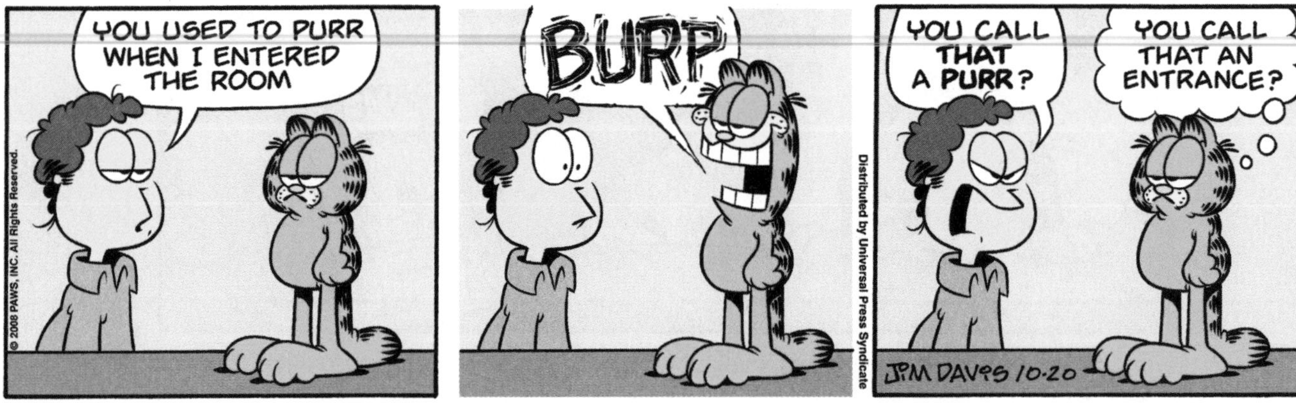
YOU USED TO PURR WHEN I ENTERED THE ROOM
BURP
YOU CALL THAT A PURR?
YOU CALL THAT AN ENTRANCE?
JIM DAVIS 10-20
© 2008 PAWS, INC. All Rights Reserved.
Distributed by Universal Press Syndicate

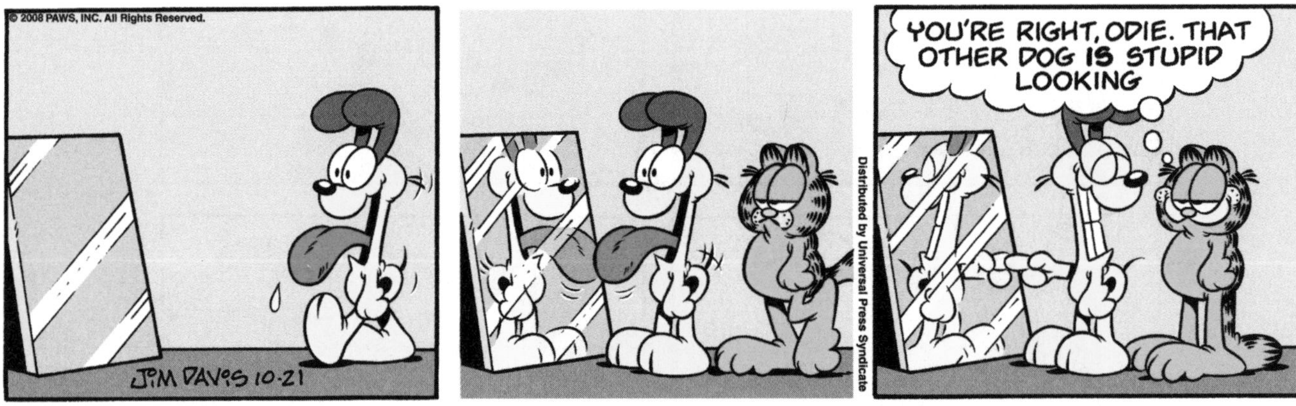
YOU'RE RIGHT, ODIE. THAT OTHER DOG IS STUPID LOOKING
JIM DAVIS 10-21
© 2008 PAWS, INC. All Rights Reserved.
Distributed by Universal Press Syndicate

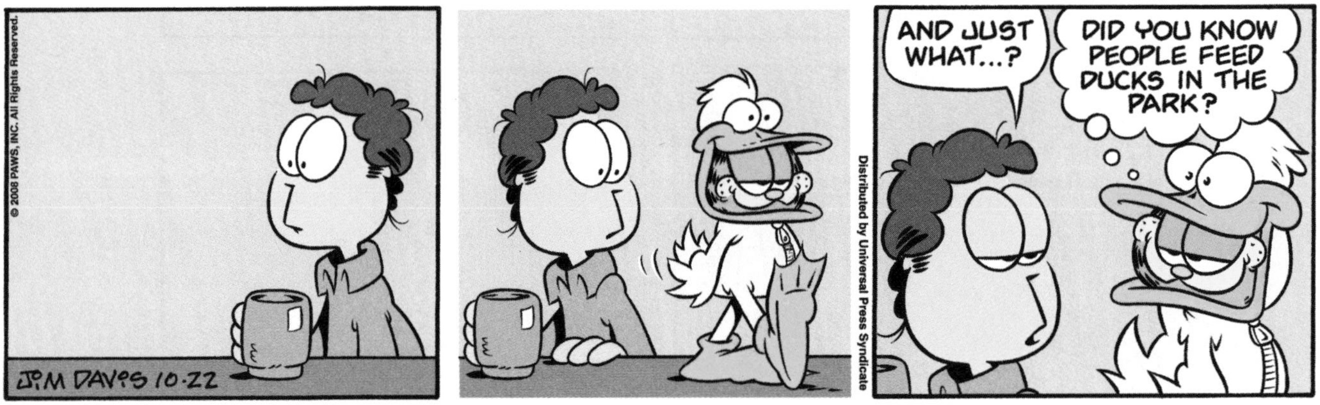
AND JUST WHAT...?
DID YOU KNOW PEOPLE FEED DUCKS IN THE PARK?
JIM DAVIS 10-22
© 2008 PAWS, INC. All Rights Reserved.
Distributed by Universal Press Syndicate

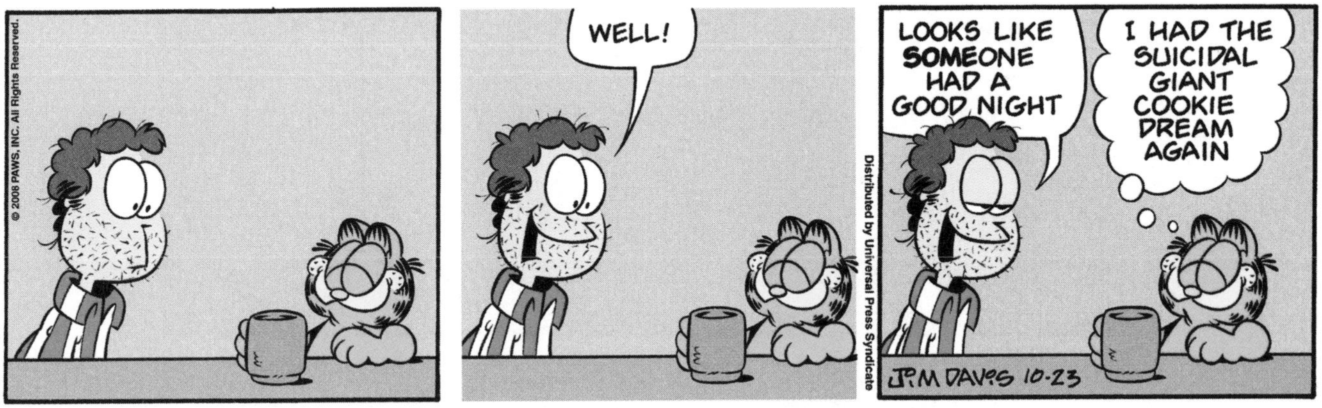
© 2008 PAWS, INC. All Rights Reserved.
WELL!
Distributed by Universal Press Syndicate
LOOKS LIKE SOMEONE HAD A GOOD NIGHT
I HAD THE SUICIDAL GIANT COOKIE DREAM AGAIN
JIM DAVIS 10-23

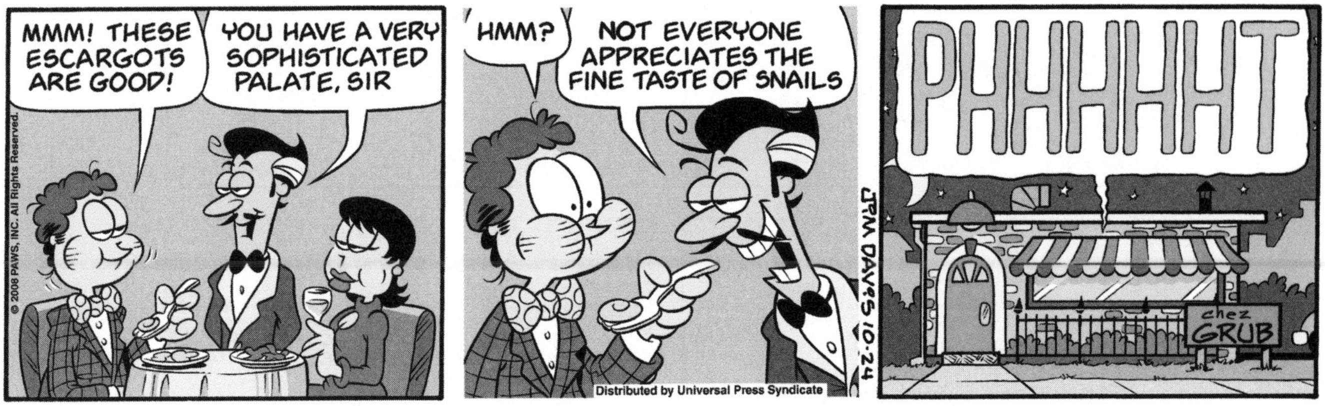
© 2008 PAWS, INC. All Rights Reserved.
MMM! THESE ESCARGOTS ARE GOOD!
YOU HAVE A VERY SOPHISTICATED PALATE, SIR
HMM?
NOT EVERYONE APPRECIATES THE FINE TASTE OF SNAILS
JIM DAVIS 10-24
Distributed by Universal Press Syndicate
PHHHHHT
chez GRUB

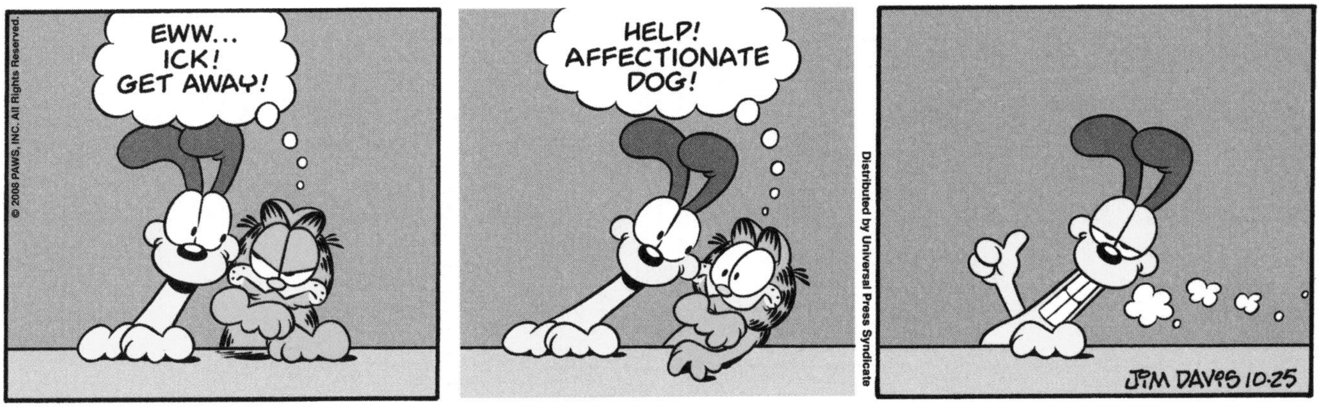
© 2008 PAWS, INC. All Rights Reserved.
EWW... ICK! GET AWAY!
HELP! AFFECTIONATE DOG!
Distributed by Universal Press Syndicate
JIM DAVIS 10-25

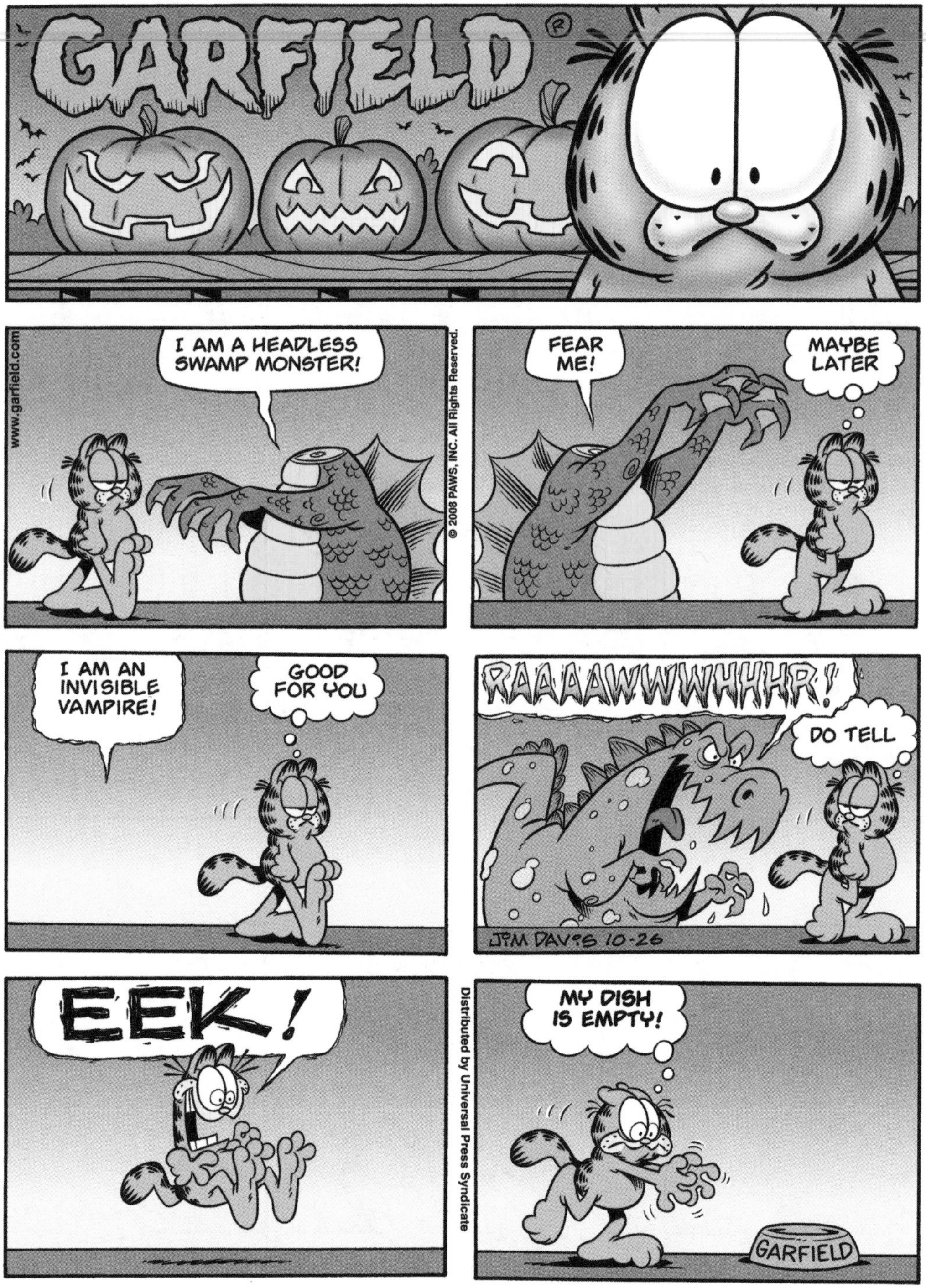
GARFIELD®
www.garfield.com
I AM A HEADLESS SWAMP MONSTER!
© 2008 PAWS, INC. All Rights Reserved.
FEAR ME!
MAYBE LATER
I AM AN INVISIBLE VAMPIRE!
GOOD FOR YOU
RAAAAWWWHHHR!
DO TELL
JIM DAVIS 10-26
EEK!
Distributed by Universal Press Syndicate
MY DISH IS EMPTY!
GARFIELD

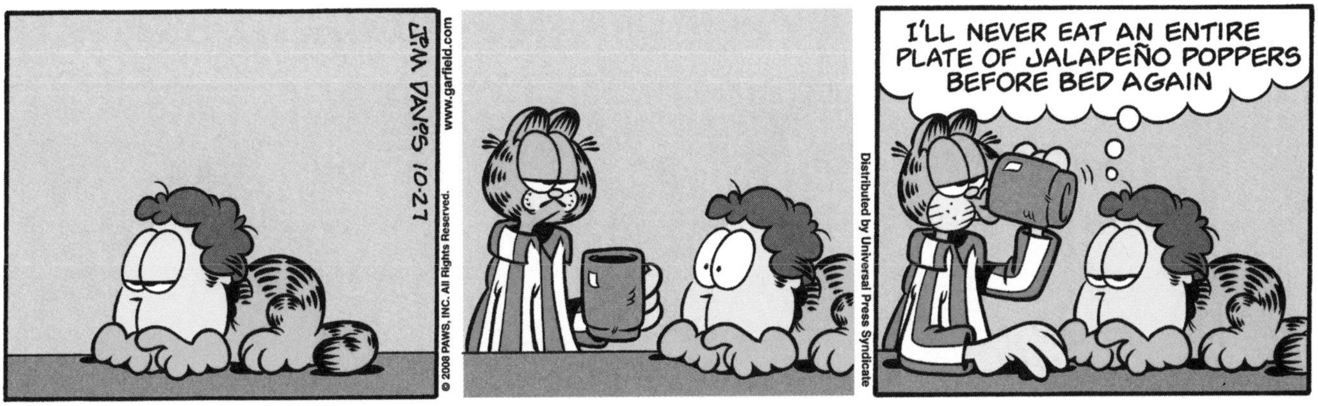
JIM DAVIS 10-27
www.garfield.com
© 2008 PAWS, INC. All Rights Reserved.
Distributed by Universal Press Syndicate
I'LL NEVER EAT AN ENTIRE PLATE OF JALAPEÑO POPPERS BEFORE BED AGAIN

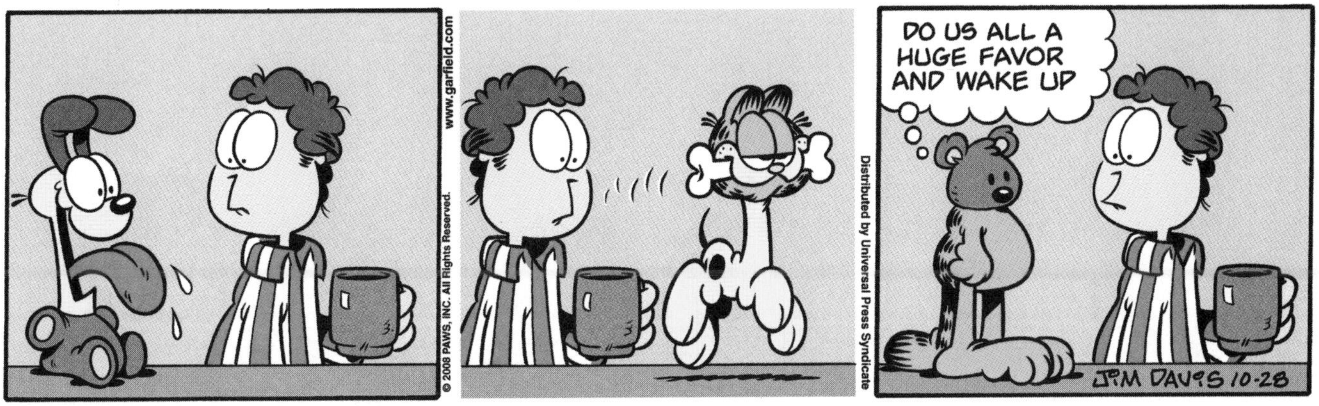
www.garfield.com
© 2008 PAWS, INC. All Rights Reserved.
Distributed by Universal Press Syndicate
DO US ALL A HUGE FAVOR AND WAKE UP
JIM DAVIS 10-28

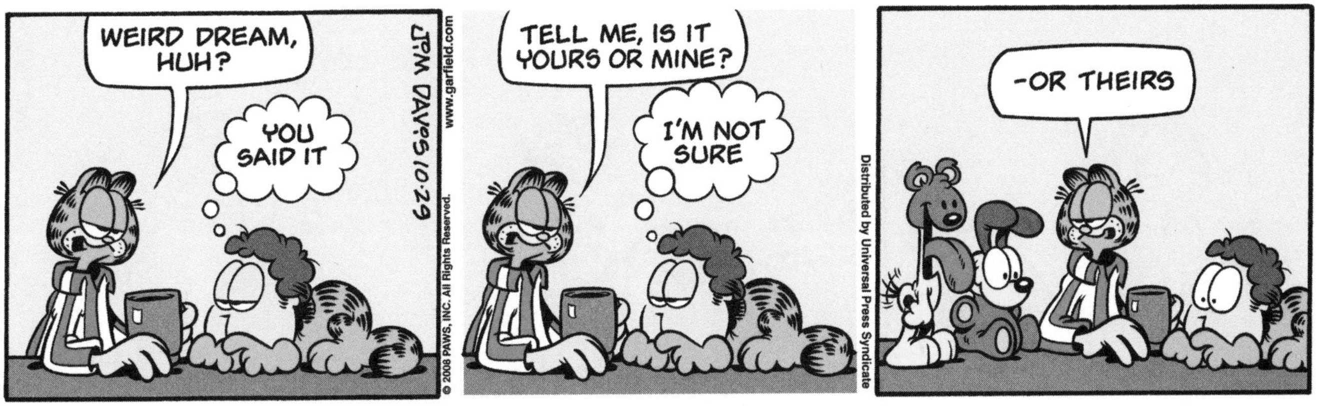
WEIRD DREAM, HUH?
YOU SAID IT
JIM DAVIS 10-29
www.garfield.com
© 2008 PAWS, INC. All Rights Reserved.
TELL ME, IS IT YOURS OR MINE?
I'M NOT SURE
Distributed by Universal Press Syndicate
-OR THEIRS

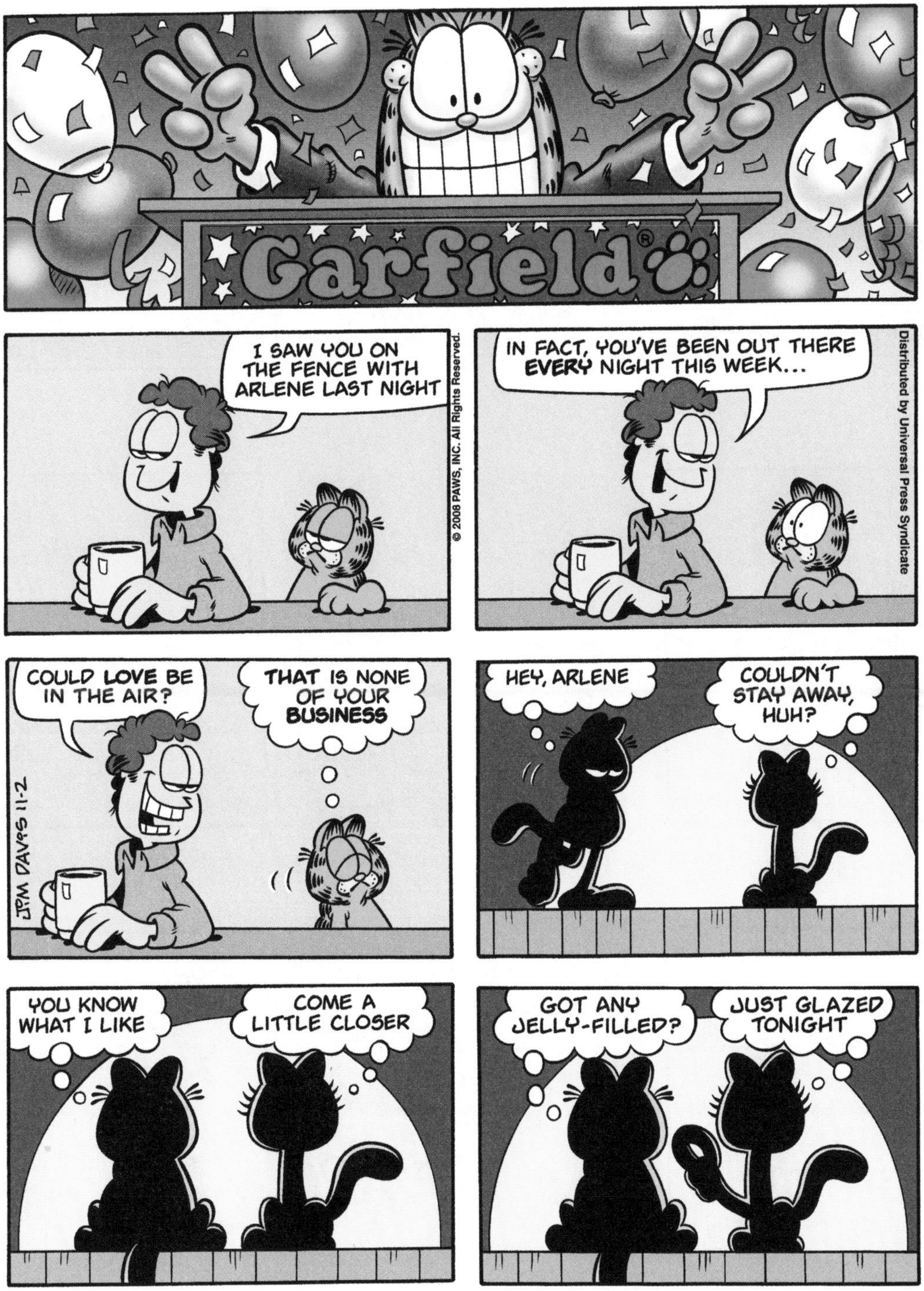
Garfield®
I SAW YOU ON THE FENCE WITH ARLENE LAST NIGHT
© 2008 PAWS, INC. All Rights Reserved.
IN FACT, YOU'VE BEEN OUT THERE EVERY NIGHT THIS WEEK...
Distributed by Universal Press Syndicate
COULD LOVE BE IN THE AIR?
THAT IS NONE OF YOUR BUSINESS
JPM DAVPS 11-2
HEY, ARLENE
COULDN'T STAY AWAY, HUH?
YOU KNOW WHAT I LIKE
COME A LITTLE CLOSER
GOT ANY JELLY-FILLED?
JUST GLAZED TONIGHT

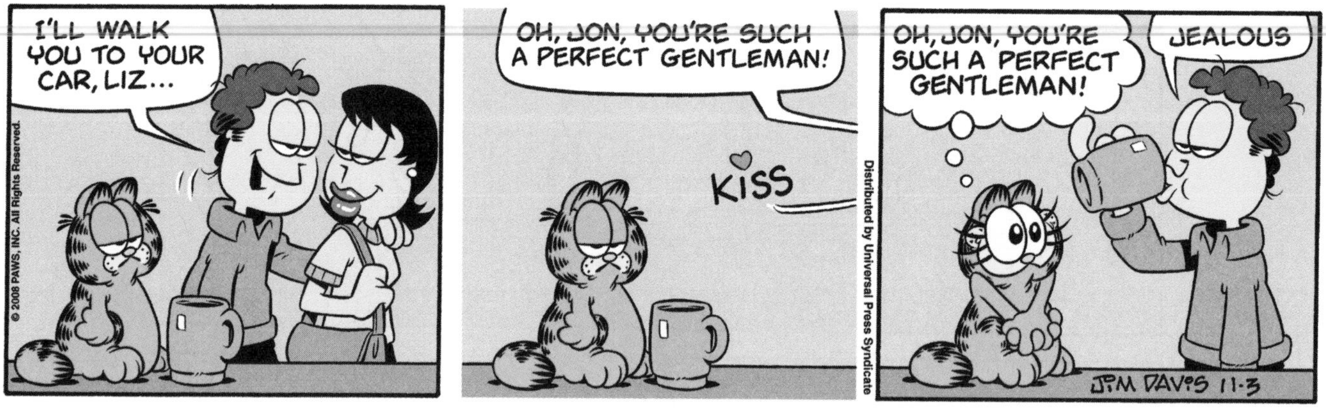
I'LL WALK YOU TO YOUR CAR, LIZ...
OH, JON, YOU'RE SUCH A PERFECT GENTLEMAN!
KISS
OH, JON, YOU'RE SUCH A PERFECT GENTLEMAN!
JEALOUS
JIM DAVIS 11-3
© 2008 PAWS, INC. All Rights Reserved.
Distributed by Universal Press Syndicate

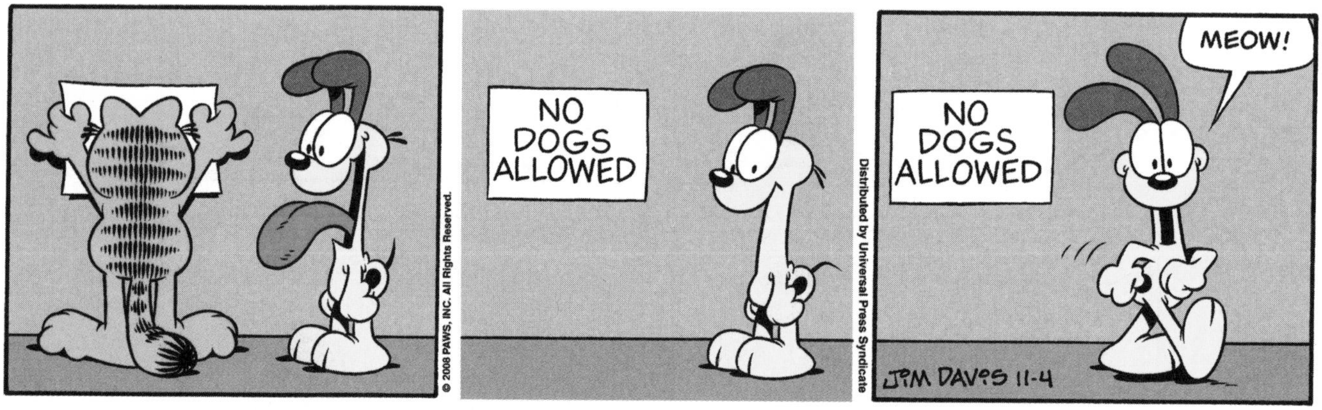
NO DOGS ALLOWED
NO DOGS ALLOWED
MEOW!
JIM DAVIS 11-4
© 2008 PAWS, INC. All Rights Reserved.
Distributed by Universal Press Syndicate

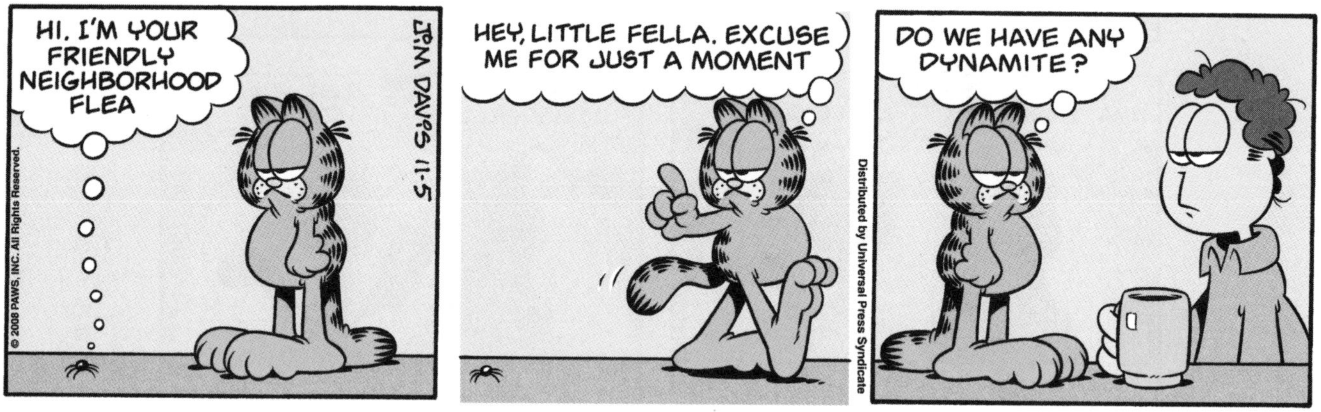
HI. I'M YOUR FRIENDLY NEIGHBORHOOD FLEA
JIM DAVIS 11-5
HEY, LITTLE FELLA. EXCUSE ME FOR JUST A MOMENT
DO WE HAVE ANY DYNAMITE?
© 2008 PAWS, INC. All Rights Reserved.
Distributed by Universal Press Syndicate

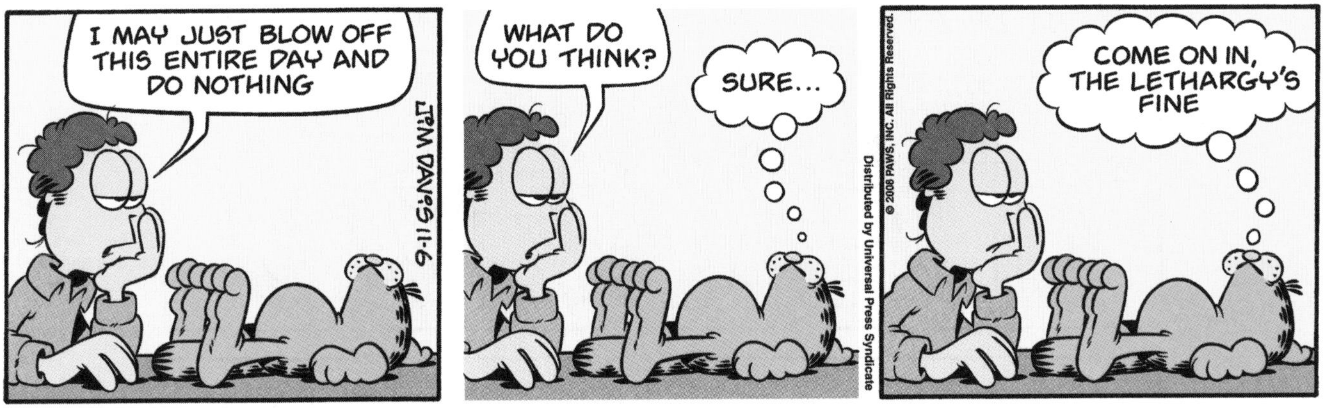
I MAY JUST BLOW OFF THIS ENTIRE DAY AND DO NOTHING
JIM DAVIS 11-6
WHAT DO YOU THINK?
SURE...
Distributed by Universal Press Syndicate
© 2008 PAWS, INC. All Rights Reserved.
COME ON IN, THE LETHARGY'S FINE

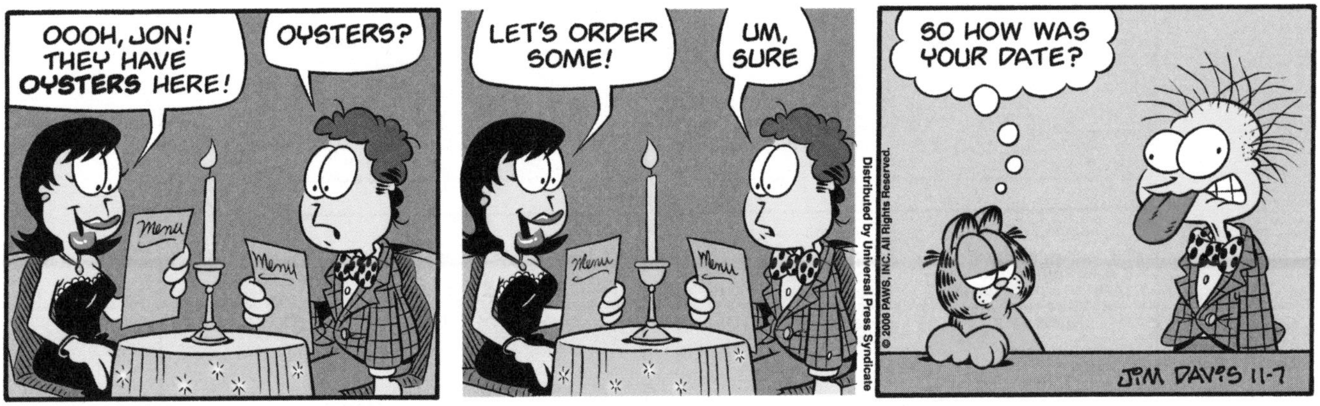
OOOH, JON! THEY HAVE OYSTERS HERE!
OYSTERS?
Menu
Menu
LET'S ORDER SOME!
UM, SURE
Distributed by Universal Press Syndicate
© 2008 PAWS, INC. All Rights Reserved.
SO HOW WAS YOUR DATE?
JIM DAVIS 11-7

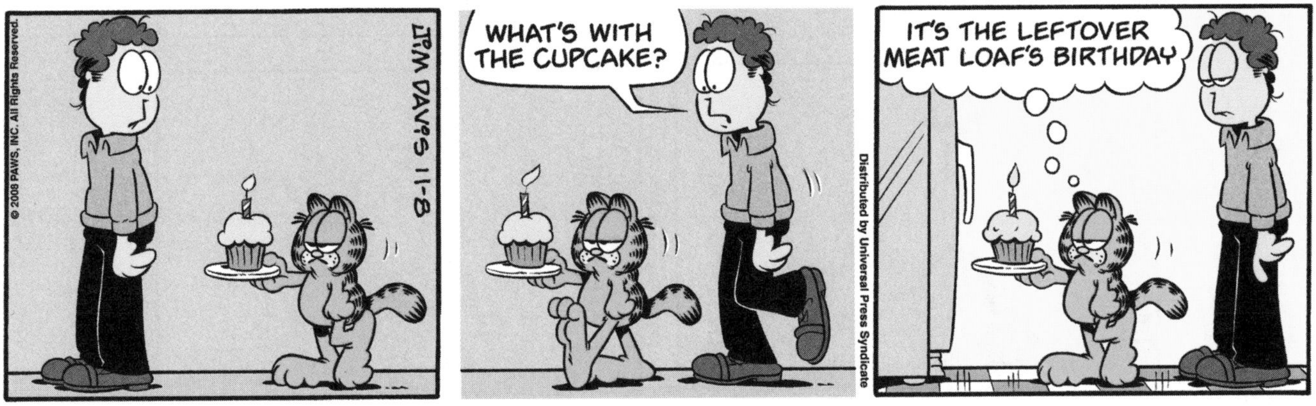
© 2008 PAWS, INC. All Rights Reserved.
JIM DAVIS 11-8
WHAT'S WITH THE CUPCAKE?
Distributed by Universal Press Syndicate
IT'S THE LEFTOVER MEAT LOAF'S BIRTHDAY

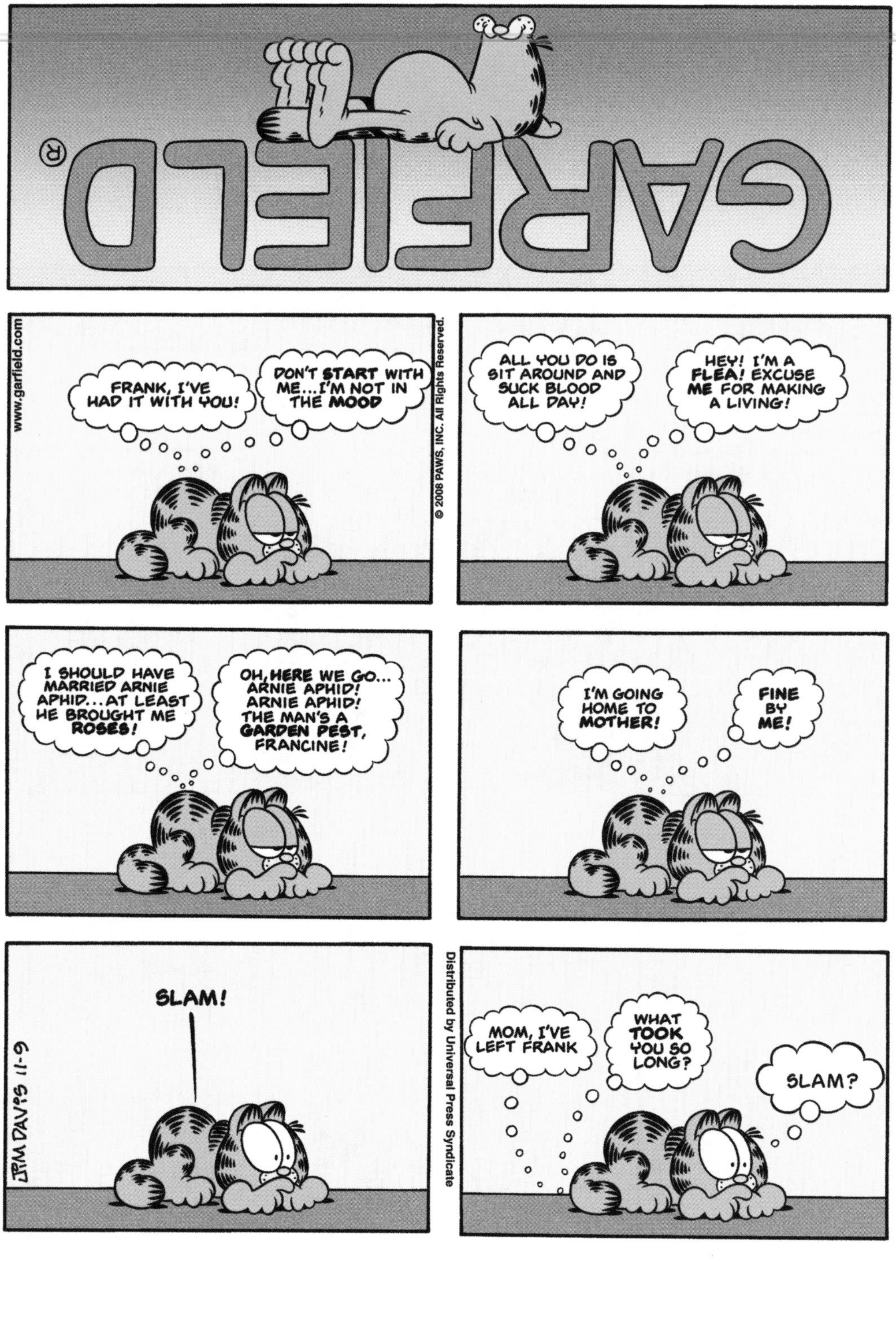
GARFIELD®
www.garfield.com
© 2008 PAWS, INC. All Rights Reserved.
FRANK, I'VE HAD IT WITH YOU!
DON'T START WITH ME...I'M NOT IN THE MOOD
ALL YOU DO IS SIT AROUND AND SUCK BLOOD ALL DAY!
HEY! I'M A FLEA! EXCUSE ME FOR MAKING A LIVING!
I SHOULD HAVE MARRIED ARNIE APHID...AT LEAST HE BROUGHT ME ROSES!
OH, HERE WE GO... ARNIE APHID! ARNIE APHID! THE MAN'S A GARDEN PEST, FRANCINE!
I'M GOING HOME TO MOTHER!
FINE BY ME!
SLAM!
JPM DAVIS 11-9
Distributed by Universal Press Syndicate
MOM, I'VE LEFT FRANK
WHAT TOOK YOU SO LONG?
SLAM?

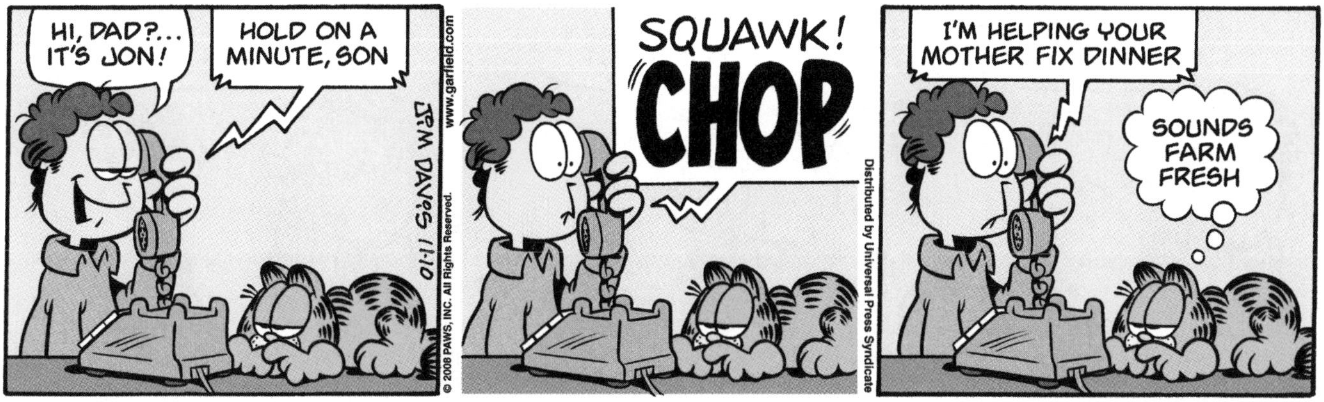
HI, DAD?... IT'S JON!
HOLD ON A MINUTE, SON
JIM DAVIS 11-10
© 2008 PAWS, INC. All Rights Reserved. www.garfield.com
SQUAWK!
CHOP
Distributed by Universal Press Syndicate
I'M HELPING YOUR MOTHER FIX DINNER
SOUNDS FARM FRESH

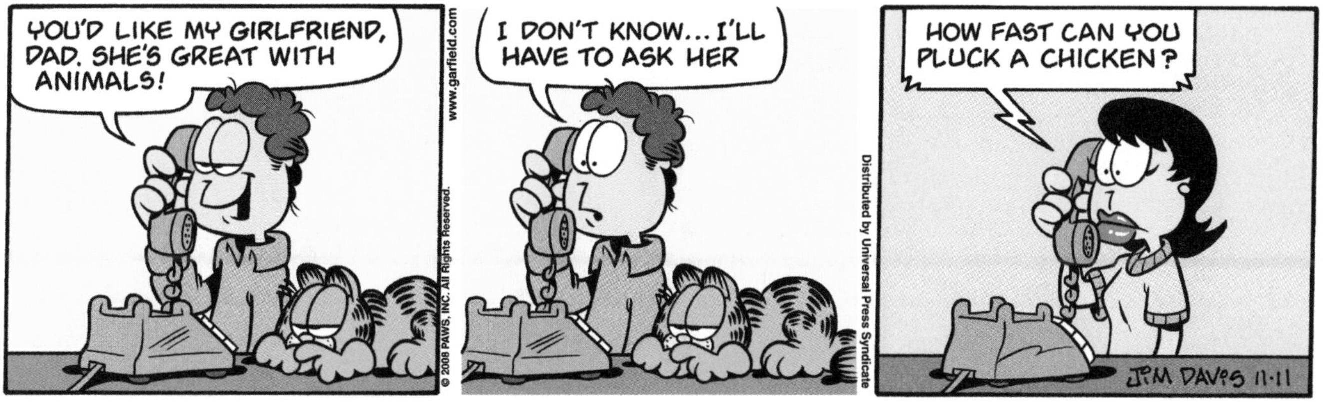
YOU'D LIKE MY GIRLFRIEND, DAD. SHE'S GREAT WITH ANIMALS!
© 2008 PAWS, INC. All Rights Reserved. www.garfield.com
I DON'T KNOW... I'LL HAVE TO ASK HER
Distributed by Universal Press Syndicate
HOW FAST CAN YOU PLUCK A CHICKEN?
JIM DAVIS 11-11

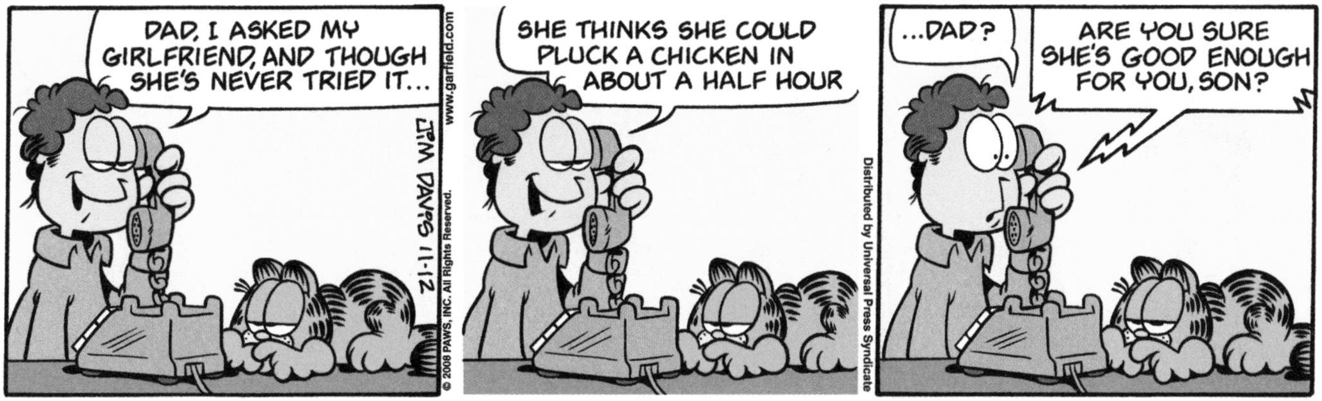
DAD, I ASKED MY GIRLFRIEND, AND THOUGH SHE'S NEVER TRIED IT...
JIM DAVIS 11-12
© 2008 PAWS, INC. All Rights Reserved. www.garfield.com
SHE THINKS SHE COULD PLUCK A CHICKEN IN ABOUT A HALF HOUR
Distributed by Universal Press Syndicate
...DAD?
ARE YOU SURE SHE'S GOOD ENOUGH FOR YOU, SON?

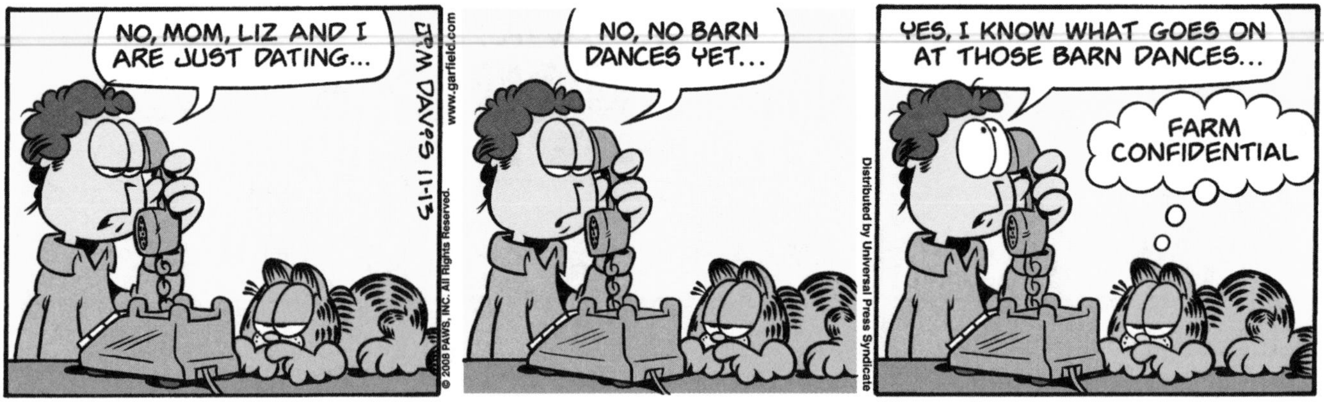
NO, MOM, LIZ AND I ARE JUST DATING...
JIM DAVIS 11-13
www.garfield.com
© 2008 PAWS, INC. All Rights Reserved.
NO, NO BARN DANCES YET...
Distributed by Universal Press Syndicate
YES, I KNOW WHAT GOES ON AT THOSE BARN DANCES...
FARM CONFIDENTIAL

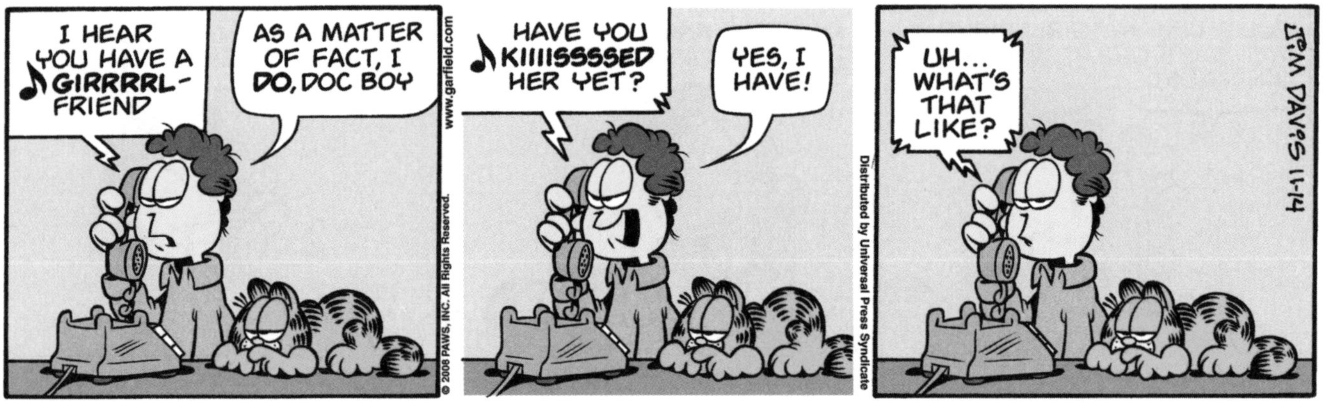
I HEAR YOU HAVE A ♪ GIRRRRL-FRIEND
AS A MATTER OF FACT, I DO, DOC BOY
www.garfield.com
© 2008 PAWS, INC. All Rights Reserved.
HAVE YOU ♪ KIIIISSSSED HER YET?
YES, I HAVE!
Distributed by Universal Press Syndicate
UH... WHAT'S THAT LIKE?
JIM DAVIS 11-14

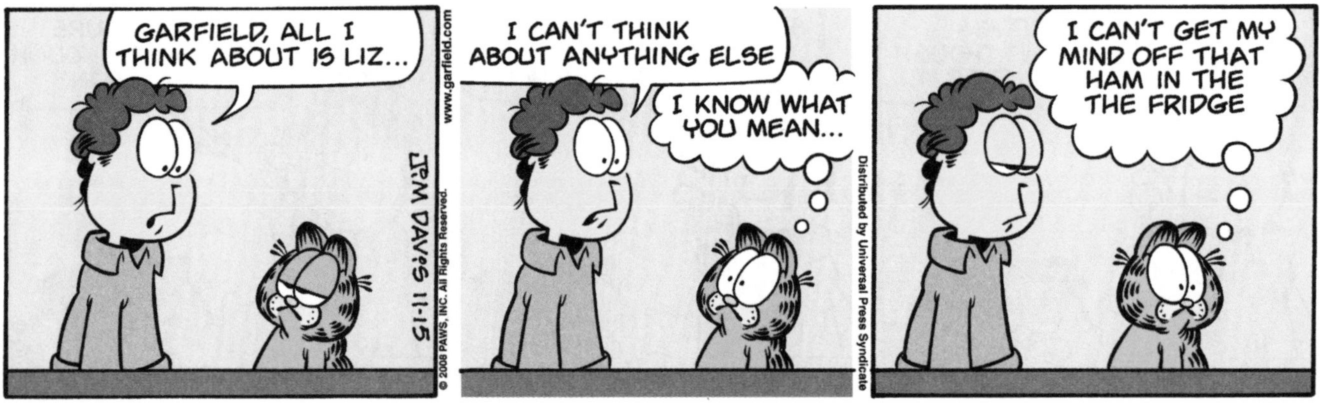
GARFIELD, ALL I THINK ABOUT IS LIZ...
JIM DAVIS 11-15
www.garfield.com
© 2008 PAWS, INC. All Rights Reserved.
I CAN'T THINK ABOUT ANYTHING ELSE
I KNOW WHAT YOU MEAN...
Distributed by Universal Press Syndicate
I CAN'T GET MY MIND OFF THAT HAM IN THE THE FRIDGE

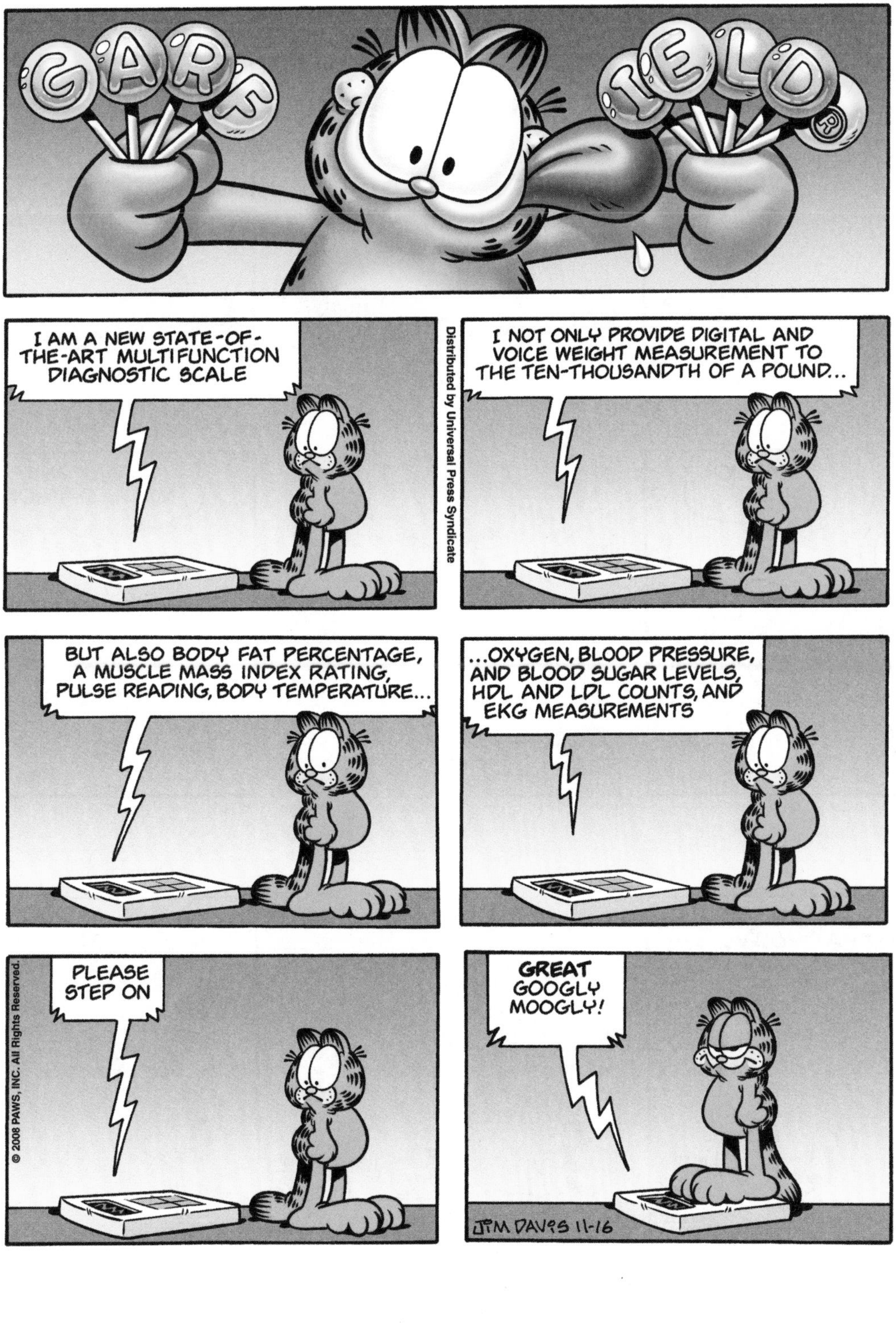
GARFIELD®
I AM A NEW STATE-OF-THE-ART MULTIFUNCTION DIAGNOSTIC SCALE
Distributed by Universal Press Syndicate
I NOT ONLY PROVIDE DIGITAL AND VOICE WEIGHT MEASUREMENT TO THE TEN-THOUSANDTH OF A POUND...
BUT ALSO BODY FAT PERCENTAGE, A MUSCLE MASS INDEX RATING, PULSE READING, BODY TEMPERATURE...
...OXYGEN, BLOOD PRESSURE, AND BLOOD SUGAR LEVELS, HDL AND LDL COUNTS, AND EKG MEASUREMENTS
© 2008 PAWS, INC. All Rights Reserved.
PLEASE STEP ON
GREAT GOOGLY MOOGLY!
JIM DAVIS 11-16

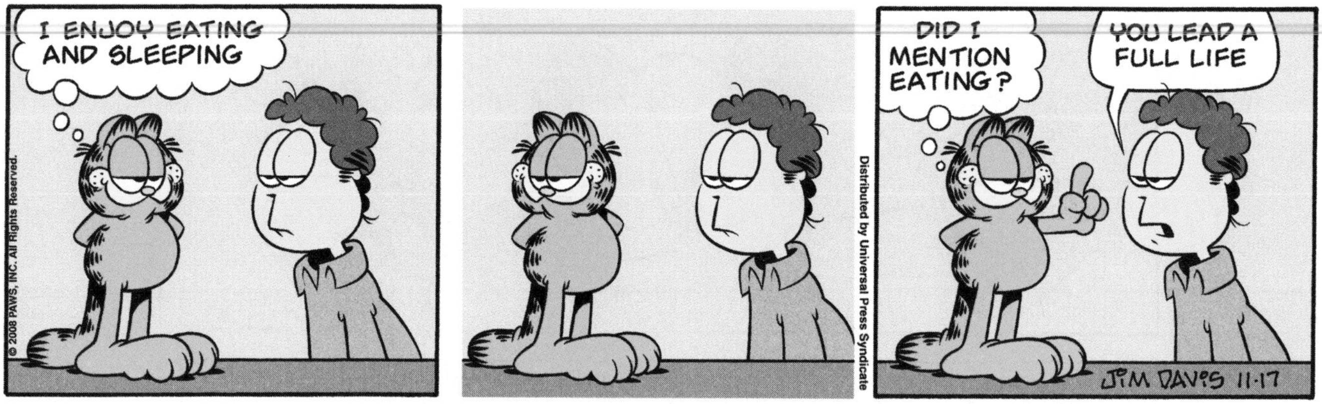
I ENJOY EATING AND SLEEPING
DID I MENTION EATING?
YOU LEAD A FULL LIFE
JIM DAVIS 11-17
© 2008 PAWS, INC. All Rights Reserved.
Distributed by Universal Press Syndicate

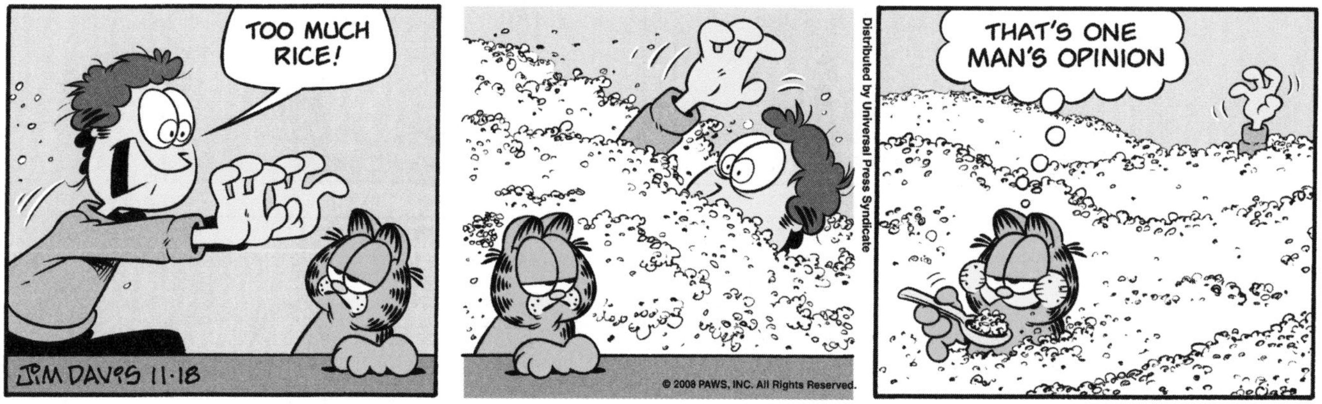
TOO MUCH RICE!
THAT'S ONE MAN'S OPINION
JIM DAVIS 11-18
© 2008 PAWS, INC. All Rights Reserved.
Distributed by Universal Press Syndicate

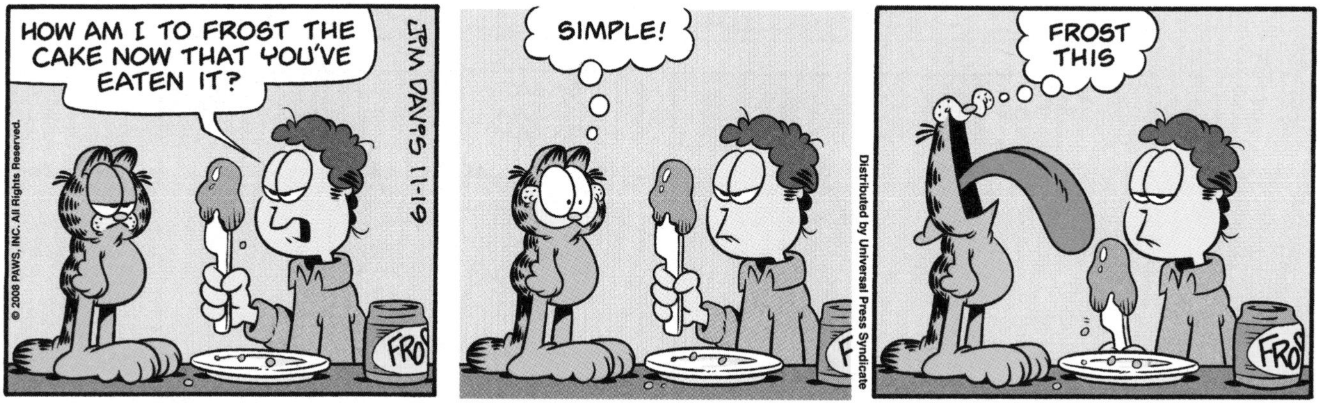
HOW AM I TO FROST THE CAKE NOW THAT YOU'VE EATEN IT?
SIMPLE!
FROST THIS
JIM DAVIS 11-19
© 2008 PAWS, INC. All Rights Reserved.
Distributed by Universal Press Syndicate

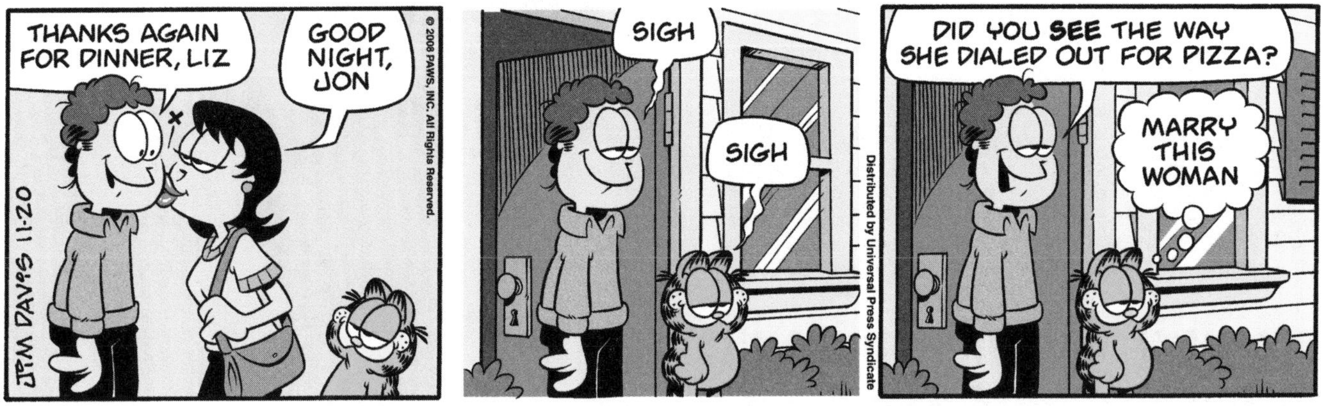
THANKS AGAIN FOR DINNER, LIZ
GOOD NIGHT, JON
JIM DAVIS 11-20
© 2008 PAWS, INC. All Rights Reserved.
SIGH
SIGH
Distributed by Universal Press Syndicate
DID YOU SEE THE WAY SHE DIALED OUT FOR PIZZA?
MARRY THIS WOMAN

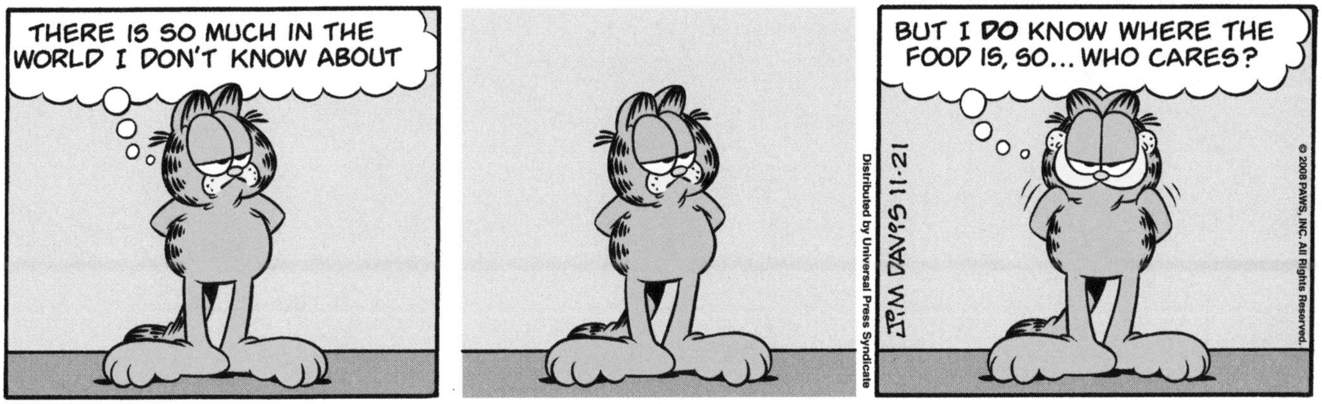
THERE IS SO MUCH IN THE WORLD I DON'T KNOW ABOUT
Distributed by Universal Press Syndicate
JIM DAVIS 11-21
BUT I DO KNOW WHERE THE FOOD IS, SO... WHO CARES?
© 2008 PAWS, INC. All Rights Reserved.

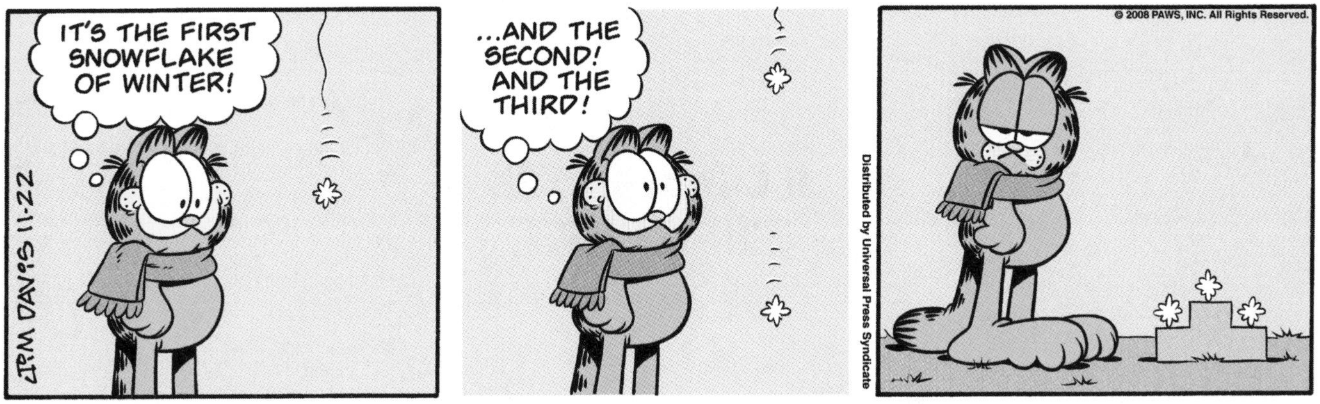
IT'S THE FIRST SNOWFLAKE OF WINTER!
JIM DAVIS 11-22
...AND THE SECOND! AND THE THIRD!
Distributed by Universal Press Syndicate
© 2008 PAWS, INC. All Rights Reserved.

More ANIMAL FUN FACTS

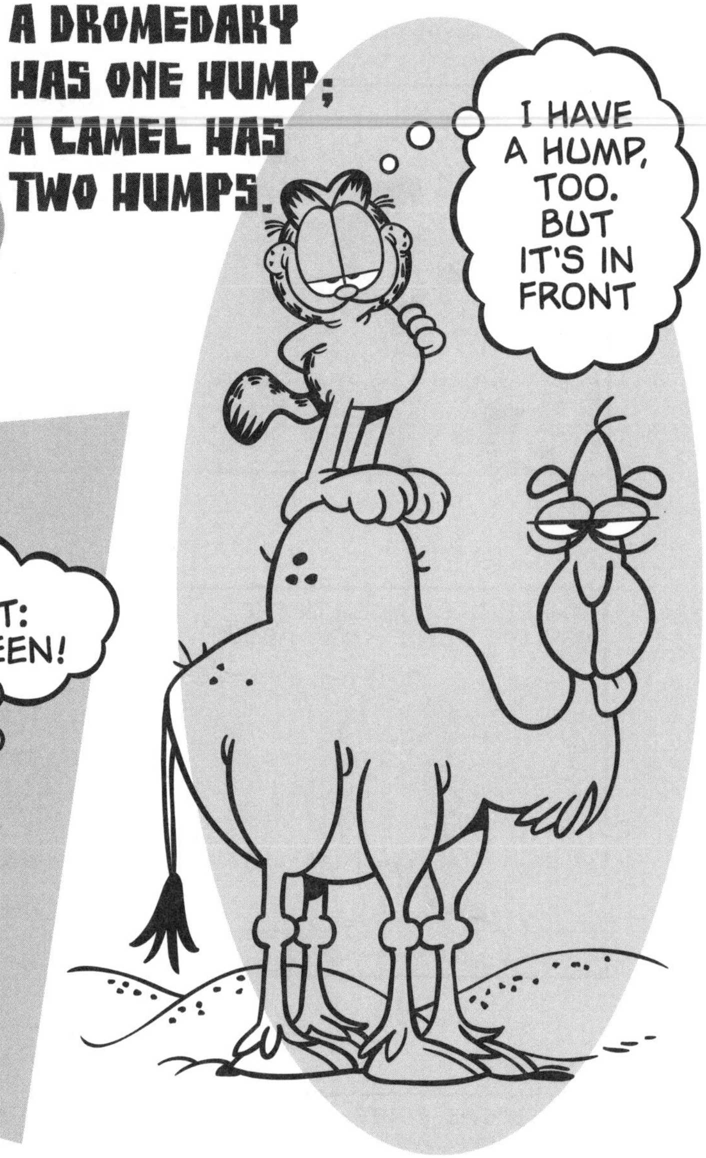
A DROMEDARY HAS ONE HUMP; A CAMEL HAS TWO HUMPS.
I HAVE A HUMP, TOO. BUT IT'S IN FRONT

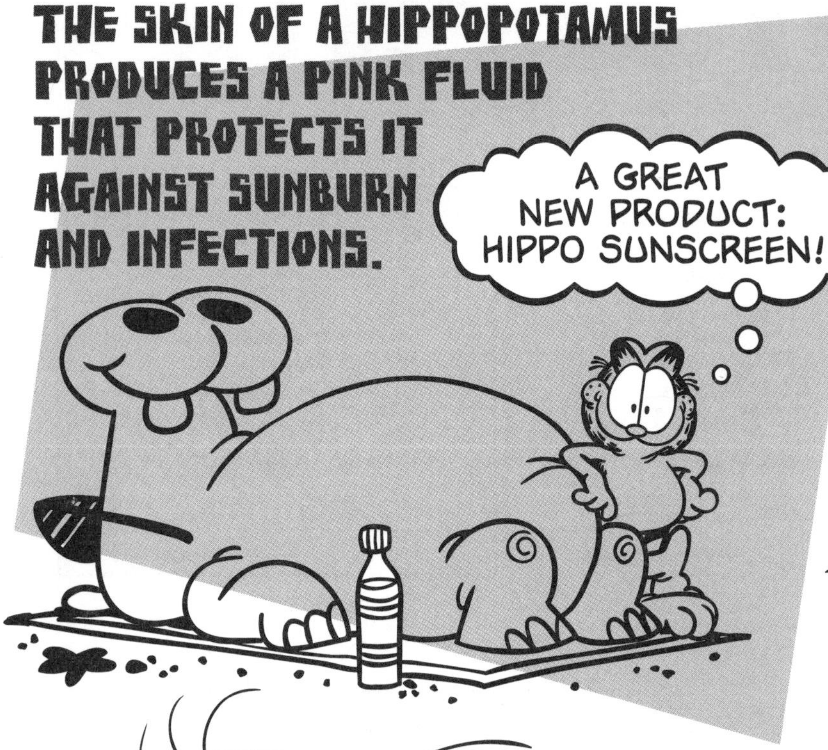
THE SKIN OF A HIPPOPOTAMUS PRODUCES A PINK FLUID THAT PROTECTS IT AGAINST SUNBURN AND INFECTIONS.
A GREAT NEW PRODUCT: HIPPO SUNSCREEN!

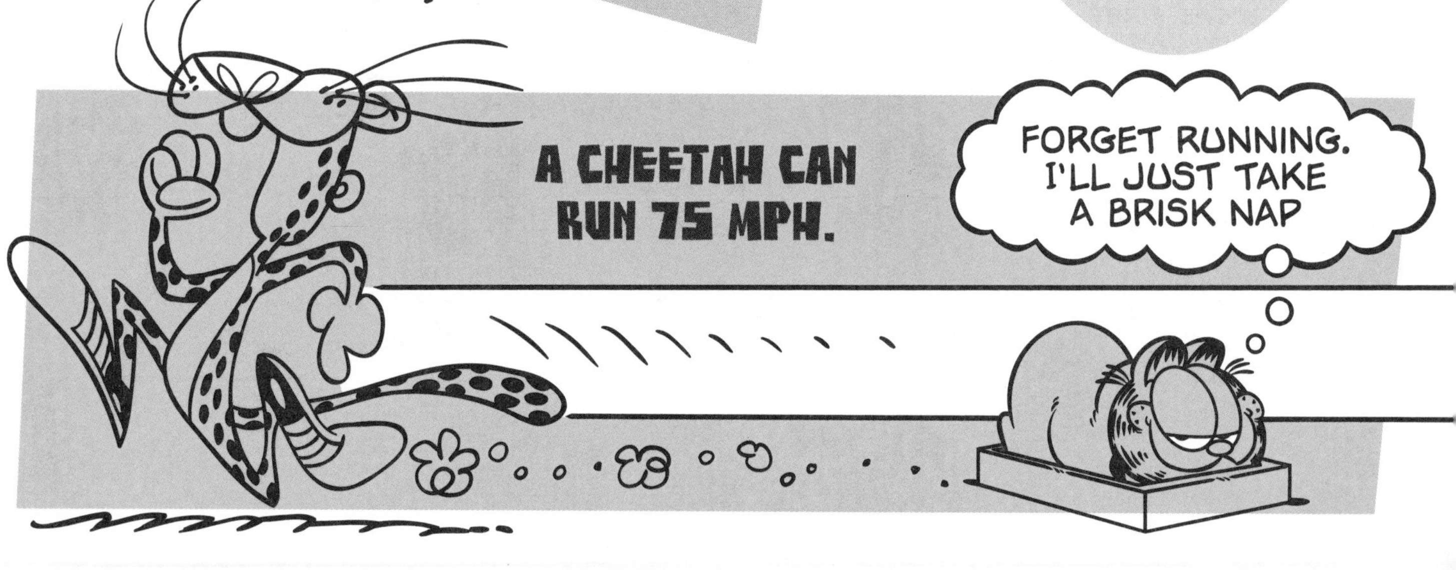
A CHEETAH CAN RUN 75 MPH.
FORGET RUNNING. I'LL JUST TAKE A BRISK NAP

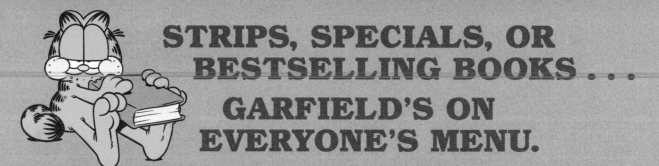

STRIPS, SPECIALS, OR BESTSELLING BOOKS . . .
GARFIELD'S ON EVERYONE'S MENU.

Don't miss even one episode in the Tubby Tabby's hilarious series!

New larger, full-color format!